Holy Bingo, the Lingo of
Eden, Jumpin' Jehosophat
and the Land of Nod

Holy Bingo, the Lingo of Eden, Jumpin' Jehosophat and the Land of Nod

A Dictionary of the Names, Expressions and Folklore of Christianity

Les Harding

McFarland & Company, Inc., Publishers

Jefferson, North Carolina, and London

LIBRARY OF CONGRESS CATALOGUING-IN-PUBLICATION DATA

Harding, Les, 1950–
Holy bingo, the lingo of Eden, jumpin' Jehosophat and the land
of Nod : a dictionary of the names, expressions and folklore
of Christianity / Les Harding.
p.   cm.
Includes bibliographical references and index.

ISBN 0-7864-2241-6 (softcover: 50# alkaline paper) ∞

1. Bible — Miscellanea — Dictionaries.   I. Title.
BS615.H37   2006   230.003 — dc22   2005031097

British Library cataloguing data are available

On the cover: Jan Brueghel the Younger,
Paradise, oil on oak, ca. 1620 *(Pictures Now)*

Manufactured in the United States of America

*McFarland & Company, Inc., Publishers
Box 611, Jefferson, North Carolina 28640
www.mcfarlandpub.com*

In memory of my mother,
Jean Harding

Table of Contents

Preface

Everyone knows that the temptress Delilah cut off Samson's hair. But everyone is wrong. A close reading of the Bible indicates that Delilah was a shrew and hired a barber to do her dirty work. Jesus and Judas were unique historical figures but they did not have unique names. Their names were among the most common for males. Jesus had a brother named Judas and the criminal Barabbas' first name was Jesus. Because of a curious mistranslation it was once assumed that Moses had horns like a goat. Jiminy Cricket's name may be blasphemous. The forbidden fruit may have been an apricot. It certainly was not an apple. A calculation was made that heaven covers exactly 3,375,000,000 cubic miles. There may have been a Pope Pig Face, and the Jesuits were once called Methodists. Stamp collectors, truss makers and gas station attendants can be comforted by their very own patron saints, as can the recruits of the mighty Andorran army and the Bolivian navy. In the dark days before computers, someone with far too much free time counted all 46,227 occurrences of the word *and* in the King James Bible. And then there was the aptly named *Wicked Bible* published in 1632. The word *not* was left out of the seventh commandment, rendering it, "Thou *shalt* commit adultery." The publisher was fined heavily and subsequently went out of business.

What you hold in your hands is a miscellany for the general reader — but a miscellany with a difference. I do not know of any other book that is like this one. There are a number of general miscellanies on library shelves, but none devoted to the curiosities of Christian lore and legend. As such, this book is intended as a companion to standard reference works rather than a replacement.

Books about Christianity are manifold and fall into three broad categories. The first is scholarly reference, including such works as concordances, histories, hagiographies, and biographical and historical dictionaries. These I used extensively, shamelessly mining them for interesting factoids. The second category is devotional. Passing no judgment upon them, these I avoided. The third, which I looked at very sparingly, is the sensational, such as the claim that the Star of Bethlehem was a U.F.O.

I have studied religion at the university level and fancy that I know something about the subject. I also fancy myself to be an intelligent general reader. If after a lifetime of eclectic reading and study I came across something that caught my interest, something that I did not know, I assumed that the reader of this dictionary would not know it either and that he or she would find it as interesting as I did. Therefore I included it. Unless they are biblical scholars or experts in Christian history, most readers will have much to learn and enjoy here. Inevitably a work of this type leaves the author open to the charge of subjectivity. I do not think entirely objective criteria exist, but I did my best to make this an interesting, useful book. I also attempted to put myself in the place of the average intelligent contemporary reader. I say contemporary, because much that was common knowledge to past generations has been forgotten or given a different and even opposite interpretation in our time.

Holy Bingo is for the reader looking for the uncommon, the odd, the unusual, the quirky, and the dramatic, things not easily found anywhere else. Information that can be readily obtained in standard dictionaries, encyclopedias and guides has been deliber-

ately avoided. The entries, nearly fifteen hundred tidbits from two thousand years of Christian lore, ranging from Aaron's Beard to Zounds, are alphabetically arranged, fully cross-referenced and often supplemented with quotations. The reader will understand that this book is a compilation of folklore, which is often based on tradition rather than on demonstrable historical fact. With this understanding in mind, most entries report the particulars of various legends without tempering phrases such as "it is said that," "reputedly," or "legend holds that." The intention is to be as varied as possible, to entertain as well as inform. Whether or not I have succeeded, I leave to the reader to judge.

Les Harding,
St. John's, Newfoundland

The Dictionary

A

Aaron's Beard

A popular name for two varieties of St. John's wort, the great St. John's wort and the Jerusalem star, or rose of Sharon. Both produce prominent yellow flowers and have beard-like stamens presumably reminiscent of Aaron's whiskers. Aaron's beard is also the name of the Kenilworth ivy which has threadlike runners. The reference is to Psalms 133:2:

> "It is like precious oil upon the head, running down upon the beard, upon the beard of Aaron, running down on the collar of his robes!"

Aaron was the elder brother of Moses, descendant of the tribe of Levi and the founder of the hereditary Jewish priesthood (Numbers 18:1–7).

Aaron's Breastplate

A richly embroidered vestment of gold, violet, purple and scarlet thread worn by the Jewish high priest (Exodus 28:15–30; 39:8–21). On it were 12 precious stones arranged in four rows, one stone for each of the 12 tribes of Israel:

First row: Zebulun — carbuncle, Is-sachar — topaz, Judah — sardius; Second row: Gad — diamond, Simeon — sapphire, Reuben — emerald; Third row: Benjamin — amethyst, Manasseh — agate, Ephraim — jacinth; Fourth Row: Naphthali — jasper, Asher — onyx, Dan — beryl.

Some attribute the custom of assigning a birth stone for each month of the year to the 12 jewels in Aaron's breastplate.

Aaron's Rod

A powerful force that overwhelms everything in its path can be called Aaron's rod. Aaron's miraculous rod or wand turned into a serpent before Pharaoh and swallowed up the rods of the Egyptians which had also turned into snakes (Exodus 7:8–12). It also produced blossoms and bore almonds signifying God's favor toward Aaron. As befitting a precious artifact, the rod was kept in the ark of the covenant. The term has also been used for a number of tall flowering plants including the goldenrod. It is also an architectural term for a decorative rod with ornamental leaves or a serpent wrapped around it.

> "[America became] a vast manufacturing nation with its Federal government eating up all the state governments like an Aaron's rod."
> — *Our Business Civilization*, James T. Adams (1879–1949).

Aaron's Serpent

Similar in meaning to Aaron's rod, Aaron's serpent is something so strong that it overpowers all opposition. Reptile, however, may be a more accurate translation than serpent.

> "Aaron cast down his rod before Pharaoh and his servants, and it became a serpent ... the magicians of Egypt did the same by their secret arts. For every man cast down his rod, and they became serpents. But Aaron's rod swallowed up their rods" [Exodus 7:10–12].

Abaddon

(*see also* Bottomless Pit)

The Hebrew word "abaddon," associated with death, destruction and Sheol, Hades, or hell, appears several times in the Old Testament where it is used as a proper noun, the equivalent of the Greek *Apollyon*, the destroyer. Its only use in the New Testament is in Revelation 9:11, where it is equated by St. John with Satan, the angel of the Bottomless Pit:

> "They have as king over them the angel of the bottomless pit; his name in Hebrew is Abaddon, and in Greek he is called Apollyon."

Abba

An Aramaic word for father. Jesus used the word in Mark 14:36: "Abba, Father, all things are possible to thee." The early Christians used Abba as well (Romans 8:15; Galatians 4:6). It has often been used, with its translation, as Abba Father, an invocation to God the Father. Abba has slipped into English by way of abbot, the ecclesiastical figure in charge of monks in an abbey.

Abbess

A woman, at least 40 years of age, in charge of a nunnery or convent. The office, which goes back to the sixth century, is elective and normally held for life, although holders are subject to dismissal for misconduct. As a female an abbess cannot carry out the spiritual functions of a priest, but can expect absolute obedience from her nuns. In Celtic lands abbesses sometimes presided over joint houses of nuns and monks.

Abbey Lubbers

Minor devils of folk belief who were thought to inhabit the wine cellars and kitchens of monasteries, tempting the monks to be greedy, gossipy, lascivious and drunken. The corrupted monks themselves could also be called abbey lubbers.

> "This is no Father Dominic, no huge overgrown abbey-lubber; this is but a diminutive sucking friar."
> —*Spanish Friar*, John Dryden
> (1631–1700).

Abecedarian

(*see also* Abecedarian Psalm)

Any person who is learning the alphabet or someone teaching it can be called an abecedarian. It was also the name of an extreme German Anabaptist sect of the 16th century whose members considered all forms of education and human learning to be contrary to religion. The Bible, they believed, contained the only learning worth having. The study of theology was considered to be idolatrous. For an extreme abecedarian even an ABC or absey book interfered with the hearing of God's true voice. An absey was a primer for children containing simple moral tales based on religious stories.

> ... that is question now;
> And then comes answer like an Absey book.
> —*King John*, William Shakespeare (1564–1616).

Abecedarian Psalm

Abecedarian hymns are those which have their lines arranged in alphabetical order. Psalm 119 is made up of 22 stanzas that correspond to the 22 letters of the Hebrew alphabet. There are eight couplets in each stanza. The couplets of the first stanza all begin with *aleph*, the first letter of the Hebrew alphabet; those of the second stanza begin with *beth*, the second letter, and so on to the end. This is completely lost in translation.

Abel

Adam and Eve's second son, the first herdsman and the first person to offer acceptable sacrifices to God. Abel was also the first human to feel the effects of sibling rivalry. He was also the victim of the first homicide when he was murdered by his brother Cain, who was envious of him (Genesis 4:2–16). The famous story of Abel's murder by his elder brother expresses an ancient tribal bias. Because herding was the occupation of nomads, Abel's sacrifice was pleasing to God while that of Cain, a farmer, was not. A question arises as to why Abel was a herdsman or shepherd before the Flood. Animals were not given to mankind for food until after the deluge. Perhaps the answer can be found in Genesis 3:21 which suggests that animals were used to make garments of skin.

Abelites

A strange fourth century heresy of North Africa. Because the Bible does not mention any children being fathered by Abel, second son of Adam and Eve, it was concluded he had none and therefore that he must have led a chaste life. The Abelites considered marriage to be obligatory, but refrained from consummating their unions. To keep their numbers up each husband and wife adopted a boy and a girl.

Abgar's Letter to Jesus and Jesus's Reply
(*see also* Mandylion; Volto Santo)

There is a legend that Abgar V Ukkama (ruled 4 B.C. to A.D. 7 and 13 to 50), king of Edessa, now in Syria, hearing of the miracles of Jesus sent him a letter begging him to come to his country, offering him asylum. The king had an affliction, probably gout or leprosy, and wished Jesus to cure him. Jesus wrote in reply that he must remain in Jerusalem to fulfil God's plan, but that after his ascension he would send a disciple to the king. St. Thomas the Apostle sent Thaddaeus, one of the apostles, who miraculously cured King Abgar. On his return, the king's messenger brought a handkerchief or veil which had been miraculously imprinted with the image of Christ's face. Copies of these letters were widely circulated but they were spurious, most likely composed in the fourth century.

Abigail

It is thought that the name goes back to Abigail, David's wife, who frequently refers to herself in 1 Samuel as, "your handmaid." At one time this was the archetypal name for a servant girl or lady's maid. From the 16th century Abigail has been a popular woman's name. In 1610 Francis Beaumont and John Fletcher named a maid or "waiting gentlewoman" Abigail in their play, *The Scornful Lady*. Jonathan Swift, Henry Fielding, William Congreve, Tobias Smollett and others used the name Abigail in the same fashion. Early in the 18th century Queen Anne (1685–1714) was attended by a Mrs. Abigail Masham (d. 1734), which served to further popularize the name as that of a maid.

Abishag *see* Shunammitism

Abomination of Desolation

A reference to Daniel 11:31: "And they shall set up the abomination that makes desolate." Other references to the abomination of desolation can be found in Daniel 9:27 and 12:11. Its exact nature remains obscure, but the abomination was probably an idol of Zeus erected in the temple in Jerusalem by Antiochus Epiphanes in 168 B.C. Others have understood the abomination to refer to the antichrist or anything profane. In the New Testament it is alluded to in Matthew 24:15 and Mark 13:14, where it may denote the fluttering standards of the occupying Roman army. "But when you see the desolating sacrilege set up where it ought not to be (let the reader understand), then let those who are in Judea flee to the mountains" (Mark 13:14).

Abracadabra

(*see also* Hocus-pocus)

Nowadays this is a harmless nonsense word much loved by magicians and conjurers. But in ancient times it was a powerful charm thought to be made up of the Hebrew words for a Christian rubric: *Ab* (Father), *Ben* (Son) and *Ruach ACadsch* (Holy Spirit). Abracadabra's earliest known occurrence was in a poem of the second century. Written in a triangular form and worn on a parchment, folded in the shape of a Christian cross, hung around the neck by a strip of linen, it suggested infinity. If the parchment was worn for nine days and then tossed into an eastward flowing river, it was believed to cure ague.

```
A B R A C A D A B R A
A B R A C A D A B R
A B R A C A D A B
A B R A C A D A
A B R A C A D
A B R A C A
A B R A C
A B R A
A B R
A B
A
```

Abraham

(*see also* Abraham-man; Terah; White-haired Man, First)

Abraham, the father of the Jewish people, was the first of the Old Testament patriarchs (Genesis 11:27–25:10). He lived early in the second millennium B.C.. Because he is traditionally depicted with white hair, legend arose that he was the first white-haired man. Abraham is, of course, a central figure in one of the Bible's best-known stories, he near-sacrifice of his son, Isaac.

Abraham-man

(*see also* Bedlam; White-haired Man, First)

The wards of the infamous Bethlehem Hospital (Bedlam) in London were named after saints or patriarchs. The lunatics in the ward named after Abraham were allowed to wander the streets begging for their keep. (There was probably a connection to the parable of the beggar Lazarus in Luke 17.) The beggars wore an identifying badges but this was soon adopted by imposters. Abraham-man, also spelled Abram-man, came to mean imposter or fraud. To sham Abraham was to pretend sickness or to fake a disability.

> The country gives me proof
> and precedent
> Of Bedlam beggars, who, with
> roaring voices,
> Strike in their numb'd and
> mortified bare arms
> Pins, wooden pricks, nails,
> sprigs of rosemary,
> And with this horrible object,
> from low farms,
> Poor pelting villages, sheep-cotes,
> and mills,
> Sometimes with lunatic bans, sometimes
> with prayers,
> Enforce their charity.
> —*King Lear*, William
> Shakespeare (1564–1616).

Abraham's Bosom
(*see also* White-haired Man, First)

By the 16th century this term was a eu-phemism for peace, rest or heaven. Al-though not mentioned in Genesis there is a tradition that the Old Testament patriarch Abraham welcomes the souls of the right-eous to paradise. When Lazarus the beggar died he "was carried by the angels to Abra-ham's bosom" (Luke 16: 22). The exact na-ture of Abraham's bosom is never defined but is probably some sort of purgatory. The Latin Vulgate translation of the Bible sug-gests the pocket of a toga. For that reason Abraham was shown holding a cloth to re-ceive souls. "There is no leaping from Delilah's lap to Abraham's bosom," is a saying which means that those who have lived and died in sin cannot expect to enter heaven.

> The sons of Edward sleep in
> Abraham's bosom.
> —*Richard II*
> William Shakespeare
> (1564–1616).

Abram-man *see* Abraham-man

Absalom's Hair

King David's ambitious third son, Ab-salom, was a handsome man known for his long hair. He cut his hair only once a year, and the cuttings weighed several pounds. Absalom raised an army and rebelled against his father. Defeated in battle, Absalom tried to flee but his hair, as is commonly believed, caught in an oak tree and he was killed by Joad, David's army commander. However, a close reading of 2 Samuel 18:9 indicates that he was not caught by his hair:

> "Absalom was riding upon his mule, and
> the mule went under the thick branches
> of a great oak, and his head caught fast
> in the oak, and he was left hanging
> between heaven and earth...."

Absey *see* Abecedarian

Abstemii

A word once used for those who refused to accept the cup of the Eucharist because they believed wine to be inherently sinful. Modern sects who hold this view maintain that the wine used by Christ was unfer-mented. They use grape juice in place of wine.

> "It ought to give pause to the most fa-natical teetotaller that the only humans worth saving in the Flood were a family of vintners."
> —*Now I Lay Me Down to Eat*, Bernard Rudofsky (1905–1988).

Acacia
(*see also* Burning Bush)

A family of about 1,200 species of shrubs and flowering trees native to warm climates. The plants produce clusters of yellow or white flowers thought by some to resemble tongues of flame. For that reason the acacia was ac-cepted as the burning bush in which the angel of the Lord appeared to Moses (Exodus 3:2). Because the bush was not destroyed by the fire, the acacia came to be symbolic of the soul's immortality. The ark of the covenant (Exodus 25–27) was constructed of acacia wood which is light, hard and durable. A leg-end arose that the crown of thorns placed upon Christ's head at the crucifixion was also fashioned from the acacia.

> Our rocks are rough, but smiling there
> Th' acacia waves her yellow hair,
> Lonely and sweet, nor loved the less
> For flow'ring in a wilderness.
> —*Lalla Rookh*, Thomas Moore
> (1779–1852).

Acacius, St. *see* Headaches

Acanthus

An ornamental plant with large scal-loped, spiny leaves common to the Mediterranean area. In Christian legend the plant was thought to grow in paradise and became symbolic of Heaven. Its thorns came to symbolize pain and punishment for sin.

Accidie
(see also Dark Night of the Soul)

A Latin word derived from the Greek for "indifference." It became the technical term for the cardinal sin of sloth. It also described a state of mental prostration to which hermits and monks, due to the outward monotony of their lives, were especially prone. Accidie is a restless inability to pray and spiritual dryness brought on by excessive fasting. Its fruit is despair.

> "There are great drynesses even in the way of meditation; the bread of prayer is often without taste."
> —*A Simple Method of Raising the Soul to Contemplation*, François Malaval (1627–1719).

Aceldama

Aceldama means "field of blood" in Aramaic, and came to be the name for any battlefield or place of horrific slaughter. Originally it was a field near Jerusalem purchased by the elders and chief priests with the 30 pieces of silver Judas Iscariot returned to them after he had betrayed Jesus. It was also known as the Potter's Field, a burial ground for strangers. Bodies, it was believed, would quickly decompose in the soil of this field. Aceldama is mentioned in Matthew 27:8 and Acts 1:19. For a thousand years, ending in the 17th century, the traditional site was used as a place of burial for Christian pilgrims.

> "What an Aceldama, what a field of blood Sicily has been in ancient times."
> —*Vindication of Natural Society*, Edmund Burke (1729–1797).

Acheiropoitos
(see also Mandylion; Volto Santo)

Images "not made by hands" but miraculously by divine intervention. Relics which claim to bear an authentic likeness of Christ fall under this category.

A.D. *see* Anno Domini

Ad Majorem Dei Gloriam *see* AMDG

Adam
(see also Adam, Not to Know Him From; Calvary and Golgotha; Eve; Tree of Knowledge of Good and Evil; Would You Adam and Eve It?)

Created by God from the dust of the earth, Adam was the first man, the father of the human race. With his wife, Eve, he was driven from the Garden of Eden because he ate the forbidden fruit from the tree of knowledge. Adam was then forced to earn his bread by the sweat of his brow and to face death. Adam's name is probably a pun, deriving from the Hebrew word for man as a species, both male and female. Until Genesis 4:25 he is simply called "the man." The four Greek letters of Adam came to stand for the four compass points and thus symbolized the entire human race. A legend arose that Adam was buried at Golgotha, the site of Christ's crucifixion. Seeds from the forbidden fruit were placed under Adam's tongue and from these grew the wood of the cross of Jesus.

> In Adam's fall
> We sinnèd all.
> —*New England Primer*.

Adam, Not to Know Him From
(*see also* Adam)

To emphatically not recognize someone. Adam was the first man. This is an 18th century expression which does not appear in the Bible.

Adamites
(*see also* Adam)

Members of various heretical sects who considered themselves children of Adam, the first man, and thereby inheritors of his primeval innocence. Accordingly, they rejected marriage and clothing as foreign to Eden. They also rejected human law and believed nothing they did could be judged good or bad. Not surprisingly they were suppressed several times. Small groups practicing "holy nudity" continue in our own times.

> "An enemy to clothes in the abstract. A new Adamite."
> —*Sartor Resartus*,
> Thomas Carlyle
> (1795–1881).

Adam's Ale
(*see also* Adam)

A humorous euphemism for water, also called Adam's wine. Adam, being the first man, had no other beverage. Water has also been called Adam's wine, or simply Adam.

> "A cup of cold Adam from the next purling stream."
> —*Works*, Tom Brown
> (1663–1704).

Adam's Apple
(*see also* Adam)

A lump at the front of the throat formed by the thyroid cartilage, prominent in adult males. It is so named from a piece of the forbidden fruit (Genesis 3:6) which presumably stuck in Adam's throat.

Adam's Arms
(*see also* Adam)

A euphemism for a spade or shovel.

Adam's Curse
(*see also* Adam; In the Sweat of Thy Face)

Work. Because he disobeyed God, Adam was expelled from the Garden of Eden and forced to earn his bread by hard labor, the sweat of his brow.

> A line will take us hours maybe;
> Yet it does not seem a
> moment's thought,
> Our stitching and unstitching
> has been naught.
> —*Adam's Curse*,
> William Butler Yeats
> (1865–1939).

Adam's Needle
(*see also* Adam; Fig Leaves; Joshua Tree)

According to Genesis 3:7, Adam and Eve, suddenly embarrassed by their nakedness, made aprons for themselves by "sewing fig leaves together." There is no mention of them having needles, so how did they fasten those fig leaves together? They must have used the needle-like spines of various spiky plants. (A species of the yucca native to the Eastern United States is called Adam's needle.)

Adam's Profession
(*see also* Adam)

Agriculture and gardening. Adam was directed to keep the Garden of Eden, and after his fall was condemned to till the soil. Even though Eve technically conducted the first harvest by picking a fruit in the Garden of Eden, Adam gets the credit for inventing agriculture.

> "There is no ancient gentlemen but gardeners, ditchers and gravemakers; they hold up Adam's profession"
> —*Hamlet*, William Shakespeare (1564–1616).

Adam's Rib

(*see also* Adam; Eve)

Now an ironic and politically incorrect name for a woman. The original meaning was anything but belittling. The intention was to demonstrate how important and how close Eve was to Adam. Contrary to the popular belief created by this Bible verse, men do not have one rib less than women.

> "And the rib which the Lord God had taken from the man he made into a woman and brought her to the man"
> (Genesis 2:22).

Adam's Wine *see* Adam's Ale

Add a Cubit to His Stature

An expression that indicates the limitations of human existence. The cubit was an inexact measure of length, the measure of a person's arm from the elbow to the tip of the middle finger, or from the elbow to the wrist, about 18 to 22 inches. Its use in the Bible is something of a mixed metaphor because a cubit measures length, not time.

> "And which of you by being anxious can add one cubit to his span of life?"
> (Matthew 6:27).

Adder *see* Serpent

Adoption

Although every Christian can be regarded as a child of God, there are only two explicit examples of adoption in the Bible. In Exodus 2:10 the infant Moses is adopted by an Egyptian princess. In Esther 2:7 Esther is adopted by her uncle Mordecai. The word *adoption* occurs five times in the King James Bible (1611). An 8th century heresy called Adoptianism taught that Christ was not the true Son of God but His adopted son. A godchild's relationship to its godparents has sometimes been called adoption by baptism.

> "Having predestinated us unto the adoption of children by Jesus Christ to himself, according to the good pleasure of his will"
> (Ephesians 1:5).

Adrian IV *see* English Pope

Adulterous Bible

An edition of the Bible, published in London in 1632, that contained an alarming misprint. The word *not* was left out of the seventh commandment, rendering it, "Thou *shalt* commit adultery." For obvious reasons it is also called the Wicked Bible. The printers were fined £300 for their carelessness and went out of business as a result.

Adultery

In the Old Testament a wife was the chattel of her husband, and adultery violated only a husband's property rights. Since a wife had no rights, it was impossible for a husband to commit adultery against her. An errant husband and his lover could still be stoned to death, but only if the woman was married. That would mean that another man's property rights had been violated. Sex with an unmarried woman was illicit, but it did not constitute adultery. Jesus expanded the definition of adultery when he declared that the desire was as bad as the act.

"But I say to you, that every one who looks at a woman lustfully has already committed adultery with her in his heart" (Matthew 5:28).

The patron saints of the victims of adultery are Catherine of Genoa (1442–1510), Elizabeth of Portugal (1271–1336), Fabiola (d. 399), and Marguerite d'Youville (1701–1771), all of whom were married to abusive and unfaithful husbands. There is one male saint associated with adultery, Gengulphus (d. 760), who was murdered by his wife's lover.

Adversary

The adversary is a literary term for the devil. Its use in English literature stems from 1 Peter 5:8:

"Be sober, be watchful. Your adversary the devil prowls around like a roaring lion, seeking some one to devour."

Advocatus Diaboli *see* Devil's Advocate

Aesop

(*see also* Stephaton; Vinegar; Wolf in Sheep's Clothing

In John 19:29 an unnamed bystander soaked a sponge in vinegar (more accurately sour wine) and put it on a reed of hyssop, a plant of the mint family, for Jesus to quench his thirst. In Byzantine art the man's name became Aesop from the Greek for hyssop. He should not to be confused with Aesop (c. 620–c. 560 B.C.) the Greek writer of animal fables. Jesus was probably familiar with Aesop's writings, however. His warning to beware of false prophets who are as wolves in sheep's clothing (Matthew 7:15) resembles a fable by Aesop.

Affinity Bible

A Bible published in 1923 which contained the following glaring error in a table of affinity:

"A man may not marry his grandmother's wife."

After Your Own Heart

Someone who closely agrees with you. The expression comes from 1 Samuel 13:14:

"But now your kingdom shall not continue; the Lord has sought out a man after his own heart."

Agapetae

In the early Middle Ages, agapetae were virgins who lived chastely with celibate monks. The virgins were consecrated to God and were supposed to be united to the monks by spiritual love. After the predictable abuses and scandals occurred, the custom was suppressed by the Lateran Council of 1139.

Agatha, St. *see* Bell-makers

Agnes, St. *see* St. Agnes's Eve

Agnus Dei

(*see also* Lamb of God; Martyrs' Paste)

"Lamb of God," in Latin; this term refers to consecrated medallions of Christ consisting of cakes of wax or dough stamped with the image of a lamb bearing a banner or cross, a symbol of the Savior. They have also been made from wax and the dust of martyrs' bones. On the obverse appear images of saints or popes. The medallions are blessed by the pope in the first year of his pontificate and every seventh year thereafter, and are distributed on the Sunday after Easter. They developed from an earlier custom of collecting the wax from Paschal candles which were stamped with an image of the lamb. The wax symbolizes the virgin flesh of Christ, and the lamb, a sacrificial victim. Agnus Dei is also that part of the Mass and the Communion service, based on John 1:29, which begins with, "O Lamb of God, that takest away the sin of the world."

> "The cross for the first time revealed God in terms of weakness and lowliness and suffering; even, humanly speaking, of absurdity. He was seen thenceforth in the image of the most timid, most gentle and most vulnerable of all living creatures — a lamb. Agnus Dei."
> — *Jesus Rediscovered*, Malcolm Muggeridge (1903–1990).

Agony in the Garden *see* Gethsemane

Agrapha

"Unwritten things." Authoritative words of Jesus which have been preserved in places other than the four Gospels. In Acts 20:35, Paul quotes Jesus saying, "It is more blessed to give than to receive." Another example can be found in 1 Corinthians 11:24–25 where Paul quotes Jesus at the Last Supper. Agrapha representing an oral tradition can be found in the apocryphal Gospel of Thomas, the writings of the Fathers of the Church, and in Islamic tradition. Further agrapha have been discovered in various manuscripts of biblical texts. These sayings are not in the Bible as we know it today.

Agur's Wish

An expression which means neither too much nor too little. Agur was a sage, the reputed author of Proverbs 30:1–33.

> "Give me neither poverty nor riches" (Proverbs 30:8).

Ah Mihi Beate Martine *see* All My Eye and Betty Martin

Ahasuerus *see* Wandering Jew

Alexander the Corrector

A name assumed by Alexander Cruden (1701–1770), the compiler of the *Concordance of the Bible*, a work upon which all later concordances are based. He was employed as a proofreader or corrector, and from this Cruden took it upon himself to improve Britain's morals, especially with regard to swearing and the keeping of the Christian Sabbath. Believing himself divinely inspired, he walked around with a sponge for the ready erasure of anything objectionable. For reasons known only to himself, one thing he found objectionable was the number 45. Cruden's petition to parliament to become corrector for the people's reformation was not granted. Alexander the Corrector was twice sent to a lunatic asylum.

Alexander the Great

The Macedonian conqueror (357–323 B.C.) who forged an empire stretching from Greece to India is mentioned in 1 Maccabees 1:1–9; 6:2, a book which Roman Catholics accept as scripture but Protestants do not. Legends portrayed Alexander either as a saintly Christian or an antichrist.

> How great was Alexander, pa,
> That people call him great?
> Was he, like old Goliath, tall?
> His spear a hundredweight?
> — *How Great Was Alexander*, Elijah Jones (?–1869).

All Creatures Great and Small

This is not a Bible quote, as is often supposed. It comes from the hymn, *All*

Things Bright and Beautiful, composed by Mrs. Cecil Alexander in 1848. In 1975 some marketing genius took two books by English veterinarian James Herriot, *If Only They Could Talk* and *It Shouldn't Happen to a Vet*, and published them in an omnibus edition under the title *All Creatures Great and Small*. It became a best-seller worldwide leading to more books, films and a television series.

All Is Vanity

(*see also* Ecclesiastes)

This famous expression occurs a number of times in Ecclesiastes (1:2; 2:11, 17, 26; 4:4, 16; 6:9, etc.). Vanity here does not mean conceit, as is often thought, but folly or emptiness.

> "All is vanity, and discovering it —
> the greatest vanity."
> — *The Sinner's Comedy*, John Oliver
> Hobbes (1867–1906).

All My Eye and Betty Martin

This 18th century expression of emphatic disbelief or complete nonsense is sometimes shortened to *all my eye*. So the story goes, a sailor went to church and heard a priest utter the Latin phrase, *Ah, mihi, beate Martine.* This is an invocation to St. Martin, but the sailor, who knew no Latin, mistook the words for, "All my eye and Betty Martin."

> "That's all my eye, the king only can
> pardon, as the law says."
> — *Goodnatured Man*, Oliver
> Goldsmith (1728–1774).

All Souls' Day

On November 2, this day of prayer and alsgiving is intended to alleviate the suffering of souls in purgatory. A pilgrim returning from the Holy Land once met a hermit who told him of a cleft on a rocky island which opened directly into the nether regions.

Flames belched forth and the groans of suffering souls were audible. When St. Odilo (962–1048), the abbot of Cluny, heard of this, he was so moved that he set aside the next day, which happened to be November 2, as a day of commemoration for the faithful departed. It has been observed every November 2 since 993. All Souls' Day spread, without official sanction, from the monasteries at Cluny throughout Europe.

All Things in Common

As attested to in Acts 2: 44–45, the first Christians lived a communal life, sharing everything as was needed.

All Things to All Men

This phrase now has a suggestion of insincerity about it. What St. Paul meant when he used it (1 Corinthians 9:22) was that when he presented the message of Jesus to the Gentiles he spoke in a manner appealing to Gentiles, and to the Jews in a manner appealing to Jews. Paul was adaptable rather than insincere.

All to Break

In the King James Bible (1611), Judges 9:53 is rendered, "And a certain woman cast a piece of millstone upon Abimelech's head, and all to brake his skull." As the Revised Standard Version (1952) makes clear, the woman's intent was, in fact, more serious than to merely inflict an injury:

> "And a certain woman threw an upper
> millstone upon Abimlech's head, and
> crushed his skull."

Allah

An Arabic word for God used by Muslims worldwide. Arabic-speaking Christians sometimes use the word as well.

Alleluia *see* Hallelujah

Almond
(*see also* Aureole; Mandorla)

A symbol of the Virgin Mary and others, who are often shown enclosed in an almond-shaped aureole or halo, sometimes called a mandorla, from the Italian for almond. The almond also signifies God's favor as witnessed by the flowering of Aaron's rod, which bore ripe almonds (Numbers 17:8). The almond, a sweet nut enclosed in a hard shell, symbolizes the spiritual and hidden reality of the incarnation of Christ.

Alms

The social duty of Christians to give charity to the needy. In past centuries it was one tenth of a monastery's income. Samuel Johnson's *Dictionary of the English Language* (1755) claims the word has no singular; the *Oxford English Dictionary* (1971) that it has no plural. The King James Bible (1611) says that he "asked an alms" (Acts 3:3).

> Not what we give, but what we share —
> For the gift without the giver is bare;
> Who gives himself with alms
>   feeds three —
> Himself, his hungering neighbor,
>   and me.
> — *The Vision of Sir Launfal*,
> James Russell Lowell (1819–1891).

Alpha and Omega

The first and last letters of the Greek alphabet. A, the first letter symbolizes the beginning of all things. Because it is made with three pen strokes, it became a symbol of the Trinity. The word *alpha* is mentioned four times in the King James Bible (1611), all in Revelation. When Jesus said, "I am the Alpha and Omega, the beginning and the end, the first and the last" (Revelation 22:13), he was signifying the totality of God. Alpha and Omega have come to mean the beginning and end of any concept. *A–Ω* was a sacred monogram suggesting Alpha and Omega. In art, Christ is often depicted holding an open book upon which this monogram is inscribed.

Alpha Mu Omega *see* AMΩ

Alphabetical Curiosity in a Bible Verse

In the King James (1611) and Revised Standard (1952) translations of the Bible, Ezra 7:21 contains every letter of the alphabet except J.

Altar
(*see also* North Side of Altar)

The table on which bread and wine are consecrated during communion. In the early church altars were made of wood. During the Roman persecutions the tombs of martyrs in the catacombs were used. From this came the custom of using stone for altars. Nowadays altars, still in the basic shape of a sarcophagus, can be of stone or wood. If they are of wood, a stone is usually inserted.

> O Thou who camest from above,
> The pure celestial fire to impart,
> Kindle a flame of sacred love
> On the mean altar of my heart.
> —*Hymn*, Charles Wesley
> (1707–1788).

Amand, Saint *see* Bartenders

Amatory Mass

A ritual which claimed to invoke the power of the Roman Catholic mass for purposes of seduction. In the Middle Ages the practice arose of performing masses for specific goals, such as better crops or rain.

Unfortunately, some corrupt priests began performing masses for more carnal ends. The amatory mass was condemned as heretical.

Am I My Brother's Keeper?

A question which has only one answer—yes! When Cain slew Abel this was Cain's inadequate reply when asked about his brother's disappearance (Genesis 4:9).

AMDG

The abbreviation for the Latin, *Ad majorem Dei gloriam*. "To the greater glory of God." The Jesuits use the phrase as their motto. A colloquial rendering of the abbreviation is, "All my duties to God."

Amen

An interjection meaning "be it so" or "may it be true." It is usually said after a prayer or as an informal expression of approval. Jesus is called "the Amen" in Revelation 3:14.

> I had most need of blessing, and "Amen"
> Stuck in my throat.
> —*Macbeth*, William Shakespeare
> (1564–1616).

Amen Corner

A sarcastic name for a section of pews near the pulpit where the most zealous and ostentatious church elders lead the responses.

AMΩ

A sacred monogram consisting of the opening letters of *Alpha, Mu, and Omega,* the first, the middle, and the last letters of the Greek alphabet. The purpose of the monogram is to remind us of Hebrews 13:8: "Jesus Christ the same yesterday, and today, and for ever."

Amphisbaena

A mythological serpent of ancient times that was used in Christian art. Sometimes depicted with feathers, it had a head at each end and eyes that glowed like candles. One head could partially swallow the other, turning the creature into a hoop which could then roll in any direction. Although it dwelt in hell and fed on the dead, it was sometimes used as a symbol of vigilance because one of its heads was always awake and it could see backwards and forwards. To wear a live amphisbaena around the neck, assuming one could be found, would help a pregnancy; a dead one would provide relief from rheumatism.

> Thus Amphisbaena (I have read)
> At either end assails;
> None knows which leads, or
> which is led,
> For both Heads are but Tails.
> —*Dunciad*, Alexander Pope
> (1688–1744).

Anabaptist

Originally the name of a 16th century sect in Germany that objected to infant baptism, insisting that its members be baptized again (*ana* in Greek) as adults. The people to whom the name was applied rejected it because for them the question was not about re-baptism but whether or not the first baptism was valid. The word was sometimes used as an uncomplimentary term for any unorthodox Protestant sect. Anabaptists practiced nonviolence and were opposed to the taking of oaths. Because they rejected the authority of the state, they were often persecuted. Mennonites are the most well-known Anabaptists of today.

Anakim *see* Giants

Ananias

Any great liar can be so called. When confronted by Peter for keeping money for himself after the sale of a piece of property and lying to God, Ananias and his wife Sapphira dropped down dead (Acts 5:1–10). There are two other people in the Bible named Ananias: a Jewish Christian who restored Paul's sight (Acts 9:10 ff; 22:12), and a high priest when Paul was arrested in Jerusalem (Acts 23:1 ff; 24:1).

Anathema

(*see also* Anathema Maranatha;
Bell, Book and Candle)

Anything condemned or accursed can be called anathema. From the ninth century a distinction was made between anathema and minor excommunication. Anathema was the most serious form of ecclesiastical curse, whereby an unrepentant sinner, heretic or relapsed apostate was irrevocably expelled from the church and consigned to Satan. A solemn ceremony was performed by a bishop and 12 priests bearing candles. At the end of the ceremony the candles were snuffed out and thrown to the ground. In excommunications the heretic was permitted, indeed encouraged, to perform penance in order to return to the church. "The pope ... has condemned the slave trade — but no more heed is paid to his anathema than to the passing wind."—*Gleanings*, William Gladstone (1809–1898).

Anathema Maranatha

A double curse based on a misinterpretation. The King James Bible (1611) translates 1 Corinthians 16:22 as "If any man love not the Lord Jesus Christ, let him be Anathema Maranatha." Anathema means something hateful and accursed. The Aramaic word which follows, really a separate sentence, *Maran atha*, means something quite different, "Our Lord, come." Most Christians, being ignorant of Aramaic, erroneously understood Anathema Maranatha to be a double curse. The Revised Standard Version (1952) makes things clearer: "If any one has no love for the Lord, let him be accursed. Our Lord, come!"

Anchor

(*see also* Dolphin)

A heavy iron implement used to hold ships and boats in place. Figuratively the word is used for something which imparts security. Thus it became a symbol of hope, in ancient times called "the sacred anchor." The traverse bar of an anchor forms a cross. Anchors became associated with the fish, a symbol of Christ, as well as with the fourth century St. Nicholas of Myra, patron saint of seafarers. Anchors used as disguised crosses were carved by early Christians on walls, monuments and graves. "We have this as a sure and steadfast anchor of the soul" (Hebrews 6: 19). Pope Clement was bound to an anchor and thrown into the sea around A.D. 99. An anchor with a dolphin is sometimes used to depict Christ on the Cross. The dolphin represents Christ as the bearer of souls over the waters of death. Anchor and anchors are mentioned four times in the King James Bible (1611). "Which hope we have as an anchor of the soul, both sure and steadfast, and which entereth unto that within the veil" (Hebrews 6:19).

Anchorite

From the Greek word meaning "to withdraw," this term is applied to a man who withdraws from the world to devote himself to prayer and a solitary life. He differs from a hermit in that the latter is free to move about but chooses to live in isolation, whereas the anchorite is confined to his cell or dwelling. In the Middle Ages the anchorite was formally enclosed at a service performed by a bishop. Cells were often attached to a parish church, and the anchorite was supported by gifts of food and other necessities from parishioners. The female equivalent was an anchoress.

The laughing dames in whom he
did delight,
Whose large blue eyes, fair locks, and
snowy hands,
Might shake the saintship of
an anchorite.
—*Childe Harold*, Lord Byron
(1788–1824).

Ancient of Days

A Hebrew phrase meaning "an old man." It is used in Daniel 7:9, 13, and 22 to mean God the judge of the world. The familiar image of God as the majestic white-haired figure holding the book of judgment comes from Daniel.

Ancient of Days, who sittest
throned in glory,
To thee all knees are bent,
all voices pray.
—*Hymn*, William Croswell Doane
(1832–1913).

Andorra *see* Army of Andorra

Andrew, St. *see* St. Andrew's Cross; X

Anemone

This plant genus of perennial herbs related to the buttercup symbolizes the Trinity and sorrow because it has three leaves and was said to have bloomed at the foot of the Cross. Red spots on the petals recall the blood from the wounds of Christ.

Angel Food Cake

A light sponge cake containing egg whites but no yolks or shortening. The white color of the cake is meant to remind the eater of angels.

Angel Wings
(*see also* Angels)

Crawford H. Greenewalt (1902–1993) in his book *Hummingbirds* speculates on how big the wings of a 170 lb. angel would need to be:

The wing from wrist to tip would be
about four feet long, its total length between six and seven feet. When folded
neatly into the body, the end of the
wings would come just below the knee —
comfortable enough for perching and
walking. The wings would beat about
once every second, a nice easy rhythm —
not too far from a normal walking pace.
The wings would, however be heavy,
perhaps a quarter of the weight of the
body and, alas, here lies the rub: the
human frame hasn't the pectoral muscles
to drive such formidable gear. Human
pectorals are barely five per cent of
the total body weight and a reasonable
aerial job would call for at least
fifteen per cent.

Angelophany
(*see also* Angels)

The material manifestation of an angel.

Angels
(*see also* Angel Wings;
Angelophany; Archangels,
Cherubim; Fallen Angel;
Haroot and Maroot)

Angels, from the Greek word for messengers, are spiritual beings endowed with free will, created prior to men and superior to them. Those who chose good are commonly called angels, while those who chose evil and rebellion against God, devils and fallen angels, were expelled from Heaven. They and their leader Satan are condemned to eternal damnation. From many scriptural references (e.g., Isaiah 6:1–2, Ezekiel 1:4–

14), it has been deduced that there are three hierarchies of angels comprising nine choirs, so called because they continuously sing the praises of God. The hierarchy of Counsellors is composed of Seraphim, Cherubim and Thrones. These beings exist to perpetually adore God. Red, the symbol of love, is their color. The Seraphim and Cherubim are sometimes depicted as bodiless heads with wings. The Governors of the Stars and Elements is the second hierarchy. Dominions, Virtues and Powers are the choirs. Remaining aloof from mankind they receive divine illumination from the first hierarchy and communicate it to the third. They are associated with the color blue, symbolizing knowledge and light. The most important hierarchy is that of the Messengers, with the choirs of Principalities, Archangels and Angels who directly intervene in human affairs. Angel is the generic name for all of these spiritual beings as well as for the last choir. From 787 it has been permissible to depict angels in art. The image of the angel as a winged figure is not biblical and was based on Nike, the Greek winged figure of victory, and the Roman god Cupid. Angels may be invoked, and every baptized person has a guardian angel. A medieval theologian somehow concluded that there are 3,472,000 angels.

Angels were also obsolete English coins stamped with the image of an angel. This was in the memory of Pope Gregory I (c. 540–604), who remarked that the pagan Angles or English were so beautiful that if only they were Christians they would surely be angels.

> Cousin, away for England, haste before,
> And, ere our coming, see thou
>   shake the bags
> Of hoarding abbots, their
>   imprison'd angels
> Set thou at liberty.
> —*King John*, William
> Shakespeare (1564–1616).

Anglo-Israelism

A conceit that the Anglo-Saxon race is descended from the lost tribes of Israel and therefore specially favored by God.

Animals *see* Ant; Antelope; Ant-lion; Ape; Asp; Ass; Balaam's Ass; Bear; Beaver; Bee; Bestiary; Bishop-Fish; Blackbird; Boanthropy; Buridan's Ass; Butterfly; Camel; Cat; Cockatrice; Crane; Crocodile; Dog; Dolphin; Dove of Peace; Dragon; Elephant and Castle; Ermine; Falcon; Fox; Frog; Goat; Goldfinch; Griffin; Hare; Hart; Hedgehog; Hen and Chickens; Horse; Ichthus; Jesus Bug; Leopard; Leviathan; Lion; Lynx; Mother Carey's Chicken; Mouse; Noah's Ark; Ostrich; Owl; Ox; Panther; Partridge; Peacock; Pearls Before Swine; Pelican; Peter's Fish; Phoenix; Poor as Job's Turkey; Quail; Rabbit; Rat; Raven; Roar like the Sparrow; Swallow; Swan and Swan Song; Tiger; Toad; Unicorn; Vulture; Weasel; Whale; Wolf in Sheep's Clothing; Woodpecker; Wyvern

Anise and Cummin

This expression means to neglect things of importance and pay attention to things of no importance. Anise and cummin are plants native to the Middle East that produce very tiny seeds used as spices. A more accurate translation would be dill and cummin. Jesus exposed the pettifogging of the Pharisees when he said,

> "Ye pay tithe of mint and anise and cummin, and have omitted the weightier matters of the law, judgment, mercy and faith" (Matthew 23:23).

Anne, St. *see* Grandparents of Jesus

Anno Domini (A.D.)

A.D. is an abbreviation incorrectly thought by many to mean "after death." It stands for the Latin *Anno Domini*, the year of the Lord, and dates the years after the birth of Christ. Of course Jesus was dead for three days before being resurrected so "after death" would not be of much use. The politically correct among us have begun to use C.E., common era. The use of A.D. to date events of history was popularized by the Venerable Bede (c. 673–735).

> "Here toddles along some old figure of fun, with a coat you might date Anno Domini One."
> — *The Fudge Family in Paris,* Thomas Moore (1779–1852).

Annunciation

The event described in Luke 1:26–38 in which the archangel Gabriel informs Mary that, though a virgin, she has been chosen to give birth to the incarnate Christ. Gabriel greeted her by saying, "*Ave Maria*" ("Hail Mary"). She replied, "*Ecce Ancilla Domini*" ("Behold, I am the handmaid of the Lord"). The apocryphal *Book of James* records a second visitation by Gabriel, while Mary was drawing water from a well. The feast of the Annunciation, or Lady Day, is on March 25, exactly nine months before Christmas, the nativity of Jesus.

Ant

Mentioned only twice in the Bible (Proverbs 6:6–8; 30:25), where it is a symbol of thrift, industry and foresight. The ant, so it was believed, could tell wheat, which it ate, from barley, which it did not eat, and thus came to symbolize the wise person who could see the difference between truth and falsehood. The ant divided its seeds into two and symbolized the difference between the letter of the law and the spirit (2 Corinthians 3:6).

Antediluvian

Before the great flood of Noah. It has come to mean anything or anyone hopelessly out of date or old fashioned.

> "From what cursed old antediluvian, who lived before the invention of spinning-jennies, she learned this craft, Heaven only knows."
> — *St. Ronan's Well,* Sir Walter Scott (1771–1832).

Antelope

When the antelope entangled its horns in a shrub it began to bleat and a hunter was able to approach and kill it. This folk belief, which is not in the Bible, was a warning to those Christians who ensnare themselves with wine and lust and are slain by the evil hunter, the devil.

Anthony, St. *see* Tantony Pig

Antichrist

In a general sense any person or group directly or hypocritically opposed to Christ. For many Christians, however, the word describes a diabolical historical and political being who will lead the powers of evil (2 Thessalonians 2:1–12; Revelation 13). In a cataclysmic battle Christ will defeat the antichrist at the Second Coming, ushering in the end of time. The antichrist has been variously identified with Caligula, Nero, Mohammed, and Napoleon. *Man of Sin* and the *Beast* are other terms for the antichrist.

Talk about the pews and steeples
And the cash that goes therewith!
But the souls of Christian peoples ...
Chuck it, Smith!
—*Antichrist, or the Reunion of Christen-
dom*, G. K. Chesterton (1874–1936).

Antidisestablishmentarianism

Opposition to the Church of England's disestablishment. At 28 letters this is considered by many to be the longest regular word in the English language.

Antimony

A metallic element used in alloys, paints and medicines which may have an unusual Christian connection. Samuel Johnson (1709–1784) wrote in his *Dictionary of the English Language* that the word was derived from antimonachos, the Greek for antimonk. A prior, so the story goes, fed some antimony to the monastery pigs and they grew fat. But when the antimony was fed to the monks they died. Modern dictionaries suggest that the word is of Arabic origin introduced to English through the study of alchemy.

Antipopes

(*see also* Avignon Captivity)

Roman Catholic popes who resided at Avignon, France, during the Great Schism of the West in the 14th century. They were selected by temporal authority rather than by being canonically elected by cardinals of the church. A pretender to the papal throne is called an antipope.

Ant-lion

A curious mythological creature that arose from a mistranslation of Job 4:11: "The strong lion perishes for lack of prey." The Greek Septuagint uses *mirmicoleon*, a rare

word for the Arabian lion. The meaning of this word was forgotten and in another translation became *formicaleon*, ant-lion. The beast had the front part of a lion and the rear part of an ant. It was both a carnivore and a vegetarian and thus perished because there was no suitable food for it. The word is also applied to various predatory dragonflies and doodlebugs.

Anxious Bench

In Methodist camp-meetings a bench was reserved for sinners, anxious mourners, who wanted to repent. After the service an anxious meeting was held to convert the sinners.

A–Ω *see* Alpha and Omega

Ape

Because of its supposed predilection for voyeurism and copulation, the ape symbolizes lust, sloth, evil, sin and cunning. It also represents drunkenness because its foolish antics resemble those of drunken men. Satan was believed to assume the form of an ape. Female apes, who tempt the males by shamelessly presenting their hind quarters, symbolize prostitutes and other immoral women. Legends have it that spinsters will be married to apes in the afterlife, while a married woman who denies her husband his conjugal rights will be violated by apes in hell. An ape with an apple in his mouth represents the fall of man, while a chained ape represents the triumph over sin. Apes are referred to in the King James Bible (1611) in 1 Kings 10:22 and 2 Chronicles 9:21.

"For where God built a church, there the
Devil would also build a chapel.... Thus
is the Devil ever God's ape."
— *Table Talk*, Martin Luther
(1483–1546).

Ape's Paternoster

(*see also* Paternoster)

To chatter uncontrollably from cold or fear is to say an ape's paternoster. A paternoster is the Lord's Prayer.

Apocalypse

(*see also* Four Horsemen of the Apocalypse; Revelations)

Greek for uncover or revelation, the name by which the last book of the New Testament is known in Catholic Bibles. In Protestant Bibles the last book is called Revelation. The revelation of St. John the Divine at Patmos tells of the decisive battle between good and evil and of the Last Judgment. Apocalypse is also used for religious and prophetic writing about the end of the world. Apocalyptic means complete disaster or total destruction. In modern usage the word is often associated with a nuclear catastrophe.

> "Wild, dark times are rumbling toward us, and the prophet who wishes to write a new apocalypse will have to invent entirely new beasts, and beasts so terrible that the ancient animal symbols of St. John will seem like cooing doves and cupids in comparison."
> —*Lutetia or Paris*, Heinrich Heine (1797–1856).

Apocalyptic Number *see* 666

Apocrypha

A Greek word meaning hidden or obscure. There are a number of ancient writings which are not part of the Hebrew scriptures and are excluded from the Old Testament. Though not part of the Bible, the books of the Apocrypha are considered worthy of study and reflection. There are also early Christian writings which run parallel to the New Testament but have been excluded from it. The Apocrypha is usually considered to be books which Protestants generally accept as related to scripture — Judith, Wisdom of Solomon, Tobit, Sirach (Ecclesiasticus), Baruch, two books of Maccabees, two books of Esdras, additions to Esther, Song of the Three Young Men, Susanna, Prayer of Azariah, Bel and the Dragon, and the Prayer of Manasseh. Roman Catholics accept all of them, except the books of Esdras and the Prayer of Manasseh, as authentic scripture. They refer to the Protestant Apocrypha as deuterocanonical, using Apocrypha for entirely noncanonical works. Protestants refer to noncanonical works as the pseudepigrapha. In common speech anything apocryphal is considered of dubious authority or authorship.

Apollonia, St. *see* Toothache

Apostle Gems

Gems associated with the Apostles: St. Peter — jasper; St. Andrew — sapphire; St. James — chalcedony; St. John — emerald; St. Philip — sardonyx; St. Bartholomew — carnelian; St. Matthew — chrysolite; St. Thomas — beryl; St. Thaddeus — chrysoprase; St. James the Less — topaz; St. Simon — hyacinth; St. Matthias — amethyst.

Apostle Spoons

Silver or silver-gilt spoons from the 16th century whose handles contained images of the apostles. It was the custom to present spoons at baptisms or to give them as gifts at other occasions. There were 13 spoons, one for each of the apostles, and the master spoon, a representation of Jesus. The souvenir spoons of today are their direct descendants.

Apostles

(see also Symbols of the Apostles; Thirteenth Apostle)

The original 12 chosen by Jesus to preach to the world. They were Peter, James and John (sons of Zebedee), Andrew, Philip, Bartholomew, Matthew, Thomas, James (son of Alphaeus), Thaddeus (or Judas son of James), Simon the Canaanite (or Zealot) and Judas Iscariot. After Judas betrayed Jesus and hanged himself, he was replaced by Matthias. Paul is sometimes called the Apostle of the Gentiles. The word apostle came to mean any Christian leader or missionary. It has now come to denote any passionate reformer or devotee to a cause. In Cambridge University the last dozen students to be awarded a B.A. were called the Apostles. The last of them was called St. Poll, a corruption of St. Paul. In the days of muzzle loading guns, marksmen, prior to a battle, would prepare a dozen charges of powder, wad and shot. These became known as "apostles."

> "Last of all, as to one untimely born, he appeared also to me. For I am the least of the apostles, unfit to be called an apostle, because I persecuted the church of God. But by the grace of God I am what I am."
> (1 Corinthians 15:8–10).

Apostles' Creed *see* Twelve Articles of the Symbol

Apostles' Deaths

Being an Apostle was a dangerous occupation. According to tradition only John died a natural death. The others met the following painful ends: Andrew — crucified; Bartholomew — crucified; James — beheaded; James (brother of Jesus) — stoned; Judas — suicide by hanging; Jude (Thaddaeus) — crucified; Matthew — stabbed; Matthias — beheaded; Peter — crucified upside down; Philip — crucified; Simon — crucified; Thomas — stabbed.

Apostolic Succession

In the Roman Catholic, Orthodox and Anglican Churches, this term refers to the notion that there must be an unbroken chain of succession for the legitimate transmission of religious authority. The succession proceeds from the Apostles of Jesus Christ to the bishops and priests of today by virtue of prayer and the laying on of hands (John 20:23; Matthew 28:19).

Apple

(see also Forbidden Fruit)

Apples are not mentioned in Genesis. It was much later that the forbidden fruit, with which the serpent tempted Eve, became the apple. It may be a pun on the Latin *malum*, (apple) and *malus* (evil). Painters in the Renaissance usually included an apple when depicting the Fall of Man. Mary and the Christ-child were often shown holding apples as symbols of human redemption from the original sin of disobedience. Apples are mentioned by name 11 times elsewhere in the Old Testament, but it is not known for sure if the fruit was grown in ancient Palestine. Lemon, citron, apricot and orange have all been suggested as more accurate translations. Charles Borromeo (1538–1584) is the patron saint of apple orchards.

> Adam so starved me I was fain accept
> The apple any serpent pushed my way.
> — *The Ring and the Book*, Robert Browning (1812–1889).

Apple of Paradise

Because of Eve's sin in the Garden of Eden, an apple missing a bite.

Apple of Sodom *see* Dead Sea Fruit

Apple of the Eye

Something or someone valued above all else. The expression occurs in Deuteronomy

32:10, Psalms 17:8 and Proverbs 7:2. The pupil of the eye was so called because it was believed to be a solid sphere like an apple.

Appolonia, St. *see* Dentists

Aquarian (Aquarii)

Third and fourth century Christians who used Holy Water instead of wine at the Eucharist. It was also the name of persecuted Christians who used water instead of wine at communion in order not to be identified by the odor of wine on their breath.

Aquinas, St. Thomas *see* Dumb Ox

Aramaic
(*see also* Languages of Jesus)

The native language of Jesus. It is a Semitic tongue spoken by the common people in Palestine at the time of Jesus. Hebrew was the language of the upper class, the priests and government officials. The mocking title placed above the cross and called "Hebrew" was probably Aramaic. Examples of Jesus speaking the language are "'Talitha cumi'; which means, 'Little girl, I say to you, arise'" (Mark 5:41), and "About the ninth hour Jesus cried with a loud voice, 'Eli, Eli, lama sabachthari?' that is, 'My God, my God, why hast thou forsaken me?'" (Matthew 27:46). The Aramaic nickname Cephas, rock, is used eight times in 1 Corinthians and Galatians to refer to Peter. The language barely survives today.

Ararat, Mount
(*see also* Arkologist)

A volcanic snow-capped mountain (16,945 ft.) in eastern Turkey where Noah's Ark is believed to have come to rest after the deluge (Genesis 8:4). It has been called

the second cradle of the human race. Expeditions have been sent to the mountain to find evidence of Noah's Ark. A close reading of Genesis indicates that the Ark came to rest on the *mountains* of Ararat rather than on any specific peak.

> But see, where Persia's beauteous
> clime extends,
> How gloriously diluvian Ararat
> Hath pinnacled his rocky beak
> in clouds ...
> Time cannot mar his glory,
> grand he swells
> As when the Ark was balanced
> on his brow.
> —*Satan*, Robert Montgomery
> (1807–1855).

Archangels
(*see also* Angels; Gabriel)

The second choir of the third hierarchy of angels. St. John the Divine writes of "the seven angels who stood before God" (Revelation 8:2), but only four are named: Michael, Gabriel, Raphael and Urial. Tradition gave the names Chamaea, Jaffle and Zadkiel to the other three. The word archangel occurs only twice in the Bible, Jude 9 and 1 Thessalonians 4:16.

Architrinculus, St.

Mistakenly believed to be the name of the chief steward at the wedding feast at Cana (John 2:9–10). At this feast Jesus changed water into wine. In paintings and stained glass windows of the event the word *Architrinculus* appears next to a fat, jolly fellow. The word is Latin for "chief steward," but the ignorant thought it was a personal name and he became St. Architrinculus.

Argentinian Pelota Players

The Basque St. Francis Xavier (1506–1522) is the patron saint of Argentinian pelota players. Pelota is a game played on a walled court with a hard ball that is struck with a curved basket-like racket fastened to the hand. Jai alai is a variant.

Ark *see* Noah's Ark

Ark of the Covenant

Also called the Ark of God, the Ark of the Law and the Ark of the Testimony. A small gilded chest of acacia wood, 3 feet 9 inches long and 2 feet 3 inches in height and width, carried by poles, which contained the two stone tablets of the law — the Ten Commandments. A tradition says that the ark also contained a vessel of manna and Aaron's rod. The ark was the material representation of the covenant, or agreement, between God and his people. The Israelites carried the ark before them into battle and it accompanied them during their wanderings into the Promised Land. It was so all-powerful that to lay a finger on it resulted in immediate death. To treat a sacred thing with disrespect is "To lay hands on the ark." Any holy thing can be called an ark of the covenant. The Virgin Mary is symbolized by the ark. Her body, the ark of the flesh, sheltered Jesus, who emerged to establish a new covenant. Does the Ark of the Covenant still exist? Christians in Ethiopia maintain that it does. According to Ethiopian tradition, the Ark of the Covenant was brought to their country for safekeeping by Menelik, a son of Solomon and the Queen of Sheba, and is currently under lock and key in the church of St. Mary of Zion in the town of Axum. The Ark has been regularly carried into battle. It is said to have brought victory over the Italians as recently as the Battle of Adowa in 1893. Others have maintained that the Ark of the Covenant is buried on Mount Nebo in Jordan, hidden in a cave near the Dead Sea, or sealed in a secret chamber beneath the temple mount in Jerusalem.

Arkologist
(*see also* Noah's Ark)

Not to be confused with an archeologist, an arkologist is someone who seeks Noah's Ark. Many people believe that the story of Noah's ark is factually correct. After a cataclysmic flood the ark came to rest on Mount Ararat. Many seekers have claimed to have discovered fragments of the ark or to have visited the ark's final resting place. In biblical times, however, Ararat may have referred to the entire country of Armenia, not necessarily Mount Ararat.

Ark's Floor Plan
(*see also* Noah; Noah's Ark)

In 1675 Athanasius Kircher (1601–1680), a Jesuit philosopher, devised a floor plan for Noah's ark with compartments for all the animals.

Deck One: Owls, exotic birds, warblers, kites and coots, starlings and wagtails, ducks, domestic and wild geese, herons, cranes and storks, ostriches, falcons, eagles, vultures, hawks, Indian and Egyptian hens, peacocks, parrots, magpies, kingfishers, partridges, pheasants and grouse, pelicans and spoonbills, birds of paradise, quail, swallows, cuckoos, chickadees, sparrows, ravens, Japeth's room, Ham's room, Shem's room, Noah's room, dining room, kitchen, larder, singing birds, nightingales, larks and chaffinches, fowl, pigeons doves and turtle doves, gyrfalcons and harpies, king birds, crakes, shrikes, titmice and wrynecks.

Deck Two: Straw for the animals, grain for animals, water casks, oats, barley, winter wheat, wheat, lentils and rice, beans and peas, chestnuts, nuts and acorns, butter, cheese, bread and smoked meats, pears and apples, seeds and berries, spices, dried fish, candles and honey, salt metal and minerals, olive oil, firewood, ropes, mechanical tools for the future world, hand mills and oven, iron tools, cloth and utensils, agricultural implements, cattle horses and asses.

Deck Three: Boars and pigs, foxes, wolves, lynxes, unicorns, panthers, tigers, bears, lions, rhinos, elephants, camels, dromedaries, horses, asses, onagers, cats, moneys, rabbits, squirrels, Indian pigs, conies, badgers, porcupines, tortoises, seals, Indian dogs, Maltese, purebreds, greyhounds, retrievers, chamois, reindeer, deer, cattle, goats, sheep, bison, elk, gazelles, bushbucks, hippos, crocodiles, otters, and beavers.

Arma Christi

Latin for "the arms of Christ." Arms, in this case, are the weapons used by Christ to defeat sin and evil — the cross, and the instruments of the passion. In art they are depicted in scenes of the Last Judgment and on shields borne by angels.

> "Put on the whole armor of God, that you may be able to stand against the wiles of the devil"
> (Ephesians 6:11).

Armageddon

Applied to the end of the word or any tremendous battle. In our times the word is frequently used in the context of a nuclear cataclysm. In the Bible, however, Armageddon is not an event but a place. It is located in Israel at Megiddo, in the Plain of Esdraelon, a major battlefield for many centuries. It is alleged to be the scene of the final battle between the forces of good and evil prior to Judgment Day. "And they assembled then at the place which is called in Hebrew Armageddon" (Revelation 16:16).

Army of Andorra

The army of the Principality of Andorra, a tiny country in the eastern Pyrenees between France and Spain (area: 174 square miles; population: 68,000) enjoys the protection of its very own patron saint — Our Lady Help of Christians. In theory all ablebodied males who own a gun must serve. Every recruit is an officer, and the force's main duty is to present the Andorran flag at official ceremonies.

> "There is a Catalan proverb in use over the border. 'Que fa l' Andorra?' This sarcasm of insignificance might be rendered: 'What is Andorra doing?'"
> — *Two Quaint Republics*, Virginia W. Johnson (1849–1916).

Arrow

A symbol of war, the arrow is the attribute of military saints such as Joan of Arc. The arrows used in biblical times were fashioned from reeds or wood tipped with iron. The best-known patron saint of archers is Sebastian (d. c. 288). During a persecution of Christians Sebastian was shot full of arrows and left for dead. Christopher (d. c. 251), George (d. c. 304), and Hubert of Liege (c. 656–727) are also patron saints of archers. A 17th century prayer for the extraction of an arrow is as follows:

> As Nicodemus, that pious and holy man, has drawn the nails from the hands and feet of Our King, which slipped out so easily, let this arrow slip out of you with equal ease; let the Man who died on the High Cross for us help you in this your beginning; repeat this prayer three times, upon the third time take the arrow with two fingers and draw it out.

Ars Moriendi

The art of dying, in Latin. These were popular works of the Middle Ages which instructed Christians on how to achieve a good death and thereby enter heaven. A dying person would usually be depicted with the devil on one hand and an angel on the other. The devil would try to convince the person of the hopelessness of his situation while the angel gave assurance that redemption through the blood of Christ was always possible.

Artist's Bill

In 1865 an art restorer presented the following bill, for work on a religious painting, to an English lord.

To filling up the chink in the Red Sea and repairing the damages of Pharaoh's host.
To cleaning six of the Apostles and adding an entirely new Judas Iscariot.
To a pair of new hands for Daniel in the lion's den and a set of teeth for the lioness.
To an alteration in the Belief, mending the Commandments, and making a new Lord's Prayer.
To new varnishing of Moses's rod.
To repairing Nebuchadnezzar's beard.
To mending the pitcher of Rebecca.
To a pair of ears for Balaam and a new tongue for the ass.
To renewing the picture of Samson in the character of a fox-hunter and substituting a whip for the firebrand.
To a new broom and bonnet for the Witch of Endor.
To a sheet-anchor, a jury-mast, and a boat for Noah's Ark.
To painting twenty-one new steps to Jacob's ladder.
To mending the pillow stone.
To adding some Scotch cattle to Pharaoh's lean kine.
To making a new head for Holofernes.
To cleansing Judith's hands.
To giving a blush to the cheeks of Eve on presenting the apple to Adam.
To painting Jezebel in the character of a huntsman taking a flying leap from the walls of Jericho.
To painting a new city in the land of Nod.
To painting a shoulder of mutton and a shin of beef in the mouths of two of the ravens feeding Elijah.
To repairing Solomon's nose and making a new nail to his middle finger.

To an exact representation of Noah in the character of a general reviewing his troops preparatory to their march, with the dove dressed as an aide-de-camp.
To painting Noah dressed in an admiral's uniform.
To painting Samson making a present of his jaw-bone to the proprietors of the British Museum.

As the Devil Loves Holy Water

A proverb which expresses the unlikeliness of something happening.

As You Sow So Shall You Reap

The evildoer will be punished, according to Galatians 6:7:

"Do not be deceived; God is not mocked, for whatever a man sows, that he will also reap."

Ash Wednesday
(*see also* Lent)

The beginning of Lent, the day after Shrove Tuesday, the seventh Wednesday before Easter. In the early days bishops would sprinkle ashes over the heads of penitents. Later, priests began to make the sign of the cross on the forehead of each parishioner using ashes made from the palms of the previous year's Palm Sunday. "Remember that you are dust, and unto dust you shall return," is recited. Ashes symbolize the transitory nature of human existence.

Ashes to Ashes, Dust to Dust

A formula in the Anglican *Book of Common Prayer* (1549) for the burial of the dead. It emphasizes the transitory nature of the physical body and is often used to indicate ultimate finality or closure. This biblical-sounding formula does not actually appear in the Bible but is based on Genesis 3:19; "You are dust, and to dust you shall return," and on Ezekiel 28:18: "I turned you to ashes upon the earth in the sight of all who saw you."

Ashtoreth
(*see also* Baal)

Hebrew name for Astarte, or Ashtoreth, goddess of fertility worshipped by the Phoenicians and Canaanites. Her worship included sacred prostitution. The "queen of heaven" mentioned in Jeremiah 8:18; 44:17, 25 is probably Ashtoreth.

Asp
(*see also* Serpent)

The asp is mentioned five times in the King James Bible (1611). It was a venomous snake, probably the Egyptian cobra. It was believed to breathe poison. There was a jewel in the asp's head which could only be collected if the asp was lulled to sleep by music. In a similar way a preacher could enchant a sinner and harvest his soul.

"There is more poison in an ill-kept drain ... than in the deadliest asp of the Nile."
— *The Queen of the Air*, John Ruskin (1819–1900).

Aspen

The cross of Jesus was supposedly made of aspen wood and ever since aspen trees have trembled in shame and horror. A common expression is "trembling like a leaf," which is derived from, "trembling like an aspen," or, "trembling like an aspen leaf." (Aspens are trees which have broad flat branches at right angles to their leaves,

which tremble in the slightest breeze.) Another legend says that because the aspen did not bow its crown when the crucifixion occurred, but remained upright and proud, it was punished by trembling.

Oh had the monster seen those lily hands.
Tremble like aspen leaves upon a lute....
— *Titus Andronicus*, William Shakespeare (1564–1616).

Asperges
(*see also* Court Holy Water; Holy Water Sprinkler)

The sprinkling of a congregation with holy water. It comes from the Latin translation of Psalm 51:7, *Asperges me, Domine....*" Purge me with hyssop and I shall be clean." The small brush or sponge on a handle used for the sprinkling is an aspergillum, and the vessel for the water is an aspersonium.

Ass
(*see also* Burial of an Ass)

An animal, also known as the donkey, which symbolizes both good and bad. It is renowned for its obstinacy. The ass came to express humility and meekness because Jesus rode the animal when he entered Jerusalem. However, at the time of Jesus the ass was considered to be an honorable mount. An ass witnessed the Nativity and Mary rode one on the Flight into Egypt. The dark stripes running down the animal's back and shoulders resembled the cross of Christ. The ass also represented those who rejected Christ and were, by extension, foolish and stupid. Because of the size of its penis, the animal represented lechery. A male ass is known as a jackass. The patron saint of asses is St. Anthony of Padua (1195–1231).

Assumption of the Virgin
(*see also* Virgin Mary)

In the Orthodox and Roman Catholic Churches the belief that upon her death the Virgin Mary, mother of Jesus, was bodily taken up to Heaven to be reunited with her soul. This was defined as an article of faith in 1950 by Pope Pius XII (1876–1958). On August 15 the Feast of the Dormition of the Blessed Virgin Mary is celebrated in the Orthodox Church and the Feast of the Assumption in the Roman Catholic.

At Ease in Zion

A euphemism for the idle rich. It comes from Amos 6:1:

"Woe to those who are at ease in Zion."

Athanasian Wench

An English slang term from the 18th century for a woman of easy virtue. It comes from the Athanasian Creed found in the *Book of Common Prayer* (1549). Some anonymous wag noticed that the opening Latin words of the creed, *Quicumque Vult*, mean "Whosoever desires." The creed of St. Athanasius (c. 296–373) states the doctrine of the Trinity and the Incarnation.

"The Athanasian Creed is the most splendid ecclesiastical lyric ever poured forth by the genius of man."
—*Endymion*, Benjamin Disraeli (1804–1881).

Atheists *see* There Are No Atheists in Foxholes

Athletes of God

An early Christian analogy comparing the disciplined Olympian athletes with the martyrs, who suffered in the Roman arenas when pitted against lions and gladiators.

"You were rubbed with oil like an athlete, Christ's athlete, as though in preparation for an earthly wrestling match, and you agreed to take on your opponent."
—*De Sacramentis*, St. Ambrose (c. 339–397).

Athos, Mount

A monastic community situated on or near Mount Athos (6,670 feet), a craggy peninsula in northeastern Greece. Founded in 963, the community has an all-male population of Orthodox monks in 20 monasteries, some of which are situated on inaccessible mountainsides. The monks observe the Julian calendar, which is 13 days behind the Gregorian. "Beardless boys," women and female domestic animals are forbidden. Male visitors are restricted to 120 per day and, without special permission, may stay no longer than four days. Mount Athos, though part of Greece, is self-governing.

"The Holy Mountain Athos, station of a faith where all the years have stopped."
— *The Station*, Robert Byron (1905–1941).

Atilla the Hun *see* Scourge of God

Audry, St. *see* Tawdry

Augustus

Caius Julius Caesar Octavianus (63 B.C.–A.D. 14), the emperor of Rome when Jesus was born. Legend has it that on the day of the birth of Jesus, Augustus asked the sibyl if there was any ruler greater than himself. The oracle replied by depicting a beautiful virgin nursing a baby. A voice then proclaimed *Hae est Ara coli*, "This is the altar of Heaven!" Augustus supposedly dropped to his knees in supplication and refused the senate's offer of deification.

Auld Clootie *see* Clootie

Auld Hornie

A name for the devil or Satan. With the rise of Christianity, Pan, the horned half man-half goat, the pagan god of forests and herds, was transformed into Satan.

Aureole

(*see also* Almond; Glory; Mandorla; Vesica Piscis)

A word derived from the Latin for "gold colored." In astronomy an aureole is a bright ring of light that surrounds the sun. In Christian art an aureole is an elliptical display of golden light which surrounds images of Jesus and the Virgin Mary symbolizing their holy radiance. It must not be confused with a halo, which surrounds only the head. The aureole originated in the Orient and was introduced to the West at the time of Alexander the Great (357–323 B.C.)

Authorized Version *see* King James Bible

Auto-da-Fé

(*see also* Sanbenito)

A phrase meaning "act of faith." The Portuguese spelling is more often used than the Spanish *auto-de-fe* even though it was the Spanish Inquisition that is most closely associated with it. Auto-da-fé was an elaborate ceremony in which victims of the Inquisition, usually apostate former Jews and Muslims, Protestants and those involved with mystical sects, were declared guilty of heresy and paraded through the streets wearing a conical hat like a dunce's cap and a yellow garment. The ceremony, usually held on All Saints' Day or a Sunday between Whitsunday and Advent, included a Mass, an oath of obedience to the Inquisition, and a solemn reading of the sentences. Those who accepted the inquisitors' penances were eventually returned to the bosom of the church. Those who did not were "relaxed," that is, turned over to the tender mercies of the "secular arm." This meant punishment, often a grisly death by public burning. The victims were burnt because the church was forbidden to shed blood. Those who had fled were burned in effigy. Those who died of natural causes were disinterred and their corpses burned. For a particularly bad sinner the faggots were dampened with water for a prolonged roasting. If the sinner repented at the final stage, he might be given the mercy of strangulation. The earliest *auto-da-fé* was in Seville in 1481, and the last was in Mexico in the 19th century.

> Christians have burnt each other,
> quite persuaded
> That all the Apostles would have done
> as they did.
> —*Don Juan*, Lord
> Byron (1788–1824).

Automatic Writing

Words, often attributed to the divine, that are written without the consent of the writer's conscious mind. An example of automatic writing occurs in 2 Chronicles 21:12. "And there came a writing to him from Elijah the prophet saying...." St. Catherine of Siena (1347–1380) was in a state of ecstasy when she wrote her *Dialogue,* and Teresa of Àvila (1515–1582) compared her writing to the speech of a parrot repeating what it had heard without understanding it.

Ave Maria

An ave is a rosary bead. The name of the Ave Maria prayer is sometimes shortened to *ave.* The word can be read backwards as Eva (Eve), symbolically reversing the sin of Eve. Ave Maria are the opening words of a Latin invocation to the Virgin Mary, and the name of the prayer itself. It is also called Hail Mary, its English translation. The prayer is taken from a greeting to Mary by the angel Gabriel, "And he came to her and said, 'Hail, O favored one, the Lord is with you!'"(Luke 1:28). At first priests said the prayer on the fourth Sunday of the Advent, but later it became a lay prayer. In 1326 Pope John XXII (1316–1334) decreed that all Catholics should recite three *aves* morning, noon and night.

> But all his mind is bent to holiness,
> To number Ave-Maries on his beads.
> —*Henry VI*, William
> Shakespeare (1564–1616).

Avignon Captivity
(*see also* Antipopes)

A name alluding to the Babylonian captivity of the Jews, given to the time (1309–1377) when the papacy was located in Avignon, a city in southeastern France. Nine popes reigned in Avignon, under the control of the French. Pope Gregory XI (1331–1378) returned the papacy to Rome in 1378. Antipopes resided in Avignon until 1408. The popes in Avignon lived in the Palais des Papes.

> The Palais [des Papes] has little or no aesthetic interest. Its interest is archaeological and social. Only one open staircase. All the many others, together with endless narrow corridors are cut in the thick walls (8 or 10 ft. thick), as it were secretly. And everywhere are little holes, through which everyone could be spied on by somebody else. An impression unpleasant, mean, and particularly mediaeval.
> —*Journal,* Arnold Bennett (1837–1931).

Axe

An attribute of the martyrs and saints who have been killed by axes, Saints Jude, Matthias, and Thomas of Canterbury, among others. St. Benedict is shown with an axe because he used one to chop down an oak dedicated to the pagan god Thor. The axe is also associated with John the Baptist because he said,

> "Even now the axe is laid to the root of the trees; every tree therefore that does not bear good fruit is cut down and thrown into the fire"
> (Luke 3:9).

B

Baal
(*see also* Ashtoreth; Beelzebub; Jezebel)

A representative of the pagan fertility worship which tempted the Israelites. Baal was the male counterpart of Ashtoreth and the name of many fertility gods. The worship of false gods and idolatry in general is Baalism. The name Baal was compounded with various personal and place names, such as Baalbeck, Baalzebub (Beelzebub), Jezebel and Hannibal (Grace of Baal).

Babel

A place of confusion and noise. Genesis 11:1–9 describes the building of a tower that was to stretch to heaven. God punished the builders for their presumption by causing them to suddenly speak many languages. In the resulting confusion, work on the tower could not continue. The story preserves confused memories of ziggurats, Babylonian step pyramids. Such a structure, 650 feet high in seven levels, was to be seen on the approaches to the city of Babylon. The Tower of Babel symbolizes humankind's towering arrogance, an arrogance to which God will put an end. Babel was a Hebrew word for Babylon. Although not derived from Babel, the usage of the English word babble probably has some connection to the story of Babel. In Sri Lankan tradition the Tower of Babel was as high as 20,000 elephants. St. Jerome (c. 342–420) said that the tower was four miles high. It is commonly assumed that God destroyed the Tower of Babel, but such was not the case. He merely scattered its builders.

> We motored ... to Birs Nimrud which is supposed to be the Tower of Babel, and I need not say isn't (because, partly, there wasn't one, and partly because the one there wasn't was not in that place; but I fear you'll fail to understand me!).
> —*Letter*, Gertrude Bell (1868–1926).

Babylon
(*see also* Rivers of Babylon; Whore of Babylon)

A city on the Euphrates River in present day Iraq. Founded c. 4000 B.C., Babylon was famed for its luxury and for the hanging gardens, one of the Seven Wonders of the World. It was the place to which the Israelites were exiled (597–538 B.C.). Today Babylon is the ultimate representation of decadence, wickedness and obscene wealth. Rastafarians, members of a West Indian sect, use the word to describe modern society in general and White civilization in particular.

> "By the waters of Babylon, there we sat down and wept, when we remembered Zion" (Psalms 137:1).

Babylonian Captivity
(*see also* Avignon Captivity)

The time (597–538 B.C.) when the Hebrews were exiled to Babylonia. After the defeat of the Babylonians by the Persians, the Hebrews were permitted to return home. It is estimated that more than forty thousand people did so. The phrase was also used for the period (1309–1377) when the popes, under French control, resided in Avignon, France.

Bachelor's Porch

A church's north door. Male servants and poor men used to sit along the north aisle of churches and use the north door. Females would sit along the south aisle.

Backward Blessing

Saying the Lord's Prayer backwards was believed to invoke the devil. A curse.

Bad Drivers

Reckless or dangerous drivers, especially cab drivers, have sometimes humorously been called "Jehu." This term comes from 2 Kings 9:20:

> "And the driving is like the driving of Jehu the son of Nimshi; for he drives furiously." (Jehu brought down the dynasty of Ahab and Jezebel, and became king of Israel.)

Balaam
(*see also* Balaam's Ass)

Journalistic slang for stories about two-headed calves and the like, kept for use when hard news is in short supply. It is derived from Numbers 22:28–30, where Balaam's ass spoke with the voice of a man. Balaam was a Gentile prophet who had intended to bring down a curse upon the Israelites. After his encounter with the ass, Balaam had a change of heart and predicted the greatness of Israel.

Balaam's Ass
(*see also* Balaam)

Balaam was a Moabite magician sent to curse the Israelites as they journeyed to the

Promised Land. Balaam's ass proved to be more perceptive than Balaam himself. She saw the angel of the Lord when her master did not. Three times the ass stubbornly refused to move and three times did Balaam beat it. "Then the Lord opened the mouth of the ass, and she said to Balaam, 'What have I done to you, that you have struck me these three times?'" (Numbers 22:28). Balaam then saw that his way was blocked by an angel with a sword. He was moved to bless the Israelites rather than curse them. A legend arose that the ass upon which Jesus rode into Jerusalem was descended from Balaam's ass.

> "[She] continued to dig her toes in like Balaam's Ass, of whom you have doubtless heard."
> —*Jeeves in the Offing*, P. G. Wodehouse (1881–1975).

Balm of Gilead
(*see also* Rosin Bible)

The Balm of Gilead, an aromatic ointment obtained from a small evergreen tree, was a famous healing ointment and perfume. It has the consistency and color of honey. To ask the question found in Jeremiah 8:22, "Is there no balm in Gilead?" is to ask "Is there no relief or consolation for the evils which befall us?"

> "Is there, is there balm in Gilead? Tell me — tell me, I implore."
> — *The Raven*, Edgar Allen Poe (1809–1849).

Balthazar *see* Jeroboam

Banns *see* Forbidding the Banns

Baptism of Fire

Originally this was a term applied to Christian martyrs who had been burned at the stake. Napoleon III (1808–1873) used it to mean a soldier's first experience of combat, and that is the meaning that has endured. The expression can also mean the first encounter with any difficult or stressful situation.

Baptism of Jesus
(*see also* Jesus Christ)

The gospels of Matthew, Mark and Luke record that when Jesus was baptized by John in the Jordan River, the heavens opened, the Holy Spirit represented by a dove descended upon him, and a voice was heard proclaiming Jesus to be God's beloved son. This was the cause of considerable theological speculation. Why was it necessary to baptize someone who was already sinless? It was concluded that Jesus was demonstrating his humanity and his humility by his baptism.

> "Would an enquiry by experimental psychology show a higher standard of conduct on the part of those 'regenerated from original sin' than appears in others not subject to baptism?"
> — *The Rise of Christianity*, Ernest William Barnes (1874–1953).

Baptism Water

Superstitions arose around the water used for baptisms. The water was believed to restore sight so the blind would bathe their eyes with it. Baptism water was used for purification and to "drown the devil." If a baby did not cry at its baptism, the devil had not been driven out.

Barabbas

A criminal who escapes the consequences of his crime is so called. It was the custom during the Roman occupation of Palestine for the people to choose a condemned man to be set free at Passover (Matthew 27:15; Mark 15:6; John 18:39).

They chose Barabbas, a murderer and bandit, over Jesus. A variant reading of Matthew 27:16 gives the criminal's full name as Jesus Barabbas.

> Barabbas with wrists unfettered stands,
> For the world has made him free.
> — *The Way of the World*,
> James Roche (1847–1908).

Barbers

A patron saint of barbers is Martin de Porres (1579–1639), who was a barber-surgeon. The only mention of barbers in the Bible is in Ezekiel 5:1:

> "And you, O son of man, take a sharp sword; use it as a barber's razor and pass it over your head and your beard."

Barlaam and Josaphat, Saints

The legendary tale of these saints is a Christianized and garbled version of the life of Gautama Siddhartha, the Buddha. Josaphat was the son of an Indian king who was confined to a luxurious tower to stop him from becoming a hermit, as was prophesied. Josaphat escaped and learned of death and suffering by meeting a leper, a blind man and an old man. Barlaam, a wandering ascetic, converted Josaphat and taught the prince that true happiness comes from resisting earthly attachments. Josaphat became king, but gave up the throne and became a wandering hermit with Barlaam.

Barnacle Geese
(*see also* Goose)

Mythical sea birds of the British Isles that were believed to be born from pine wood soaked in sea water. When fully developed, the birds fell into the water. Because they did not originate in eggs, people thought that it was permissible to eat them during Lent, if any could be found. However, a papal bull of the 13th century ex-pressly forbade the eating of barnacle geese during Lent. The bird was a symbol of baptism because to be born it was necessary for it to be immersed in water. The legend of the barnacle geese is probably an explanation of migration, since the creatures only appeared in northern lands when fully grown.

Bartenders

Bartenders may be relieved to learn that they have their own patron saint in the form of St. Amand (c. 584 – c. 679). Amand spent most of his life in brewing and wine-making regions.

Bartholomew Doll
(*see also* Bartholomew Pig)

Any tawdry, flashy woman is so named because of her supposed resemblance to the gaudy dolls offered for sale at the fair on St. Bartholomew's Day, September 3. Bartholomew Fair was held in London from 1133 to 1855. The doll or the woman could also be named a Bartholomew baby or a Bartholomew puppet.

Bartholomew Pig
(*see also* Bartholomew Doll)

Someone who is very fat. At the St. Bartholomew Fair it was the custom to roast whole pigs. In William Shakespeare's, *Henry IV, Part II* (1597), Falstaff refers to himself as

> "A little tidy Bartholomew boar-pig."

Basilian Order

The Basilian Order named after St. Basil (c. 329–379) the founder of monasticism, claims to have produced the most high-ranking church leaders: 14 popes, more than 1,800 bishops, more than 300 abbots, and 1,085 martyrs.

Basilisk *see* Cockatrice

B.C. *see* Before Christ

Be Fruitful and Multiply
(*see also* Lord of Creation)

In Genesis 1:28 humanity's reproductive powers are sanctified by God. This verse has sometimes been used as an argument against contraception:

> "Be fruitful and multiply, and fill the earth and subdue it."

Beadsman
(*see also* Rosary)

Someone, often expressly hired for the purpose, who says prayers for others, either living or dead. Beadsmen were usually residents of almshouses who prayed for the soul of the house's founder. A female would be a beadswoman. The beads the beadsman attended to were strung together to form a rosary, each bead standing for a prayer.

Beans

St. Jerome (c. 340–420) forbade nuns to eat beans because he believed them to be aphrodisiacs.

Bear

A symbol of lust because it was believed to mate face to face like humans. Also a symbol of greed because of its appetite for sweet honey.

Bear One's Cross, To

To shoulder misfortune or suffering without complaint. It comes from the gospel accounts of Jesus who was forced to carry his own cross to the place of crucifixion (John 19:17), and of Simon the Cyrene, who was also forced to carry the cross (Matthew 27:32; Mark 15:21; Luke 23:26). Nowadays the expression is often used lightheartedly.

Beard the Lion

To face up to a dangerous opponent is to beard the lion. The expression comes from 1 Samuel 17:35. The shepherd David confronted a lion which had carried off a lamb:

> "I went after him and smote him and delivered it out of his mouth; and if he arose against me, I caught him by the beard, and smote him and killed him."

Bearded Women
(*see also* Uncumber)

Stories are told of St. Paula the Bearded (fourth century) and St. Wilgefortis (Uncumber) who, when faced with the lustful advances of men, sprouted beards and mustaches, thus deterring their would-be ravishers.

Beast, The *see* Antichrist

Beatific Vision

A vision of God granted to a person at the instant of death. Reports of near-death experiences seem to support this belief. Some theologians such as Thomas Aquinas (c. 1225–1274) thought that beatific vision was granted to the likes of Moses and St. Paul throughout their earthly lives. Acts 7:55 reads,

> "But he, full of the Holy Spirit gazed into heaven and saw the glory of God, and Jesus standing at the right hand of God."

Beating the Air

An expression which means useless work, or striking out at nothing. It comes from 1 Corinthians 9:26:

> "Well, I do not run aimlessly, I do not box as one beating the air."

Beating the Devil's Tattoo

Tapping your foot or drumming your fingers to the degree that they annoy others.

Beatitudes

(*see also* Sermon on the Mount)

A common literary form in the Bible consisting of a statement of blessedness. Any supreme happiness or blessings can be called a beatitude. What are commonly called the Beatitudes are short verses of the Sermon on the Mount (Matthew 5:3–11), each beginning with "blessed." In Latin they are *beatus,* blessed, and from that come beatitudes. There is a ninth beatitude if Matthew 5:11 is considered apart from Matthew 5:10:

> "Blessed are you when men revile you and persecute you and utter all kinds of evil against you falsely on my account."

Beaver

A symbol of Christian chastity, asceticism and triumph over lust. In former times the male beaver was killed for its testicles, believed to have medicinal value. When pursued by a hunter, it was believed, the beaver would bite its testicles off. The hunter would stop to collect the desired objects and the animal would escape.

> "The beaver being hunted, biteth off his stones, knowing that for them only his life is sought."
> —*Power and Providence of God,* George Hakewell (1578–1649).

Becket, St. Thomas à *see*
Will No One Free Me of this Turbulent Priest?

Bedlam

(*see also* Abraham-man)

The popular name for an infamous madhouse in London. Founded as a priory in 1247, it became the Hospital of St. Mary of Bethlehem in 1330, and a hospital for the insane in 1547. It was the first such hospital in England and the second in Europe. It has now been officially renamed Bethlehem Royal Hospital. Bedlam has come to mean loud confusion or general uproar. In the 17th century, for a twopence admission, anyone could enter Bedlam and be "entertained" by the antics of the inmates.

> "It's a mad world. Mad as Bedlam."
> —*David Copperfield,* Charles Dickens (1812–1870).

Bee

(*see also* Beehive)

Bees were associated with honeyed words and thus were shown in paintings as coming out of the mouths of great preachers such as St. John Chrysostom (c. 347–407). The bee was also the symbol of vigilance because it was thought never to sleep. Because it stored honey, it represented diligence. The bee is mentioned four times in the Bible (Deuteronomy 1:44; Judges 14:8; Psalms 118:12; and Isaiah 7:18). One of the patron saints of beekeepers is St. Ambrose of Milan (c. 340–397), known as the honey-tongued doctor.

Beehive

(*see also* Bee)

A symbol of the incarnation and the virgin birth because it was believed that bees reproduced by parthenogenesis, that is, without fertilization. The beehive represented the entire Christian community because its members were as united as the bees in the hive.

> "A beehive's hum shall soothe my ear."
> —*A Wish*, Samuel Rogers (1763–1855).

Beelzebub
(*see also* Fly)

A name for the devil or Satan. Beelzebub was a heathen deity called the "prince of demons" (Matthew 12:24). The name means "lord of the flies," and is probably a contemptuous Hebrew corruption. In 1954 William Golding titled his famous novel of the breakdown of civilization *Lord of the Flies*.

> Once early in the morning,
> Beelzebub arose,
> With care his sweet person adorning,
> He put on his Sunday clothes.
> — *The Devil's Walk*, Percy Bysshe Shelley (1792–1822).

Befana, St.
(*see also* Epiphany; Santa Claus)

A mythical saint of Italy, the female counterpart of Santa Claus. The name comes from Epiphany. On Epiphany, or Twelfth Night, January 6, Befana fills the stockings of good children with presents. Naughty children have to make do with bags of ash or lumps of coal.

Before Christ

Abbreviated as B.C., the years dated from before the birth of Christ. The custom of using B.C. was popularized by the Venerable Bede (c. 673–735). The politically correct have begun to use B.C.E., before the common era.

Begats *see* Most Boring Chapters in the Bible

Begorra

An Irish variety of "begad," or, "by God." It is used as a mild oath and in the form of "faith and begorra," has become a comic Irish stereotype.

Behemoth
(*see also* Leviathan)

A great beast mentioned in Job 40:15–24. It was formerly thought to be an elephant but is now identified as a hippopotamus. Anything large and powerful can be termed a behemoth.

> "Behold, Behemoth, which I made as I made you; he eats grass like an ox. Behold, his strength in his loins, and his power in the muscles of his belly" (Job 40:15–16).

Belfry

Although it is the bell tower of a church, the belfry did not receive its name because it houses bells. The name is derived from the Middle English word for a moveable siege-tower. Originally a belfry was a battle tower pushed against the walls of an enemy fort or castle. Sometimes belfries were used as watchtowers and equipped with bells to warn of the approach of an enemy. The church tower resembles the military structure.

> Alone and warming his five wits,
> The white owl in the belfry sits.
> —*Song: The Owl*, Alfred Lord Tennyson (1809–1892).

Belial *see* Sons of Belial

Bell, Book and Candle
(*see also* Anathema)

A literary expression for Anathema, the

severest form of excommunication in the Roman Catholic church. The ceremony includes the solemn reading of a formula. "Cursed be they from the crown of the head to the sole of the foot. Out be they taken from the book of life and as this candle is cast from the sight of men, so be their souls cast from the sight of God into the deepest pit of hell. Amen." A bell is tolled as if in mourning for the dead, the book (of life) is closed and 12 candles, signifying the end of grace, are extinguished. The ceremony demonstrates how the person has been excluded from worship, the sacraments and the society of the faithful.

> The Cardinal rose with a dignified look,
> He call'd for his candle, his bell,
> and his book!
> In holy anger, and pious grief,
> He solemnly cursed that rascally thief! ...
> Never was heard such a terrible curse!
> But what gave rise to no little surprises,
> Nobody sem'd one penny the worse!
> — *The Jackdaw of Rheims*, Richard
> Harris Barham (1788–1845).

Bell-makers
(*see also* Ring the Changes)

St. Agatha was a third-century virgin. Because she refused the lewd advances of a Roman consul she was tortured and had her breasts cut off. In art she is depicted as carrying her breasts on a plate with tongs, pincers or a knife. Because her inverted breasts were mistaken for bells, she became the patron saint of bell-makers. She is also invoked against earthquakes and fires. According to legend, the carrying of a veil from Agatha's tomb has averted eruptions on Mount Etna.

> "Bells, the music bordering
> nearest heaven."
> —*Elia*, Charles Lamb
> (1775–1834).

Belly Button

Adam and Eve probably had no belly buttons. As the first people, they were created fully formed by God. They had no mother to give birth to them and therefore had no need for umbilical cords.

Belly God

Gluttons and others who live to satisfy their gross appetites are said to worship the Belly God. The expression comes from Philippians 3:19:

> "Their end is destruction, their god is the belly, and they glory in their shame, with minds set on earthly things."

Belphegor

The Greek form of the Moabite divinity Baal-Peor, worshipped by the Israelites in Numbers 25:3. In medieval times Belphegor was one of the devil's demons sent into the world to investigate the possibility of happiness in marriage. After a thorough examination Belphegor fled to a place where there were no females. A belphegor is a misogynist or a licentious man.

Belshazzar's Feast
(*see also* Belshazzar's Palsy; Eat Drink and be Merry for Tomorrow We Die; Writing on the Wall)

Belshazzar (fl. 550–539 B.C.) was the last king of Babylon, son of Nebuchadnezzar. In Daniel 5 we read how the king was slain the night after a great feast. Someone who indulges in Belshazzar's Feast is of the opinion that it is wise to eat, drink, and be merry, for tomorrow we die.

Belshazzar's Palsy
(*see also* Belshazzar's Feast; Writing on the Wall)

A fever or palsy. It was at a feast that the handwriting on the wall appeared, an apparition which caused Balshazzar (fl. 550–539 B.C.) to be shaken by palsy.

Bénédictine
(*see also* D.O.M.)

A liqueur originally made in the 16th century by the Benedictine monks at their monastery in Fécamp, France. The secret recipe, which includes 27 spices and plants, was almost lost in the French Revolution. The distilling of benedictine was revived in the 1870s and continues today. Among the known ingredients are cloves, arnica flowers, lemon peel, angelica, hyssop, cardamoms, cinnamon, nutmeg, thyme and peppermint.

Benefit of Clergy
(*see also* Neck Verse)

Centuries ago a member of the clergy was exempt from the jurisdiction of civil courts and was under the protection of the church. Since few but clergymen could read, it came to pass that anyone who was literate and therefore a potential clergyman could claim "benefit of clergy." Under a law passed in 1087, any literate person guilty of a crime could save himself from execution if he could prove that he could read. Of course an illiterate would be without benefit of clergy. The first verse of Psalm 51, the so-called neck-verse, was the chosen passage for the reading test: "Have mercy on me, O God, according to thy steadfast love; according to thy abundant mercy blot out my transgressions." Although it had long fallen into disuse, the law was not repealed until 1700. Benefit of Clergy was based on I Chronicles 16:22 and Psalms 105:15, wherein the anointed were not to be harmed.

> "May you die without benefit of clergy; may there be none to shed a tear at your grave, and may the hearthstone of hell be your best bed forever."
> — Irish Curse.

Benjamin
(*see also* Mess of Pottage)

A pet or the youngest can be so called. The reference is to Benjamin, the youngest son of Jacob (Genesis 35:18). Benjamin's mess is the biggest portion. When Benjamin, the viceroy of Egypt, gave a banquet for his family,

> "Benjamin's mess was five times so much as any of theirs"
> (Genesis 43:34).

Bestiary

A type of medieval book containing allegorical descriptions and moral instruction based on the lives of animals. It was customary for bestiaries to describe the characteristics and symbolism of one hundred beasts. These fanciful accounts of the habits of real and mythical beasts became important sources of symbolism in religious art and literature sometimes rivaling the Bible in popularity.

Betrothal

In former times an engagement required a formal ceremony performed before a priest. Rings were exchanged, which explains the modern engagement ring. The engagement could be broken but the church could excommunicate either party if there was no good reason for its termination. Girls between seven and 12 years of age and boys between seven and 14 could be betrothed but not married.

> "And I will betroth you to me in righteousness and in justice, in steadfast love, and in mercy. I will betroth you to me in faithfulness; and you shall know the Lord"
> (Hosea 2:19–20).

Betrothal and Marriage of the Virgin Mary
(*see also* Divine Cuckold)

In the New Testament a virgin named

Mary was betrothed to Joseph, a man from Nazareth (Matthew 1:18; Luke 1:26). The Apocrypha purports to give further details. Mary was raised in the temple, and when she reached puberty at the age of 12 was deemed ready for marriage. All the widowers in Judea were instructed to assemble at the temple bringing rods or wands. The rod of Joseph, an old man with sons, flowered and a dove emerged from it, signs that he was divinely chosen to be Mary's husband. Joseph was reluctant to marry so young a girl, but he was obedient to God's command, although he did not consummate the union. Pictures of the wedding show the high priest of the temple conducting the ceremony. Seven maidens accompany Mary. Joseph is attended by the rejected suitors holding their rods, some breaking them in bitter disappointment.

Better to Marry than to Burn

St. Paul's opinion of marriage in the King James Bible (1611) was not very complimentary. "I say therefore to the unmarried and widows, It is good for them if they abide even as I. But if they cannot contain, let them marry: for it is better to marry than to burn" (I Corinthians 7:8–9). Some have interpreted burn to mean burn in hell for fornication. The Revised Standard Version (1952) substitutes "to be aflame with passion."

> "Marriage is distinctly and repeatedly excluded from heaven. Is this because it is thought likely to mar the general felicity?"
> —*Notebooks*, Samuel Butler (1835–1902).

Between the Devil and the Deep Blue Sea

When you are faced with choosing between two evil possibilities, you are said to be between the devil and the deep blue sea. The expression is often thought to derive from Matthew 8:28–34, which recounts the miracle in which Jesus cast out devils from two men and sent the evil spirits into a herd of swine. The maddened animals then plunged over a cliff and drowned in the sea. In fact, the expression is probably nautical in origin. The seam in the hull of a wooden sailing ship was the devil. Thus, the distance between the devil and the deep blue sea was not very large.

Beulah Land

When a Christian's faith is so strong that he is entirely without doubt, then he is said to reside in Beulah Land or the Land of Beulah. This phrase comes from Isaiah 62:4, in the King James translation of 1611, which reads, "Thou shalt no more be termed Forsaken; neither shall thy land any more be termed Desolate: but thou shalt be called Hephzibah, and thy land Beulah." Beulah is Hebrew for "married woman," and symbolizes the marriage of Palestine with God. Hephzibah means "my delight."

Bible *see* Abecedarian Psalm; Alphabetical Curiosity in a Bible Verse; Bible-backed; Bible-carriers; Bible-tripe; Bibliolatry; Bibliomancy; Books of the Bible; Chapters in the Bible; Clidomancy; Godless Books; Holystone; Identical Bible Chapters; Identical Bible Verses; King James Bible; Letters in the Bible; Longest Chapter in Bible; Longest Verse in Bible; Middle Book of Bible; Middle Chapter of Bible; Middle Line of Bible; Middle Verse of Bible; Most Boring Chapters in the Bible; Revised Standard Version; Shortest Chapter in Bible; Shortest Verse; Verses in the Bible; Vulgate; Words in the Bible

Bible, Authorship of *see*

Shakespeare the Author of the Bible?

Bible, Unusual Editions of *see*

Adulterous Bible; Affinity Bible; Biblia Pauperum; Bowdlerized Bible; Breeches Bible; Denial Bible; Devil's Bible; Discharge Bible; Ears to Ear Bible; Fool Bible; Forgotten Sins Bible; He Bible; Idle Bible; Incunabula Bible; Large Family Bible; Leda Bible; More Sea Bible; Murderers' Bible; Printers' Bible; Rebekah's Camels Bible; Rosin Bible; Sin-on Bible; Standing Fishes Bible; Sting Bible; To-remain Bible; Treacle Bible; Unrighteous Bible; Vinegar Bible; Wife-hater Bible

Bible-backed

Round shouldered. A condition presumably caused by too much Bible study.

Bible Belt

A term invented by H. L. Mencken (1880–1956) in the 1920s for parts of the Southern United States where belief in the literal truth of the Bible was widespread. Bible Belt has since been applied to other places with conservative social values, and is usually mildly pejorative.

> "Driving around the state [Georgia], one sometimes gets the impression that there are more churches than houses…. There cannot be many other places where one is likely to be confronted by a billboard that says 'God Makes House Calls.'"
> —*New Yorker*, E. J. Kahn, Jr.
> (6 February, 1978).

Bible-carriers

An unkind term for the overtly pious.

Such people liked to be seen carrying the Bible to church.

Bible-tripe

A dialect word from Northumberland, in England. The name for a cow's third stomach, which is thought to resemble the pages of a Bible. There are recipes which actually call for its use.

Biblia Pauperum

The Bible of the poor. Said to have been invented by St. Anschar of Bremen (801–865), these were picture books for the illiterate. Consisting of 40 to 50 pages, they illustrated important Bible stories. Typically each page illustrated a New Testament event with related Old Testament stories on either side. Suitable Latin inscriptions appeared in the margins. Such works were among the earliest printed books, produced first from wooden blocks and later from movable type.

Bibliolatry

Reverence for the words, the syllables, even the punctuation of the Bible carried to the level of idolatry.

Bibliomancy

Idolatrous usage of the words or verses of the Bible for purposes of divination. With eyes closed the seeker opens the Bible at random. The seeker then opens his eyes and the first words he sees are believed to provide the sought-after guidance. Sometimes a finger stabbed randomly on a page is believed to provide the same result.

Bilocation

The ability to be in two places at the

same time. St. Alphonsus Maria de Liguori (1696–1787) was seen at the sickbed of Pope Clement XIV in 1774, despite being confined in a prison four days' journey away. Saints Anthony of Padua (1195–1231) and Ambrose of Milan (c. 340–397) are also said to have been able to bilocate.

Bingo *see* Holy Bingo

Birthdate of Jesus
(*see also* Jesus Christ; Nativity of Jesus)

Jesus was not born in the year 1 as is popularly supposed. Luke records that Jesus was born during the reign of Herod the Great, who died in 4 B.C. The Roman census, the reason for Mary and Joseph to travel to Bethlehem, occurred in 6 or 7 B.C.

Birthstone *see* Aaron's Breastplate

Bishop
(*see also* Metropolitan; Mitre; Nolo Episcopari)

A high-ranking priest who presides over a diocese and who has the authority to ordain lesser clergy. A bishop is also the name of a chess piece, originally called the archer, which moves diagonally. There is a liqueur called bishop consisting of sugared and spiced red wine poured over orange or lemon slices.

> Bishops vary just as much as books. Some are like eagles, soaring high above use, bearing important messages; others are nightingales who sing God's praises in a marvellous way; and others are poor wrens, who simply squawk away on the lowest branch of the ecclesiastical tree, trying to express the odd thought on some great subject.
> —*Letter to Mark Twain*, Pope John Paul I (1912–1978).

Bishop Fish

There was a tradition that everything on land had its parallel in the sea. Thus a bishop fish, in a less than complimentary view of ecclesiastical authority, had a scaly body, mitred head, and in place of arms, two clawlike fins.

Bishop Hath Put His Foot in It *see* Cheese

Bitter End

An expression which means to see something through to the conclusion, no matter what. The bitter end is also a nautical term meaning the shipboard end of an anchor cable. The term may have originated in Proverbs 5:4, "but in the end she is bitter as wormwood."

> ... for 'tis a physic
> That's a bitter to sweet end.
> —*Measure for Measure*, William Shakespeare (1564–1616).

Black

The symbol of primordial darkness, evil, Hell and death. Black is the color used for masses for the dead and Good Friday. Used in the habits of some monastic orders, black symbolizes humility, abstinence and penance.

> "Nay, then, let the devil wear black, for I'll have a suit of sables."
> —*Hamlet*, William Shakespeare (1564–1616).

Black Madonnas

Images of the Virgin Mary and the infant Jesus that have turned black because of centuries of candle smoke or chemical reactions in paint. They are found all over Europe and are often associated with places that were pre-Christian pilgrimage sites.

Other black Madonnas are found in countries where the population is dark skinned.

Blackbird

Because it was black, it was a symbol of sinfulness. Because it also sang sweetly it represented the allure of unchastity. Blackbirds have their own patron saint in the person of St. Kevin (d. c. 618).

> The birds have ceased their songs,
> All save the blackbird, that from
> yon tall ash,
> 'Mid Pinkie's greenery, from his
> mellow throat,
> In adoption of the setting sun,
> Chants forth his evening hymn.
> —*An Evening Sketch*, David
> Moir (1798–1851).

Blasphemy
(*see also* Marked with a B)

Offensive speech concerning matters of religion and disrespectful use of religious symbols. Laws against blasphemy remain on the books, but are seldom, if ever, enforced. In 1968 a judge in Maryland, discovering that the state's 1723 blasphemy statute was still in force, encouraged police to charge drivers with blasphemy if they said "God damn" when receiving speeding tickets. A higher court overruled the judge.

> "Men blaspheme what they
> do not know."
> —*Pensées*, Blaise Pascal (1623–1662).

Blessed Virgin *see* Virgin Mary

Blessing

Among clergy of the Roman Catholic and Orthodox Churches the thumb and first two fingers, representing the trinity, are used in ceremonial blessing. The thumb, being the strongest, symbolizes the Father, the long second finger represents the Son, and the first finger, the Holy Spirit, which proceeds from the Father and the Son.

> "Let the blessing of St. Peter's Master be
> ... upon all that are lovers of virtue, and
> dare trust in his Providence, and be
> quiet and go a-angling."
> —*The Complete Angler*,
> Izaak Walton (1593–1683).

Blind Leading the Blind

In this short, humorous parable Jesus was condemning the Pharisees. The expression has come to denote any stupid or misguided leadership.

> "And if a blind man leads a blind man,
> both will fall into a pit"
> (Matthew 15:14; Luke 6:39).

Blood of St. Januarius

St. Januarius was martyred in 305. In the cathedral at Naples is preserved about an ounce of his blood in two vials. Three times a year, it is claimed, the first Sunday in May, September 19 (the anniversary of the saint's death), and on December 16, the blood liquefies. The earliest record of the saint's blood is in 1389. On September 19, 1799, the blood of St. Januarius refused to liquefy. This angered General Championnet, commander of an invading French army. In a message to the officiating priest of the cathedral he said, "Tell his reverence that if the blood does not liquefy in five minutes I will order the bombardment of Naples." Within the allotted time the blood liquefied and Naples was spared destruction. The blood of St. Januarius has never been scientifically evaluated and the saint may never have existed. Some have speculated that the "blood" may be some combination of blood, beeswax, olive oil and red pigment; the product of a 14th century manufacturing process now lost. St. Januarius is the patron saint of bloodbanks.

Bloodsucker *see* Daughter of
the Horse Leech

Blow One's Horn

To brag. A paraphrase of Matthew 6:2:

> "Thus, when you give alms, sound no
> trumpet before you."

Blue

(*see also* Blue Laws)

Blue symbolizes truth, wisdom and
chastity. Blue is the color associated with
the Virgin Mary, possibly because it is the
color of the sky and thus heaven. Mary is
frequently depicted wearing a blue gown.
The deepest and therefore the best blue was
obtained from lapis lazuli, an expensive pigment. Its very expense was considered to be
an expression of devotion. Blue is also associated with drunkenness. Blue Monday was
the Monday before Lent, a day popularly
spent in dissipation.

Blue Laws

(*see also* Church Organs; Coffee)

Any puritanical law or strict regulation
of Sunday observance is a blue law. The
name comes from laws enacted by the Puritans of New Haven, Connecticut (1638–
1665), which were reputedly printed on blue
paper. In the name of combating heresy,
adornments, clothing and even kissing between husband and wife were regulated.
Work, commerce, sports, traveling and en-
tertainment were all forbidden on Sundays.
A man and woman were sent to trial for the
crime of "sitting together on the Lord's Day
under an apple tree...." A former soldier
was heavily fined for "netting a piece of old
hat to put in his shoe." A sea captain, who
had returned from a three-year voyage on
the Sabbath, was sent to the stocks for the
"lewd and unseemly behaviour" of kissing
his wife on his doorstep.

> "The Puritan hated bear-baiting, not
> because it gave pain to the bear, but be-
> cause it gave pleasure to the spectators."
> —*History of England*, Thomas
> Babington Macaulay (1800–1859).

Boanerges

In Mark 3:17 this was a surname given
by Jesus to James and John, sons of Zebedee, because of their fervid spirit. The
word means "sons of thunder." It also came
to be applied to loud orators in general and
preachers in particular.

Boanthropy

A madness in which a person believes
himself to be an ox. It comes from Daniel
4:33, in which King Nebuchadnezzar was
driven mad and began eating grass like an
ox. Nebuchadnezzar's illness was a specific
form of *Insania zoanthropica*, a madness in
which a person thinks himself to be an animal.

> "Then that's the waters of Babylon.
> Great snakes, that I should have lived to
> see the fields where King Nebuchadnez-
> zar grazed!"
> —*Greenmantle*, John Buchan
> (1875–1940).

Bodysnatching *see*
Resurrection Men

Bog

Bog is the Russian word for God. In
1930 a new schoolbook was issued containing a poem in which the word was used.
The atheists in the Kremlin were horrified
to discover that the word had been capital-
ized throughout. One million copies of the
book had to be recalled and 16 pages re-
typeset so that Soviet children would not
be "contaminated" by exposure to Bog with
a capital.

Bolivian Navy

Despite the fact that Bolivia has been a landlocked country since its defeat in the War of the Pacific (1883), it has a navy. The sailors who operate patrol craft on Bolivia's rivers and on Lake Titicaca enjoy the protection of their own patron saint, Our Lady of Charity.

> "It has never been easy to find many Bolivians who have seen the sea."
> —*Bolivia: Land, Location and Politics Since 1925*, Joan Fifer (1972).

Bonanza

A rich stratum of ore or any source of immense profit. The word comes from the Spanish where it means calm, fair weather, or prosperity. Matthew 8:26 records how Jesus stilled the wind and the sea, "and there was a great calm." In the Spanish translation this is rendered as "una grande bonanza."

Bone of My Bones
(*see also* Adam's Rib; Eve)

The closest possible relationship. The fact that Eve was made of Adam's body emphasizes this relationship between husband and wife.

> "This at last is bone of my bones and flesh of my flesh" (Genesis 2:23).

Boniface, St. *see* St. Boniface's Cup

Book Borrowers
(*see also* Libraries)

Borrowing books from medieval monastery libraries was actively discouraged. Monks were driven to pen curses against the borrower of books.

> "The lending of books ... the smaller without pictures, as the larger with pictures, is forbidden under the penalty of excommunication."
> — Ingulf, Abbot of Croyland (d. 1109).

> Even popes felt threatened by the book borrower:
> "Whoever writes his name here in acknowledgment of books received on loan out of the Pope's Library, will incur his anger and his curse unless he return them uninjured within a very brief time."
> — Pope Nicholas V (c. 1397–1455).

Book First Printed in English
(*see also* Books)

The first book printed in the English language appeared in 1474. It was not the Bible, contrary to what one might expect. At the time the possession of an English-language Bible was seen as evidence of Protestant heresy. The first printed book in English was *Recuyell of the Historyes of Troye* published by William Caxton (c. 1422–1491). William Tyndale (d. 1536) was the first to print parts of the Bible in the English vernacular. He published the New Testament in 1525, the Pentateuch (the first five books in the Bible) in 1530 and Jonah in 1531. He was declared a heretic, strangled and burned at the stake for his troubles. The first complete English Bible was published by Miles Coverdale (c. 1488–1568) in 1535.

Books
(*see also* Book First Printed in English; Libraries)

During the first centuries of Christian Europe manuscripts were very expensive and difficult to reproduce. Only the very rich could afford to buy a Bible, and books were as prized as they were rare. Monastery books started out plain but became more elaborate with the passage of time. Margins were decorated and title pages added with ornamental borders and miniature paintings. The parchment might be dyed purple or green and the entire work lettered in gold and silver.

> "A monastery without a book-chest is like a castle without an armory."
> —12th century aphorism.

Book of Life

A registry in which is written the names of those to be saved on Judgment Day. To be erased from the Book of Life means to die and suffer eternal damnation. The Book is mentioned in Revelation 3:5; 20:12–15; 21:27.

> "And I saw the dead, great and small, standing before the throne, and books were opened. Also another book was opened, which is the book of life"
> (Revelation 20:12).

Books, Banned *see* Index Librorum Prohibitorum

Books of the Bible

(see also Ecclesiastes; Enoch; Godless Books; Middle Book; New Testament Books in Rhyme; Old Testament Books in Rhyme)

There are 39 books in the Old Testament, 27 books in the New Testament and 14 in the Apocrypha.

Boots

The unofficial name given to the bishop in the House of Lords with the least seniority. In order to be appointed to the chamber he had to wait for someone to die; that is, to walk in a dead man's boots.

Born on Good Friday

The power of communing with the spirit world was believed to be given to those born on Good Friday or Christmas.

Born Within the Sound of Bow Bells

The traditional sign of a true Cockney is being born within the sound of the bell-peal of St. Mary-le-Bow Church in London.

Bottomless Pit
(see also Abaddon)

In Revelation 20:1 the name for hell. Today the expression is used to denote something or someone who insatiably consumes all your resources and energy. It is also used for someone who has a huge appetite for food. A nickname given to William Pitt (1759–1806), referring to his extreme thinness, was Bottomless Pitt.

Bounden Duty

A very strong obligation. The expression appears in the *Book of Common Prayer* (1549). Despite the antique language the expression remains in use:

> "We beseech thee to accept this our bounden duty and service."

Bowdlerized Bible

In the 18th century the Rev. Edward Harwood (1729–1794) set out to clean up the New Testament, or, as he put it, "to clothe the genuine ideas and doctrines of the apostles with that propriety and perspicuity in which they themselves, I apprehend, would have exhibited them, had they now lived and written in our language." Every word that was remotely vulgar was replaced with a genteel equivalent. Thus Salome was described as "a young lady who danced with inimitable grace and elegance."

Paul's warning to the church in Laodicea comes out as, "Since, therefore, you are now in a state of lukewarmness, a disagreeable medium between the two extremes, I will, in no long time, eject you from my heart with fastidious contempt." Peter, upon witnessing the Transfiguration, exclaims, "Oh, sir! What a delectable residence we might fix here." Rev. Harwood was proud that his translation of the New Testament "leaves the most exacting velleity without ground for quiritation."

Bowels of Compassion

Mercy or sympathy. In ancient times the bowels were considered to be the seat of the emotions. "Bowels of compassion" is now translated as "heart."

> "Who hath this world's good, and seeth his brother have need, and shutteth up his bowels of compassion from him, how dwelleth the love of God in him?"
> (1 John 3:17).

Boxing Day

The day when alms-boxes in churches were opened and their contents distributed to the poor. It has nothing to do with the sport of boxing. Boxing Day is now held on December 26, but was originally held on the first weekday after Christmas.

> "Poetry's unnat'ral; no man ever talked poetry 'cept a beadle on Boxin' Day."
> —*Pickwick Papers*, Charles Dickens (1812–1870).

Boy Bishop
(*see also* Feast of Fools)

On December 6, the feast day of the fourth century St. Nicholas, patron saint of children, it was the custom to elect choir boys as mock-bishops and other clergy. The other children had to obey the boy bishop until Childermas on December 28. The pseudo-clergy would undertake a burlesque of clerical duties with the authentic clerics taking on the boys' roles. The festivities which developed around this custom grew scandalous and the practice was suppressed during the Reformation.

Boy Pope

An unflattering term given to an extremely young pope. John XII (c. 937–964) became pope at the age of 18 and died at 27.

Boyhood of Jesus
(*see also* Jesus Christ)

Apart from the incident of his debating the priests in the temple at age 12, the Bible has little to say about the childhood of Jesus. Inevitably legends arose to fill the gap. The boy Jesus reputedly stilled a storm at sea, defeated a sorceress, played with lions, walked across a pond, walked up a sunbeam, made live sparrows from clay and healed boys bitten by a serpent.

Boz

A nom-de-plume used by Charles Dickens (1812–1870). Moses was the nickname of a younger brother. As Dickens wrote in the preface to *The Pickwick Papers*, Boz "facetiously pronounced through the nose, became Boses, and being shortened, became Boz. Boz was a very familiar household word to me, long before I was an author, and so I came to adopt it."

Braid St. Catherine's Tresses
(*see also* Catherine Wheel; Mystical Marriage of St. Catherine)

St. Catherine was a pious virgin who died a martyr's death. To braid St. Catherine's tresses is to choose to remain a virgin.

"Thou art too fair to be left to braid
St. Catherine's tresses."
—*Evangeline*, Henry Wadsworth
Longfellow (1807–1882).

Bramble
(*see also* Burning Bush)

Believed by some to be the burning
bush, the miracle by which God was revealed to Moses. The bramble symbolizes
the Virgin Mary's perpetual virginity because

"the bush was burning, yet it was
not consumed"
(Exodus 3:2).

Bread *see* Bread of Affliction;
Break Bread; Not by Bread Alone;
Worst Metaphor

Bread Cast Upon the
Waters *see* Worst Metaphor

Bread of Affliction

Suffering. "Feed him with the bread of
affliction and with water of affliction" (I
Kings 22:27). The verse is now translated as
"bread and water."

Break Bread

The Eucharist. To break bread is to
share a meal.

"And they devoted themselves to the
apostles' teaching and fellowship, to the
breaking of bread and the prayers"
(Acts 2:42).

Breath of Life

The human soul, described as physical
breath given by God:

"Then the Lord God formed man of
dust from the ground, and breathed into
his nostrils the breath of life; and
man became a living being"
(Genesis 2:7).

Breeches Bible

A Bible published by English exiles in
Geneva, Switzerland in 1560 and named
after a peculiar translation of Genesis 3:7.
"The eyes of them both were opened, and
they knew that they were naked; and they
sewed fig-tree leaves together and made
themselves breeches." In modern Bibles,
Adam and Eve sew themselves aprons. The
Breeches Bible is more properly referred to
as the Geneva Bible.

Brendan the Navigator
(*see also* Earthly Paradise)

St. Brendan (c. 485–575) was a monk
and abbot who established monasteries in
Ireland. A ninth century cult arose from stories of Brendan's seven-year voyage in a
leather boat or curragh, to an island in the
mid–Atlantic in search of paradise on earth.
Even the birds and animals he found were
practicing Christians. At one point Brendan celebrated Easter on the back of a whale
thinking it to be an island. Some have
identified Brendan's Isle as Newfoundland.
The wondrous tales of St. Brendan partially
inspired Christopher Columbus (1451–
1506) to sail west in search of Asia. Brendan
is the patron saint of whales.

And we came to the Isle of a Saint who
had sailed with St. Brendan of yore,
He had lived ever since on the Isle and
his winters were fifteen score.
— *Voyage of Maeldune*, Alfred,
Lord Tennyson (1809–1892).

Bricks Without Straw

Unreasonable or impossible labor.
Pharaoh placed such conditions on the cap-

tive Israelites when he made them gather the straw necessary for brick making with no reduction in the quota of bricks to be made (Exodus 5:7–8).

> "And how,' demanded Mr. Brandibal, spearing a kidney, 'was the new Ibsen?' 'Bricks without Shaw,' said Mr. Gloom, dissecting a kipper."
> —*Don't Mr. Disraeli*, Caryl Brahms (1901–1982) and S. J. Simon (1904–1948).

Brothers and Sisters of Jesus
(*see also* Jesus, Family of;
Jesus Christ)

The family of Jesus consisted of James, Joseph, Judas and Simon, as well as four sisters who are unnamed. This posed a problem for those who believed in the perpetual virginity of Mary and that she had but one child, conceived by the Holy Spirit. The explanation was that Joseph had an earlier marriage. The males were half-brothers of Jesus and the sisters were cousins. At first Jesus' siblings were not convinced that he was the Messiah. They went so far as to mock him (John 7:3–5) and for a time thought that he was mad (Mark 3:21–31). But after his crucifixion and resurrection they came to believe in his divinity and joined the early Christian community.

Brown

The color brown stands for simplicity. As used in the clothing worn by some religious communities, it symbolizes death to the world, abstinence, humility, mortification and mourning.

Buddha, The *see* Barlaam and Josaphat, Saints

Bug Bible

An edition of 1535 that translates Psalm 91:5 as, "Thou shalt not need to be afraid for any bugs by night." It is now translated as, "You will not fear the terror of the night." Bug meant bogie and was similar in meaning to terror. Bugs are not mentioned in the King James Bible (1611).

Bugger

A sodomite. The word comes from Bulgarus, a Latin word which means both Bulgarian and sodomite. Later the word came to apply to the Bulgarian Albigenses, an 11th century heretical Bulgarian sect, the members of which were accused of practicing sodomy. The word has come to be used as a term of abuse for an unfair person or a difficult task.

> "We've done the bugger."
> —*Attr.*, Tenzing Norkay (On climbing Mount Everest, 1953).

Bulrush

A symbol of salvation. Baby Moses was hidden in the bulrushes until saved by Pharaoh's daughter.

Burial of an Ass
(*see also* Ass)

To be thrown in a garbage heap, to suffer indignity:

> "With the burial of an ass he shall be buried, dragged and cast forth beyond the gates of Jerusalem" (Jeremiah 22:19).

Buridan's Ass

A person who is indecisive. Dr. Jean Buridan (c. 1292–1358), the rector of the University of Paris, is credited with this famous problem of Christian free-will. A hungry ass is placed between two identical and equidistant piles of hay. Does the animal choose one of the hay piles over the other or does he find it impossible to choose between equals and thus dies of starvation? Many thought that the ass, having no rational basis for choosing, must die of indecision, while others denied that absolute equality was possible. A human being, of course, has free will and can choose. The animal mentioned in Buridan's commentary was, in fact, a dog.

Burning Bush
(*see also* Acacia; Bramble)

A symbol of God's immanence in nature. In Exodus 3:1–6 Moses encounters the angel of the Lord as a flame of fire in a bush that was not consumed. The angel of the Lord is not a separate being but an embodiment of God himself.

Burying at the Crossroads

In the Middle Ages suicides could not be buried in consecrated ground, or with the rites of the church. They were buried at a crossroads.

Butter

Butter was unknown in biblical times, although there are 11 references to it in the King James Bible (1611). A more accurate translation would be goat curd or milk from cows.

> "She brought forth butter in a lordly dish" (Judges 5:25).

Butterfly

A beautiful insect that emerges from a chrysalis and is a symbol of the Resurrection. Its short life and beauty, however, also symbolize futility and vanity. The butterfly is nowhere mentioned in the King James Bible (1611). Angels in the Middle Ages were sometimes depicted with butterfly wings.

> Much converse do I find in thee,
> Historian of my infancy!
> Float near me; do not yet depart!
> Dead times revive in thee.
> — *To a Butterfly*, William
> Wordsworth (1770–1850).

By and By

An expression which now means in the near future. However, when the King James Bible was published in 1611, it meant *immediately*. Mathew 13:21 was translated as, "For when tribulation or persecution ariseth because of the word, *by and by* he is offended." The Revised Standard Version (1952) makes the meaning clearer for modern readers by using the word *immediately*.

By Cock and Pie

A solemn declaration. Cock is an oath which stands for God. Pie is the table or chart which indicated the church service for each day.

> "By cock and pie, sir, you shall not away to-night."
> —*Henry IV, Pt. II*, William
> Shakespeare (1564–1616).

By George

A mild exclamation or oath. It comes from "St. George!" the battle cry of English soldiers in the Middle Ages. St. George (fl. third century) is the patron saint of England.

By Jingo

A euphemism for "by Jesus." Stemming from a 19th century music hall song, Jingo now refers to a bellicose warmonger.

We don't want to fight, but, by jingo,
if we do,
We've got the ships, we've got the
money, too.
—*Song*, George Ward Hunt
(1825–1877).

By the Skin of Your Teeth

The narrowest escape possible. The expression comes from Job 19:20:

"My bones cleave to my skin and to
my flesh, and I have escaped by the skin
of my teeth."

By the Sweat of One's Brow

Hard labor. The expression comes from Genesis 3:19 where Adam was punished for eating the forbidden fruit by being expelled from the Garden of Eden:

"In the sweat of your face you shall eat
bread till you return to the ground, for
out of it you were taken; you are
dust, and to dust you shall return."

C

Cain *see* Abel; Cain-colored
Beard; Cain's Wife; Cainites;
Mark of Cain; Raise Cain

Cain-colored Beard
(*see also* Mark of Cain)

A yellowish or reddish beard has long been considered a symbol of betrayal. Although there is no biblical basis for it, Judas and Cain are usually depicted with yellow beards.

"He hath but a little wee face, with a
little yellow beard, a Cain-
colored beard."
—*Merry Wives of Windsor*, William
Shakespeare (1564–1616).

Cainites
(*see also* Mark of Cain)

A strange group of heretics from the second century. They believed that Cain was innocent of the murder of Abel, and they even justified the betrayal of Judas, the crucifixion, and the inhabitants of Sodom. They even had an apocryphal *Gospel of Judas Iscariot*. Not surprisingly, they were suppressed.

Cain's Wife
(*see also* Mark of Cain)

According to Genesis 4:17, Cain, Adam and Eve's eldest son, had a wife. Who was she and where did she come from? Since Adam's family constituted the first human population, Cain's wife can only have been an unnamed sister.

Caladrius

A magical white bird, also known as the charadrius, with a long neck like that of a swan. Although it is non-biblical, the caladrius is frequently found in the religious art of the Middle Ages. If a sick person was destined to die the bird turned its back, but if the patient was destined to live, the caladrius took the illness onto itself, flew toward the sun and vomited it harmlessly into the air. Because of its bright yellow legs and beak, the bird's intervention was especially good against jaundice. Its dung, applied to the eyes, cured blindness. The bird's whiteness represented the purity of Jesus, who turns his back on nonbelievers and attends to us in our sickness.

Call Me Ishmael

"Call me Ishmael" is one of the most famous openings in literature. The phrase appears in Herman Melville's *Moby Dick*, (1851). The Ishmael of the novel and the

Ishmael of the Bible (son of Abraham) were restless wanderers, the one at sea, the other in the wilderness.

Calvary and Golgotha

The crucifixion is described four times in the Bible, but only in Luke 23:33 does the word Calvary appear. Elsewhere, in Matthew 27:33, Mark 15:22, John 19:17, Golgotha is used. Both words mean "place of the skull." Legend says that Adam's skull was buried there. Golgotha comes from the Aramaic and Calvary comes from the Latin translation of the Greek. Whatever its name, the traditional place of the crucifixion, now occupied by the Church of the Holy Sepulchre, was located near Jerusalem. There is no support for the common assumption that Calvary/Golgotha was on a hill that resembled the dome of a skull.

> When one stands where the Savior was crucified, he finds it all he can do to keep it strictly before his mind that Christ was not crucified in a Catholic Church. He must remind himself every now and then that the great event transpired in the open air, and not in a gloomy candle-lighted cell in a little corner of a vast church, upstairs — a small cell all bejewelled and bespangled with flashy ornamentation, in execrable taste.
> — *The Innocents Abroad*,
> Mark Twain (1835–1910).

Calvary Clover
(*see also* Four-leaved Clover)

A low plant of the pea family. The common three-leaf clover was supposed to have grown in the wake of Pontius Pilate as he traveled to the site of the crucifixion. In each of the three leaves is a small red spot which gives the appearance of a cross. The plant produces a small yellow flower resembling the crown of thorns.

Calvin, John

Because of the common rendition of his name, John Calvin (1509–1564), the great Protestant reformer, is often thought of as English. In fact he was French by birth, and moved to Switzerland. His name is more properly Jean Calvin or Cauvin. Other variants are Chauve, Calvus or Calvinus.

> " ... that Calvinistic sense of innate depravity and original sin from whose visitations, in some shape or other, no deeply thinking mind is always and wholly free."
> — *Hawthorne and His Mosses*,
> Herman Melville (1819–1891).

Camel
(*see also* Eye of a Needle)

A symbol of humility because the animal has to kneel to receive its burden, and a symbol of prudence because it stores water. Because it was believed that camels would mate for an entire day they also symbolized lust. The lust of the female camel came to represent nymphomania. The camel of the Bible is probably the one-humped dromedary. In the Old Testament the camel is a beast of burden and transport, a gift and a form of wealth. In the New Testament the camel is a figure of speech for something impossible or nearly so.

> "You blind guides, straining out a gnat and swallowing a camel"
> (Matthew 23:24).

Camel Through a Needle's Eye *see* Eye of a Needle

Can Anything Good Come Out of Nazareth?
(*see also* Nazarene)

An expression of surprise and mocking disbelief. The reference is to John 1:46.

Nathaniel asked, if Jesus was so great why did he come from an insignificant place like Nazareth?

Can the Leopard Change His Spots?
(*see also* Leopard)

It is impossible to change human nature, is today's meaning of this phrase. Jeremiah (13:23) used it to answer those who denied his prophecies of destruction.

Cana, Wedding Feast at *see*
Water Into Wine

Canaan

Ham, the father of Canaan, looked upon his father Noah's nakedness and he and his lineage were rebuked. "Cursed be Canaan; a slave of slaves shall he be to his brothers" (Genesis 9:25). Since Africans were traditionally considered to be descendants of Canaan this passage has sometimes been used as a justification of slavery. Canaan was also the name of the land promised to the Hebrews and hence came to be used for any land of refuge or for heaven.

Candle

In modern translations of the Bible candles are not mentioned. The King James Bible (1611) has 70 references to candles and candlesticks. These are mistranslations of lamps or lamp stands.

> "Neither do men light a candle, and put it under a bushel, but on a candlestick; and it giveth light unto all that are in the house" (Matthew 5:15).

Candle-holder

Someone who assists to a slight degree.

The reference is to the Roman Catholic Church, where a candle is held for the reader.

> "I'll be a candle-holder and look on."
> — *Romeo and Juliet*, William Shakespeare (1564–1616).

Candlemas Day
(*see also* Virgin Mary)

A Roman Catholic festival commemorating the purification of the Virgin Mary, when she presented the baby Jesus in the Temple. It is held 40 days after Christmas, February 2. The name Candlemas was introduced when candles came into use during the procession honoring Mary. Church candles for the upcoming year, representing Jesus as the light of the world, are consecrated. The festival has been celebrated since the sixth century.

Candy Cane

A 19th century candy maker in Indiana introduced the candy cane as a familiar Christmas treat. He took a stick of white peppermint (white being the symbol of Christ's purity), added three small red stripes (symbolizing Christ's suffering on the cross), one bold red stripe (for the blood Christ shed for mankind), and bent the top. The cane resembled a shepherd's crook because Christ is the shepherd of mankind. Turn the cane upside down and it resembles a *J*, the first letter of Jesus.

Cannibalism

The practice of eating human flesh. References to cannibalism in the Bible include Leviticus 26:29, where it is used as a threat, "You shall eat the flesh of your sons, and you shall eat the flesh of your daughters"; 2 Kings 6:28–29, "This woman said to me, 'Give your son, that we may eat him today, and we will eat my son tomorrow.' So we boiled my son, and ate him. And on the next day I said to her, Give your son, that we may eat him'"; and Lamentations 4:10, "The hands of compassionate women have boiled their own children; they became their food."

> "Is it progress if a cannibal uses knife and fork?"
> —*Unkempt Thoughts*, Stanislaw Lec (1909–1966).

Canonical Age

Ecclesiastical law stated that fasting became an obligation at the age of 21, religious vows could be taken at 16, and that a bishop must be at least 30 years of age.

Canter

The easy gait of a horse that is somewhere between a gallop and a trot. It comes from Canterbury gallop, the relaxed pace maintained by pilgrims as they rode to the shrine of St. Thomas à Becket (1118–1170) at Canterbury.

Cardinals

Constituting the Sacred College, or Conclave, the highest dignitaries in the Roman Catholic Church, next to the pope. Since 1179 the cardinals have had the privilege of electing popes, who always come from their ranks. They wear a red hat as a reminder that they are willing to shed their blood in defense of the Church. Cardinals retire from administrative duties at the age of 75 and cease to be papal electors at the age of 80. The name cardinal comes from the Latin *cardo*, hinge, because the pope's election hinges on them. The common red bird known as a cardinal obtained its name from the red hat worn by the cardinals of the Church.

Carnation
(*see also* Virgin Mary)

A large many-petaled flower associated with the Virgin Mary, brides and bridegrooms. White carnations symbolize pure love; pink carnations, the tears of the Virgin Mary and motherhood; red carnations, marriage and passionate love; and the yellow carnation, rejection. The flower is not mentioned in the King James Bible (1611).

Carol
(*see also* Christmas)

A joyous Christmas hymn. Originally the word meant a round dance and the song that accompanied it. The earliest known Christmas carol in English dates from the 13th century, and the oldest printed book of Christmas carols from 1521.

> It is not a carol of joy or glee,
> But a prayer that he send from his heart's deep core …
> I know why the caged bird sings!
> —*Sympathy*, Paul Laurence Dunbar (1872–1906).

Carriage

In 1611 when the King James Bible was published, carriage meant luggage or burden, not a means of conveyance.

> "And after those days we took up our carriages, and went up to Jerusalem" (Acts 21:15).

Cartaphilus *see* Wandering Jew

Cast One's Bread Upon the Waters *see* Worst Metaphor

Cast the First Stone

To be the first to find fault with someone else when one is equally to blame. The law called for a woman caught in adultery to be stoned to death. Jesus replied with a call for mercy and a warning against those who are self-righteous:

> "Let him who is without sin among you be the first to throw a stone at her" (John 8:7).

Cast the Moneychangers Out of the Temple
(*see also* Den of Thieves)

Any challenge to unbridled commercialism, particularly when associated with religion. Birds were sold in the Jerusalem temple for ritual sacrifices. The moneychangers were there to change Roman money into Hebrew, so the temple taxes could be paid.

> And Jesus entered the temple of God and drove out all who sold and bought in the temple, and he overturned the tables of the moneychangers and the seats of those who sold pigeons. He said to them, It is written, My house shall be called a house of prayer; but you make it a den of robbers (Matthew 21:12–13).

Cat

One of the common forms taken by the devil or Satan. As a cat toys with a mouse so Satan toys with the souls of men. She-cats symbolize promiscuous and lascivious women who ensnare men. The cat, especially the black cat, became associated with death, evil and witches. An exception to the aura of evil surrounding the cat was the medieval *gatta della Madonna*— the cat of the Madonna — which, according to legend, had its litter in the stable as Mary gave birth to Jesus. The *gatta della Madonna* had the mark of a cross on her back. There is no mention of cats in the King James Bible (1611). Gertrude of Nivelles (626–659) is the patron saint of cats as well as of travelers and gardeners.

> Confound the cats! All cats — away —
> Cats of all colours, black, white, grey;
> By night a nuisance and by day —
>   Confound the cats!
> —*A Dithyramb on Cats*, Orlando Thomas Dobbin (19th century).

Catechumens

In the early church this word applied to converted Jews and heathens not yet baptized but receiving Christian instruction. They had a special place in the congregation but were not permitted to be present during communion. The word was later used for any young Christian receiving instruction prior to confirmation.

Catherine, St. *see* Braid St. Catherine's Tresses; Catherine Wheel; Mystical Marriage of St. Catherine; Virgins

Catherine Wheel
(*see also* Braid St. Catherine's Tresses; Mystical Marriage of St. Catherine; Virgins)

This pinwheel, common in displays of fireworks, commemorates St. Catherine, a pious virgin, who was martyred for her faith in 309. Catherine was destined to be torn to pieces when she was lashed to a wheel with hooks in its rim. But in a blinding light the wheel shattered and Catherine was freed. Her escape was brief, however, and she was beheaded. St. Catherine is the patron saint of wheelwrights.

Catholic

Prior to the Protestant Reformation, Catholic referred to the entire community of Christians, the universal church. Since the Reformation the term has referred to the Church of Rome, the Roman Catholic Church.

"He was of the faith chiefly in the sense that the church he currently did not attend was Catholic."
— *One Fat Englishman*, Kingsley Amis (1922–1995).

Cedars of Lebanon

Cedars are found in many places but those of Lebanon are best known because of their frequent mention in the Old Testament. They are symbolic of the Virgin Mary because of their beauty and the healing powers of their sap. The cedar towers over other trees as Mary is exalted over all other women. Today only a few groves of cedars remain in the mountains of Lebanon. A cedar is displayed on the flag of Lebanon where it is a symbol of holiness, eternity and peace. The cedar is also the symbol of Lebanon's Maronite Christians. Describing Lebanon's cedars, one author wrote,

After having been told so often that they are ragged and ugly, I am agreeably disappointed in them. There are about 400 of them, some very fine old trees, grass and flowers growing under them — a heavenly camping ground. At this moment it is too delicious: a low sun, birds singing in the great branches and the pale brown, snow-sprinkled hills gleaming behind.
— *Letter*, Gertrude Bell (1868–1926).

Censorship *see* Index Librorum Prohibitorum

Census

There are two censuses in the Bible. Because they were the basis for taxation, military service and forced labor, they were not popular. When David undertook a census (2 Samuel 14; 1 Chronicles 21), it was seen as a challenge to God, an expression of pride deserving of punishment. For those reasons some Christian sects today refuse to participate in censuses. In Luke 2:1 we learn of a census of people in their birthplaces. This was the reason for Joseph and Mary's journey to Bethlehem where Jesus was born.

"A census ... treats people as if they were units, whereas they are not. Each is a universe."
— *Good Work*, Ernst Schumacher (1911–1977).

Centaurs

Centaurs were monstrous creatures of Greek mythology, horse below the waist and man above, infamous for their drunkenness, violence and licentiousness. In Christian art they represented all things that are lustful. When depicted as a hunter, the centaur reminded the viewer of the devil who hunted souls. But when depicted as an archer the centaur symbolized virtue overcoming evil.

Centaur, n. One of a race of persons who lived before the division of labor had been carried to such a pitch of differentiation, and who followed the primitive economic maxim, "Every man his own horse."
— *The Devil's Dictionary*, Ambrose Bierce (1842–1914).

Centos *see* Mosaics

Cephas
(*see also* Peter, St.; Peter's Fish; Peter's Pence)

Aramaic for rock. A nickname for St. Peter, given to him by Christ (John 1:42). It is equivalent to the Greek *Petros,* Peter.

Chadband

A religious hypocrite. It comes from a character of that name in Charles Dickens's *Bleak House* (1852), an illiterate, gluttonous minister of an unspecified sect.

Chamber Pot *see* Jordan

Chapter and Verse

Detailed proof or an established set of regulations. It comes from the Bible which is divided into chapters and verses and is considered to be the ultimate authority.

Chapters in the Bible

(*see also* Identical Bible Chapters; Longest Chapter in Bible; Middle Chapter in Bible; Most Boring Chapters in the Bible; Shortest Chapter in Bible)

There are 929 chapters in the Old Testament, 260 chapters in the New Testament and 183 chapters in the Apocrypha. The modern division of the books of the Bible into numbered chapters is attributed to Stephen Langton (c. 1150–1228), an archbishop of Canterbury. He may have consulted an earlier system of chapters.

Charadrius *see* Caladrius

Charcoal Burners

The patron saint of all the world's charcoal burners is the aptly named Alexander the Charcoal-burner, who was burned alive c. 275.

Chariot of Fire

In the middle of a whirlwind, Elijah was taken bodily to heaven in a chariot of fire (2 Kings 2:11). A chariot of fire became a poetic device to describe a miraculous transcendence or the overcoming of impossible odds. A popular use of the term occurred in the title of the 1981 movie, *Chariots of Fire*, about two Olympic runners who overcome great obstacles.

Charity Begins at Home

(*see also* Daily Bread)

Before worrying about other people you must provide for yourself and your family. This expression is a paraphrase of 1 Timothy 5:4:

"If a widow has children or grandchildren, let them first learn their religious duty to their own family and make some return to their parents; for this is acceptable in the sight of God."

Charlemagne

Founder of the Holy Roman Empire, ruler of most of Western Europe, and defender of the Church. According to legend, Charlemagne (c. 742–814) will rise crowned and armed on the day the antichrist appears.

Cheating the Devil

To use ill-gained riches for a good purpose.

Cheese

In the *Five Hundred Points of Good Husbandry* (1573), by Thomas Tusser (c. 1524–1580), for a cheese to be perfect it must not be salty like Lot's wife, poor like Lazarus, hairy like Esau, full of whey like Mary Magdalene, full of maggots or gentils like the Gentiles or made of burnt milk like a bishop. The last refers to an old expression for burnt milk, "The bishop hath put his foot in it." Cheese is mentioned three times in the King James Bible (1611).

Cherubim

(*see also* Angels)

The second highest order of angels, celestial beings who carried or supported God's throne. It is only since the 16th century that they have been depicted as beautiful, innocent babies with wings (hence the adjective, cherubic). In Ezekiel 10:1–12 the Cherubim have four faces: human, lion, ox and eagle. Two cherubs, armed with a flaming sword, stood guard at the east side of Eden to prevent sinful mankind's return (Genesis 3:24).

> "Patience, thou young and rose-lipped cherubin...."
> — *Othello*, William Shakespeare (1564–1616).

Chi-rho *see* Labarum; XP

Chickens Into Turtles

When St. Hugh of Grenoble (1053–1132) discovered monks eating roast chicken in defiance of the rules of his order, he made the sign of the cross and the fowls were instantly transformed into turtles. Turtles were considered to be a variety of fish and the monks were allowed to eat them.

Child Blessed by Jesus

Tradition says that the child Jesus placed in the midst of his disciples, to teach them humility (Matthew 18:1–6; Mark 9:33–37), grew up to be St. Ignatius, Bishop of Antioch. Because he refused to sacrifice to idols Ignatius was martyred in the Roman Colosseum c. 107. He is depicted standing between two lions.

Childbirth

St. Margaret of Antioch was a legendary virgin martyr. When she refused a powerful man's sexual advances because she was a Christian, he had her tortured and thrown into prison, where she was swallowed by a dragon. When she made the sign of the cross, a cross materialized, grew large and split open the belly of the dragon, allowing Margaret to emerge unharmed. St.

Margaret is the patron saint of women in childbirth.

> "At the moment of childbirth, every woman has the same aura of isolation, as though she were abandoned, alone."
> — *Doctor Zhivago*, Boris Pasternak (1890–1960).

Childermas

(*see also* Massacre of the Innocents)

This festival held on December 28 commemorates the slaughter of innocent children by Herod (Matthew 2:16). It was long considered an unlucky day. It is now called Holy Innocents' Day. The custom in former times was to whip children on this day, for their own good, of course.

Children's Crusade

Any farfetched scheme. In the summer of 1212 thousands of children from France and Germany set out to liberate Jerusalem from the Muslims by love rather than force. They had answered the call of a couple of shepherd boys who had seen miraculous visions. As many as 50,000 children may have taken part. Some marched to ports in the south of France; others crossed the Alps into Italy. Some of the children returned home but most vanished, probably sold into slavery. It was not a true crusade in that the civil and church authorities did not support it.

Children's Teeth Set on Edge

To set your teeth on edge is to become very uncomfortable. There was a proverb which claimed that family members had a joint moral responsibility (Ezekiel 18:2–3). Jeremiah rejects this and proclaims individual moral responsibility.

> "In those days they shall no longer say: 'The fathers have eaten sour grapes, and the children's teeth shall be set on edge.' But every one shall die for his own sin;

each man who eats sour grapes, his teeth shall be set on edge" (Jeremiah 31:29–30).

Chimaera *see* Chimera

Chimera

An improbable or wild fancy. A chimera was a fire-breathing female monster from Greek mythology. It had the head of a lion, the body of a goat and the tail of a serpent or dragon. It appeared in Christian art and came to mean anything impossible or absurd. It was sometimes depicted as having three heads.

"What a chimera, then, is man! What a novelty, what a monster, what a chaos, what a subject of contradiction, what a prodigy!"
— *Thoughts*, Blaise Pascal (1623–1662).

Chosen People

The Jews were the instrument chosen by God to fulfill his earthly purpose. The expression has been used, sometimes facetiously, by other groups of people who felt they have been marked by God, or some other authority, for a special purpose.

"To be a Jew is a destiny."
— *And Life Goes On*, Vicki Baum (1888–1960).

Chrism

The name for the consecrated oil used in the Roman Catholic, Orthodox, Anglican and Lutheran Churches for confirmation, ordination and extreme unction. Pure olive oil is used for the latter, a mixture of oil and balsam for the others. The oil represents spiritual strength and grace. The balsam suggests virtue.

Chrisom *see* Chrism

Christ
(*see also* Jesus Christ; Messiah; Nativity of Jesus)

Derived from the Greek *Christos*, a transliteration of the Hebrew *Messiah*, "the Anointed One." In ancient Israel to anoint with oil, a very valuable commodity, was to endow a person with superior powers or exalted office. Gradually the Christ came to be seen as the redeemer. The word was originally used as a noun and was the title given to Jesus of Nazareth, *the Christ*, by his disciples. After his death it was used as a proper name and the followers of Jesus Christ were called Christians.

"All history is incomprehensible without Christ."
— *Life of Christ*, Ernest Renan (1823–1892).

Christ of the Trades
(*see also* Jesus Christ)

Christ was reputed to have followed the trade of Joseph, his earthly father, and worked as a carpenter. The Christ of the Trades is a depiction of Jesus surrounded by the tools of various occupations. It is meant to emphasize the dignity of labor.

"Sweet is the sleep of a laborer, whether he eats little or much" (Ecclesiastes 5:12).

Christian

The name applied to the followers of Christ (Acts 11:26) in the first century. It was first used by the heathens of Antioch, a city now in Turkey. To begin with, it was probably an insulting nickname.

Onward, Christian soldiers!
Marching as to war,
With the Cross of Jesus
Going on Before.
— *Onward, Christian Soldiers*, Sabine Baring-Gould (1834–1924).

Christian Imagery on Flags
(*see also* Crosses on Flags; St. Andrew's Cross; Union Jack)

The flag of the Vatican features the keys of St. Peter, which are the keys of the kingdom of heaven; the Irish tricolor has a green stripe for Roman Catholics, orange for Protestants and white for peace between the two groups. The flag of Malta is red and white, the colors of the Knights of St. John of Jerusalem; it also has a St. George's cross. The Greek flag displays a white cross as a symbol of the country's Christian faith. The shield in the center of the Portuguese flag features five white dots representing the five wounds of Christ. A yellow symbol on the flag of Vanuatu represents the peace and light of Christianity. The Dominican Republic's flag has a white cross for Roman Catholicism and a shield with a cross and a Bible. The flag of the British Virgin Islands contains a shield with St. Ursula the wise virgin, after whom the islands were named. A bishop's mitre and crosier appear on the flag of Andorra. The motto "Our Faith is Our Strength" is on the flag of Tristan da Cunha.

Christian Name

A person's first name. The term was originally *christened name*, the name given at christening.

Christmas
(*see also* Carol; Christmas Card; Christmas Tree; Holly; Nativity of Jesus; Xmas)

Christ's Mass, the festival of Christ's nativity, is celebrated by the majority of Christians on December 25. The Orthodox Church celebrates on January 6. The Bible gives no specific date for Christ's birth. April 19, May 20 and November 17 have all been suggested. The earliest mention of Christmas on December 25 is in 325. It was probably an attempt to syncretize pagan beliefs and festivities associated with the rebirth of the sun at the winter solstice with Christianity. Since one of Christ's titles is "the true sun," the date was a natural fit. It is exactly nine months from March 25, the date of the Incarnation.

> At Christmas play, and make good cheer,
> For Christmas comes but once a year.
> — *Five Hundred Points of Good Husbandry*, Thomas Tusser (c. 1524–1580).

Christmas Card
(*see also* Christmas)

The first Christmas card was designed in 1843. It featured a happy family toasting the holiday season with wine. About one thousand Christmas cards were sold that year.

Christmas Island

Christmas Island is an Australian external territory in the Indian Ocean southwest of Java. The uninhabited island, 52 square miles, received its name because it was discovered by Europeans on December 25, 1643. It now has a population of approximately 1,280, 30 percent of whom are Christians.

Christmas Tree
(*see also* Christmas)

The custom of decorating an evergreen tree—a symbol of immortality and resurrection, originated in the 16th-century Germany. The Germans adorned the tree with apples, roses and colored paper. The custom was popularized in England by Prince Albert of Saxe-Coburg-Gotha (1819–1861), the consort of Queen Victoria (1819–1901). Isaiah 60:13 says, "The glory of Lebanon shall come to you, the cypress, the plane and the pine, to beautify the place of my sanctuary." Martin Luther (1483–1546) may have been the first to decorate trees with candles. Coming home one evening, he was struck by the beauty of the starry night sky and decided to duplicate it indoors. Christmas trees were brought to America by German immigrants. Americans at first thought the custom of a decorated tree idolatrous until they realized that their German neighbors were not worshipping it. The earliest recorded use of the term Christmas tree by English speakers was in 1838.

Christmas of the Gentiles *see* Epiphany

Christopher, St.

The patron saint of travelers. The name originally meant Christ-bearer for that was literally what Christopher was. Christopher was a giant with immense strength who stood by a river bank to help travelers cross safely. One day he carried a child on his shoulders, a child who seemed to grow heavier with each step. Christopher complained that he could carry no greater weight. The child replied that Christopher had borne all the world upon him and all its sins. The child was Christ, of course, and the stream was the river of death. According to tradition, Christopher was beheaded in the third century for refusing to renounce his faith. Before he died, he prayed that all who saw him would be safe from storms, earthquakes and fires. Though St. Christopher is probably fictitious, his image, in the form of medallions, is still popular.

Church a Woman, To

When a woman has given birth and returns to church to give thanks for a safe delivery. The custom is based on the Jewish rite of purification (Leviticus 12:6).

Church Organs
(*see also* Blue Laws; Coffee; Puritan Names)

Because the Puritans so strongly disapproved of music in churches, they removed the organs. The action of the Puritans backfired because it led to the tradition of the music hall. When the surplus instruments were purchased cheaply by tavern keepers, they began offering musical evenings. An anonymous French tourist, writing in 1659 did not approve:

> That nothing may be wanting to the height of luxury and impiety of this abomination, they have translated the organs out of the churches to set them up in taverns, chaunting their dithyrambics and bestial bacchanalias to the tune of these instruments which were wont to assist them in the celebration of God's praises.

Churchwarden

A long clay pipe supposedly favored by churchwardens.

> "I was teetering on my heels the other evening before our fireplace, quaffing a tankard of mulled ale, puffing on a churchwarden, and waiving both in unison to a rousing stave...."
> —*Chicken Inspector no. 23*, S. J. Perelman (1904–1979).

Churchyard Cough

A loud, hacking cough suggesting imminent death and burial in the churchyard.

> 'Tis now the very witching time of night,
> When churchyards yawn, and hell itself breathes out
> Contagion to this world....
> —*Hamlet*, William Shakespeare (1564–1616).

Circle
(*see also* Ring)

Because it has no end or beginning the circle stands for eternity. Three intertwined circles symbolize the Trinity.

> I'm up and down and round about,
> Yet all the world can't find me out;
> Though hundreds have employed
>   their leisure,
> They never yet could find my measure.
> —*On a Circle*, Jonathan Swift
>   (1667–1745).

Circumcision of Jesus
(*see also* Foreskin of Christ)

Jesus was raised according to Jewish tradition and was circumcised "at the end of eight days" (Luke 2:21). Where the procedure was carried out and by whom was a matter of some speculation. Some said that the circumcision was done in the stable by Joseph, Jesus' earthly father. Others, interpreting Leviticus 12 to mean that the mother should perform the act, said that Mary circumcised her baby. The latter image was too shocking to be commonly depicted in art. The usual artistic rendering has the circumcision performed by a temple priest, with Joseph and Mary in attendance.

> "He is a Jew who is one inwardly, and real circumcision is a matter of the heart" (Romans 2:29).

Cities of Refuge

Six walled cities in ancient Palestine, three on either side of the Jordan River, intended as places of refuge for those guilty of unintentional manslaughter. Within the cities and for 1,000 yards around them the guilty person was safe from blood revenge. If the refugee was found guilty of premeditated murder, the right of refuge was revoked.

> "Say to the people of Israel, 'Appoint the cities of refuge, of which I spoke to you through Moses'" (Joshua 20:2).

Clay in the Potter's Hand

Someone who is easily lead or dominated.

> "Behold like the clay in the potter's hand, so are you in my hand, O house of Israel" (Jeremiah 18:6).

Cleanliness is Next to Godliness

Contrary to popular opinion, this sentiment is not directly expressed in the Bible. Religious reformer John Wesley, in his journal of February 12, 1772, writes, "Cleanliness is indeed next to godliness," in quotation marks. He was probably quoting a current saying. Similar ideas that physical cleanliness supports religious purity can be traced to Aristotle and the Talmud.

Clergyman's Throat

Chronic inflammation of the throat, an occupational ailment of preachers, teachers, street hawkers and others who must constantly use their voices.

Clerk

A word derived from the slurred pronunciation of cleric. Clerks were originally considered to be scholars and clerics were scholars, because they could read and write.

> "The greatest clerks be not the wisest men."
> —*The Reeve's Tale*, Geoffrey Chaucer (c. 1343–1400).

Clidomancy
(*see also* Key and Bible)

The use of a key, a Bible and a virgin's

index finger for divination. The name of a crime was inscribed on a key. The key and a Bible were then suspended from the finger of a virgin. The movement of the key and the Bible "proved" innocence or guilt when the name of the culprit was read out.

Climb the Walls

Driven to frenzy by boredom or frustration. The expression comes from Joel 2:7, where the wall referred to was a town's defensive perimeter. In contemporary usage what is climbed is always plural:

> "They shall run like mighty men; they shall climb the wall like men of war."

Clootie

Also Auld Clootie. Scottish dialect for the devil or the old devil. A clootie is a cloven hoof. There is also a clootie dumpling.

> O thou! Whatever title suit thee
> Auld Hornie, Satan, Nick, or Clootie.
> —*Address to the Deil*, Robert
> Burns (1759–1796).

Cloud Like a Man's Hand, A

A small thing which foreshadows a momentous event.

> "Behold, a little cloud like a man's hand is rising out of the sea ... And in a little while the heavens grew black with clouds and wind, and there was a great rain" (1 Kings 18:44–45).

Cloven Hoofed

An attribute of the satanic or grotesque. Moses declared that animals with cloven hoofs were the only ones fit to be eaten or sacrificed (Leviticus 11:3, 7, 26; Deuteronomy 14:7). A tradition of the Middle Ages gave the devil cloven hoofs. No matter how cleverly Satan disguised himself, his cloven hoofs would give him away. Pagan gods were sometimes bovine creatures with cloven hoofs.

Clover *see* Calvary Clover

Clowns

The patron saint of clowns, actors and comedians is Genesius of Rome (d. c. 303). In the middle of a play mocking Christianity he received the word of God and was converted on stage.

Coals of Fire

To heap coals of fire on someone's head is an Old Testament expression meaning to return good for evil. It has nothing to do with warfare or punishment. By forgiving an enemy you will make him uncomfortable in his sinfulness.

> "If your enemy is hungry, give him bread to eat; and if he is thirsty, give him water to drink; for you will heap coals of fire on his head, and the Lord will reward you" (Proverbs 25:21–22).

Coat of Many Colors

According to Genesis 37:3, as found in the King James Bible (1611), Joseph, Rachel's first born, was given a "coat of many colors." This expression of preference aroused such jealousy in his brothers that they had him sold into slavery. To hide their crime the coat was smeared with blood as "proof" that Joseph had been killed by a wild animal. The Revised Standard Version (1952) translates the phrase less memorably as "a long robe with sleeves."

Cock *see* Cock Crows at Dawn

Cock and Bull Story

Any long-winded, incredible or absurd tale. Various explanations have been given for the origin of this term but one has it that it comes from official statements of the pope. Seals or *bulla* were attached to such documents. The seals contained the image of St. Peter and the cock that crowed three times when he denied Jesus. After the Protestant Reformation any empty discourse came to be called a cock and bull story.

Cock Crows at Dawn

The cock is the male of the common domestic fowl. It is associated with the passion of Christ because St. Peter denied Christ three times before the cock's crow (John 13:38). That ghosts vanish at the crow of a cock is an old superstition. The cock was placed on a church steeple as a watcher where it symbolized the Christian's need to be alert against the devil's temptations. An old superstition had it that ghosts would vanish at cock's crow.

> But even then the morning cock
> crew loud,
> And at the sound it [the ghost of Ham-
> let's father] shrunk in haste away,
> And vanished from our sight.
> — *Hamlet*, WilliamShakespeare
> (1564–1616).

Cockatrice
(*see also* Weasel)

A mythical creature also called a basilisk, the cockatrice was a small, feathered, lizard-like creature whose glance and breath were said to be fatal. In Isaiah 11:8 the creature symbolizes the conquest of evil: "The weaned child shall put his hand on the cockatrice' den." In Jeremiah 8:17 it symbolizes the devil or torment: "For, behold, I will send serpents, cockatrices, among you,

which *will* not *be* charmed, and they shall bite you, saith the Lord." The cockatrice had fierce red eyes, yellow and black skin, the tail of a snake, and the head, legs and wings of a cock. It was said to be hatched by a serpent from a yokeless egg laid by a seven-year-old cock. It was hatched by a toad on a bed of dung. A weasel (which always died), a crowing cock, or the sight of its own reflexion in a mirror were the only things which could kill a cockatrice.

> It is a basilisk unto mine eye;
> Kills me to look on't.
> — *Cymbeline*, William Shakespeare
> (1564–1616).

Cockle

A weed found in fields of grain. Since a weed can infiltrate barley (Job 31:40), the cockle symbolizes the evil which can insidiously destroy a Christian community.

Cockney *see* Born Within the Sound of Bow Bells

Coffee
(*see also* Blue Laws; Church Organs; Puritan Names)

In 17th century England the drinking of coffee, especially in coffeehouses, became all the rage. The Puritans were against the consumption of coffee because it led to idleness and loose talk. The drinkers would

> "Trifle away their time, scald their
> chops, and spend their money, all for a
> little base, black, thick, nasty, bitter,
> stinking, nauseous puddle water"
> — *The Women's Petition Against
> Coffee* (1674).

Collop Monday

The day before Shrove Tuesday, so named from the custom of eating eggs and salted meat. A collop was a small piece of fried meat.

> It is a dear collop
> That is cut out of th' own flesh.
> —*Proverbs*, John Heywood
> (c. 1497–c. 1580).

Colors *see* Black; Blue; Brown; Green; Orange; Red; Sacred Purple; White; Yellow

Columbine

A common flowering herb, of at least 40 species, found throughout Eurasia and North America. Because its name is reminiscent of the Latin *columba* (dove), the plant symbolizes the Holy Spirit. The seven flowers on the stalk represent the Seven Gifts of the Holy Spirit: wisdom, understanding, counsel, fortitude, knowledge, righteousness and fear of the Lord.

Columbus, Christopher

Christopher Columbus (1451–1506) drew upon a passage in the Apocrypha to estimate the width of the Atlantic Ocean:

> "The seventh part, namely where the water was gathered" (2 Esdras 6:50).

Come Let Us Reason Together

Hope for the sinful.

> "Come now, let us reason together, says the Lord: though your sins are like scarlet, they shall be as white as snow; though they are red like crimson, they shall become like wool" (Isaiah 1:18).

Come to Pass, To

Something that must happen.

> "And it came to pass in those days, that there went out a decree from Caesar Augustus that all the world should be taxed" (Luke 2:1).

Common Names

The name Jesus was not unique to Jesus Christ. During the lifetime of Jesus of Nazareth, Jesus was a common name in Palestine. By one modern study it was determined to be the eighth most common name for males. Flavius Josephus (c. 37–100) in his books *The Jewish Wars* and *Jewish Antiquities*, mentions no fewer than 21 people named Jesus. A variant reading of Matthew 27:16 gives the full name of the criminal released at Passover in place of Jesus of Nazareth: Jesus Barabbas. There are others named Judas beside Judas Iscariot, including a Judas who was the brother of Jesus.

Communal Life *see* All Things in Common

Conclave

The name for a set of small cells in the Vatican where cardinals gather in strict seclusion to choose a pope. It is also the name of the assembly of cardinals itself. The word is derived from the Latin for "with key." When a pope dies, the cardinals are locked away until, by at least a two-thirds vote, they choose a new pope. The conclave system was put in place in 1271 to force a papal election after a three-year deadlock. The term more generally refers to an exclusive assembly or discussion.

Concordance, Bible *see* Alexander the Corrector

Concordat

A formal agreement between a government and the pope concerning religious matters. The Concordat of 1929 between the papacy and the government of Italy established the Vatican City State.

Conscience *see* Still Small Voice

Consummatum Est

The last words of Christ on the cross, in Latin. "It is finished" (John 19:30).

> Mep.: O, what will I not do to obtain
> his soul?
> Faust.: Consummatum est; this
> bill is ended.
> —*Doctor Faustus*, Christopher
> Marlowe (1564–1593).

Conventicle

An unauthorized or secret meeting, especially a religious one. Originally the word was used by the early Christians for their meeting places. Their persecutors used the word in a derisive sense.

Conversion *see* Road to Damascus

Coral

When the Christ child holds a piece of coral, it symbolizes protection from Satan. It was believed that red coral protected from witchcraft and the evil eye. Christian babies had bells of coral placed on their cribs to scare away the devil. The coral is mentioned in Job 28:18 and Ezekiel 27:16.

Cordon Bleu

Originally this was a medal suspended from a blue ribbon. It was awarded to the Knights of St. Esprit (Holy Spirit). The knights became known for the fine cuisine they served and it is from this that the modern meaning of cordon bleu arose — excellence in cooking.

> "The discovery of a new dish does more
> for the happiness of man than the
> discovery of a star."
> —*Physiologie du Gout*, Anthelme
> Brillat-Savarin (1755–1826).

Corn in Egypt

Abundance. The expression comes from the story of Joseph in Egypt (Genesis 42:2):

> "Behold I have heard that there is grain
> in Egypt; go down and buy grain for us
> there, that we may live, and not die."

Cornerstone

A stone which traditionally completes the construction of a building. It is laid at the base of a building at the intersection of two walls. Christ is so called in Ephesians 2:20 because he completed the prophecies of the Old Testament. In Psalms 144:2 daughters are likened to cornerstones because as wives and mothers they unite families.

> "The stone which the builders refused is
> become the head stone of the corner"
> (Psalms 118:22).

Corruptio Optimi Pessima

The better a thing is the worse it becomes when corrupted. A phrase used by the Latin Fathers of the Church about bad priests. Afterwards it came to be used to describe the sins of all those who had received grace.

Corsned *see* Ordeals: Ordeal of the Eucharist

Court Holy Water
(*see also* Asperges; Holy Water Sprinkler.)

Flattering speech that means nothing. Holy water is water blessed by a priest and used to convey blessings and symbolically cleanse from sin.

> "O nuncle, court holy-water in a dry
> house is better than this rain-water
> out o' door."
> —*King Lear*, William Shakespeare
> (1564–1616).

Courteous Spaniard, The

St. Lawrence was a Christian deacon from Spain, martyred in 258. Four centuries after his death, Lawrence's tomb was opened to receive the body of another saint. Lawrence is reputed to have moved aside to make room for the newcomer, thus earning the title of "the Courteous Spaniard." He was renowned for his humility and his miraculous cures. It was said that he was given the power to release one soul from Purgatory every Friday. Lawrence was roasted to death on a gridiron in the presence of Emperor Valerian (d. 269). Before he died he said to Valerian, "You have done me on one side, turn me over so that you may eat me well-done on the other." Christians saw this as an example of fortitude. Lawrence's torturers saw it as an example of the saint's laziness, giving rise to the expression, "As lazy as Lawrence."

Crane

A family of long necked, long-legged birds distributed throughout the world. For Christians they came to symbolize loyalty because of a legend that they gather in a circle to protect their leader from danger. A crane also personified vigilance because it stood on one leg and held a stone in the other. If the bird fell asleep it would drop the stone and thus wake itself up. The bird is mentioned in Isaiah 38:14 and Jeremiah 8:7.

Creation, The

Everyone knows that God created the world in six days and rested on the seventh (Genesis 1). But did He? A close reading of Genesis gives a second story of the Creation (Genesis 2:4–25). In this account no period of time is given and the order in which things were created differs. Scholars worked to determine the precise date of the creation of the world. When God divided day from night (Genesis 1:4), it was deduced that he made them of equal duration. The vernal equinox, March 25 in the Julian calendar, marks the division. An Irish bishop, James Ussher (1581–1656) came up with noon October 23, 4004 B.C. as the exact time and date of Creation. The bishop arrived at his date after meticulously comparing ancient historical records, Old Testament events and calendars. He assumed that light must have been created at midday.

> Light was first
> Through the Lord's word
> Named day:
> Beauteous, bright creation!
> —*Creation*, Caedmon
> (seventh century).

Creature
(see also Drunkard; Hangover; Martin Drunk)

A facetious reading of I Timothy 4:4 — "For every creature of God is good and nothing to be refused, if it be received with thanksgiving."—was used to justify the consumption of alcohol. Wine and other spirits came to be euphemistically called the creature.

> "I find my master took too much of the creature last night, and now is angling for a quarrel."
> —*Amphitryon*, John Dryden (1631–1700).

Credence Table

Nowadays a table near a church altar upon which the bread and wine of the Eucharist are placed before being consecrated. In earlier times the credence table had a more sinister association. Food was placed there for a food taster to sample before being served, it was hoped, poison-free. Credence means belief.

Cretin

A person suffering from severe mental retardation. It is related to the French word for Christian, *Chrétien*, the sense of which is that all baptized Christians, no matter how unfortunate, are brothers and sisters. The word originally meant man, then fellow, then poor fellow. A cretin is incapable of intentional sin.

Crikey

A euphemism for Christ. A mild oath.

Cripes

A euphemism for Christ. An oath used when the speaker wishes to avoid swearing.

Crispin and Crispinian, Saints
(*see also* St. Crispin's Holiday;
St. Crispin's Lance; Shoemakers)

Patron saints of shoemakers and tanners. Crispin was a common name given to shoemakers. Crispin and Crispinian were brothers and shoemakers from Rome who settled in France where they devoted themselves to spreading Christianity until beheaded c. 286. William Shakespeare in *Henry V*, (1599), confused the saints and made them one.

"And Crispin Crispinian shall ne'er
go by ...
But we in it shall be remembered...."

Criss Kringle *see* Kriss Kringle

Crisscross

A Maltese cross ✳, a cross formed from four arrow points. It was the symbol of the Knights of Malta. Nowadays a crisscross is a pattern of crossed lines. It was originally Christ's cross. Before and after the alphabet in hornbooks, children's readers of the 16th and 17th centuries, it was the custom to print a crisscross or Maltese cross. The same symbol was sometimes used in place of XII on clocks. Noon was called crisscross. Oddly enough the crisscross or Maltese cross does not appear on the flag of Malta. Its only use is on the flag of the Wallis and Futuna Islands, a remote French overseas territory in the central Pacific Ocean and on the flag of the Australian state of Queensland.

Crocodile
(*see also* Leviathan)

The crocodile inhabited Palestine as late as the 19th century and has been identified with the mythological Leviathan in Job 41, and with the "great dragon" of Ezekiel 29:3; 32:2. Because of its supposed sexual impulses it symbolized lust. It also represented hypocrisy because it was said to sob and sigh to make men take pity on it and draw close enough to be eaten. Then it sobbed insincere crocodile tears over its victims.

"She's false, false as the tears
of crocodiles."
— *The Sad One*, Sir John
Suckling (1609–1642).

Crocus *see* Rose of Sharon

Crooked Shall be Made Straight

When the Messiah comes the established order will be overturned.

"The crooked shall be made straight,
and the rough places plain"
(Isaiah 40:4).

Crosier

Also crozier. The pastoral staff of an abbot or bishop, in use since the fifth century. It is shaped like a crook and symbolizes the good shepherd. A bishop turns his crosier outwards to indicate his wide authority. An abbot turns his staff inwards to indicate his lesser authority. When an abbot and a bishop walk together the abbot covers his staff with a veil to show that his authority has been veiled in the presence of a superior.

Cross *see* Wood of the Cross

Cross Over Jordan

A metaphor for going to heaven. In order for the Israelites to pass into Canaan they first had to cross the Jordan River. Joshua 3 describes how the Jordan waters stopped flowing and were piled in a heap until all the people had crossed.

Cross-dressing

Transvestitism is condemned in Deuteronomy 22:5:

> "A woman shall not wear anything that pertains to a man, nor shall a man put on a woman's garment; for whoever does these things is an abomination to the Lord your God."

Cross-mark

The X that illiterates make in place of their signature is actually a cross. Among the Saxons it was the sign of a holy oath and it was customary to add a cross to the signatures of those who could write, as well as using it as a sign of good faith for those who could not. Illiterate Jews signed their names with a small circle to avoid using a Christian symbol.

Crosses on Flags
(*see also* Christian Imagery on Flags; St. Andrew's Cross; Union Jack)

The following countries and territories have a cross, the symbol of Christian faith on their flags: Alberta, Denmark, Dominica, Dominican Republic, England, Faeroe Islands, Fiji, Finland, Guernsey, Greece, Liechtenstein, Malta, Manitoba, Marshall Islands, Moldova, Montserrat, Netherlands Antilles, New South Wales, Northern Ireland, Norway, Ontario, Quebec, Queensland, St. Pierre et Miquelon, Slovakia, Spain, Sweden, Switzerland, Tonga, and Victoria. The flag of the Red Cross organization, a red cross on a white field, is the reverse of the Swiss. The Danish flag, *Dannebrog*, a white cross on a field of red, is the world's oldest flag and a model for many of the others. According to legend it fell from the sky in 1219. A beleaguered Danish army picked up the flag and with cries of "Forward to victory under the sign of the cross," won the day.

Crossing the Red Sea

Divine intervention and miraculous escape. When the Hebrews were led out of Egypt by Moses, they came to the barrier of the Red Sea. God caused a mighty wind to blow the waters apart allowing the Hebrews to escape. When Pharaoh's army tried to follow the waters closed over them (Exodus 14:1–31).

Crossroads *see* Burying at the Crossroads

Crown of Glory

Any great victory, especially a spiritual one, can be called a crown of glory. The expression is found in 1 Peter 5:4:

> "And when the chief Shepherd is manifested you will obtain the unfading crown of glory."

Crown of Thorns
(*see also* Jew's Myrtle; Thistle; Thorns)

A symbol of humiliation and suffering.

In Matthew 27:29 (also Mark 15:17 and John 19:2,5) Roman soldiers took Jesus "and plaiting a crown of thorns they put it on his head." Then they kneeled before him and "mocked him, saying 'Hail, King of the Jews!'" Most depictions of this scene show a caplet of rose vines placed upon Jesus' head with the thorn spikes digging into his head. Unfortunately such vines are not common in the Holy Land. The common species of thorn is too long for plaiting. Most likely the crown of thorns was an imitation of the crown worn by Hellenistic kings, with the thorn spikes rising from the head to resemble rays of the sun. This powerful image is often debased in our own time, applied as it to quite trivial afflictions.

> "Every noble crown is, and on earth will forever be, a crown of thorns."
> —*Past and Present*, Thomas Carlyle (1795–1881).

Crozier *see* Crosier

Crucifixion

(*see also* Crucifixion Relics; Two Thieves, Names of)

Death by crucifixion was not unique to Jesus. Crucifixion was the standard Roman method of execution for common criminals who were not citizens. There were several different types of crosses used. The likelihood that Jesus was crucified on a †-shaped cross can be inferred from Matthew 27:37, where a mocking sign was set up over Jesus' head. "This is Jesus King of the Jews." Even so, the cross of Jesus is sometimes depicted as a tau or T-shaped cross. The crucifixion of Jesus followed the usual pattern. The victim was forced to carry the crossbeam to the place of his execution where the upright beam was already in place. Contrary to most representations there was no platform for the feet and the victim's body weight was not supported by

nails. Elevated only a couple of feet above the ground the victim, always nude, would be fastened astride a peg projecting from the upright. Ropes and nails would be used to keep the victim from squirming free. An agonizing death by thirst and hunger would ensue. Sometimes the victim's legs would be broken to hasten the process.

> "Everyone in the world is Christ and they are all crucified."
> —*Winesburg, Ohio*, Sherwood Anderson (1876–1941)

Crucifixion Relics
(*see also* Crucifixion)

Supposed relics from the crucifixion of Jesus include the bandage, the blood, the cross, the crown of thorns, the cup, the grave clothes, the handkerchief, the nails, the reed, the robe, the spear, the sponge, the staircase, the table, the title, the tunic or shirt and the whipping post.

Cruden, Alexander *see* Alexander the Corrector

Crux of the Matter, The

The essence or most important point of a problem. Crux is Latin for the cross used in the crucifixion. Crux is also an English word used for a puzzle or perplexing problem.

Crystal Clear

Something that is obvious and unambiguous. It comes from Revelation 21:11.

> " ... having the glory of God, its radiance like a most rare jewel, like a jasper, clear as crystal."

Cubit *see* Add a Cubit to His Stature

Cummin *see* Anise and Cummin

Curate and Vicar

The English word curate, an assistant to a pastor, is the French *vicaire*, and the English word vicar, a priest in charge of a church dependent on a larger church, is the French *curé*.

> "Like so many vicars, he had a poor opinion of curates."
> —*Mr. Mulliner Speaking*, P. G. Wodehouse (1881–1975).

Curate's Egg

Something that is partly good and partly bad. It refers to a catch phrase introduced by *Punch*, the English humor magazine on November 9, 1895. A cartoon by George du Maurier (1834–1896) depicted a nervous curate eating breakfast with his bishop. "I'm afraid you've got a bad egg, Mr. Jones," said the bishop. The curate, not wanting to say that it was stale, said, "Oh, no, my Lord, I assure you that parts of it are excellent."

Cut My Stick

To be on the way home. Pilgrims in the Holy Land would cut a walking stick from palm wood to prepare for the long journey homeward.

Cyclamen

Plants of the primrose family with heart-shaped purple, crimson or pink flowers. Because they have red markings at the heart, they symbolize the Seven Sorrows of the Virgin Mary—Simeon's prophecy, flight into Egypt, Jesus lost in Jerusalem, meeting Jesus on the road to Calvary, crucifixion, descent from the cross and entombment.

To the question, "what is a primrose?" several valid answers may be given. One person says: "A primrose by the river's brim. A yellow primrose was to him, and it was nothing more." Just that and no more. Another person, the scientist, says "A primrose is a delicately balanced biochemical mechanism, requiring potash, phosphates, nitrogen and water in definite proportions." A third person says "A primrose is God's promise of spring." All three descriptions are correct.

> —*Science and Christian Belief*, C. A. Coulson (1910–1974).

Cypress

A dark-colored evergreen tree that represents mourning. It symbolizes death because it will not grow after it has been cut down. A cypress branch surmounted by a palm, the symbol of victory, suggests Christ's victory over death.

> Here lies below, correct in cypress wood, And entertains the most exclusive worms.
> —*Epitaph for a Very Rich Man*, Dorothy Parker (1893–1967).

D

Dad

A euphemism for God the father. It is used in mild swear words such as *dadblame*, *dadburn* and *dadblast*. The second syllables of these words are themselves euphemisms for damn.

> "By dad! Andy, you've made a mistake this time that I'll forgive you."
> —*Handy Andy*, Samuel Lover (1797–1868).

Dagger

† Also called a long cross. Used in printing as a reference for a footnote. It was orig-

inally used in Roman Catholic books to remind the priest where to make the sign of the cross.

Daily Bread

(*see also* Charity Begins at Home)

Physical needs. "Give us this day our daily bread" (Matthew 6:12). People are entitled to pray that their physical needs are fulfilled. Matthew 6:25–34 suggests that we should trust in the Lord and not be overly concerned with the future and with our material requirements.

> "… in the Lord's Prayer the first petition is for daily bread. No one can worship God or love his neighbor on an empty stomach."
> —*Speech*, Woodrow Wilson (1856–1924).

Daisy

A symbol of modesty and innocence. It is associated with Jesus, "The sun of righteousness" (Malachi 4:2). Through a popular etymology the flower is the sun or the day's eye.

> Thou unassuming commonplace Of Nature.
> — *To the Daisy*, William Wordsworth (1770–1850).

Damned If You Do, Damned If You Don't

No matter what you do you will be blamed. The expression was coined by an American evangelist who used it to condemn preachers who made the Bible contradict itself.

> You can and you can't,
> You will and you won't;
> You'll be damn'd if you do,
> You'll be damn'd if you don't.
> —*Chain (Definition of Calvinism)*, Lorenzo Dow (1777–1834).

Dan to Beersheba

An expression which means from one end of a country to the other, or to the ends of the earth. It is used in Judges 20:1. Dan was in the extreme north of ancient Israel and Beersheba in the extreme south, about 150 miles.

> "I pity the man who can travel from Dan to Beersheba and cry, 'Tis all barren!'"
> —*A Sentimental Journey*, Laurence Sterne (1713–1768).

Dance and Pay the Piper

To have to do everything yourself. The reference is to Matthew 11:17.

> "We piped to you, and you did not dance."

Dance of Death *see* Danse Macabre

Dancing Mania

(*see also* St. Vitus's Dance)

A religious frenzy of the 13th to the 17th century in Europe, characterized by delirious dancing to the point of exhaustion or even death. It was called the leaping ague in Scotland. In Italy, because it was believed to be caused by the bite of the tarantula spider, it was known as tarantism. Music and cold water allayed the dancing frenzy. Dancing mania is not to be confused with the nerve disease chorea, or St. Vitus's Dance, which causes involuntary twitching. The cause is unknown but it might have originated with ergot, a fungus found in rye flour, the ingesting of which can cause hallucinations and convulsions.

Dandelion

A pernicious weed which became symbolic of grief because of its bitter taste. It may have been the bitter herb eaten by the Israelites on the Passover night (Exodus 12:8). The word comes from the French *dent de lion*, lion's tooth.

> The dandelion's pallid tube
> Astonishes the grass
> And winter instantly becomes
> An infinite alas.
> —*Poem #1519*, Emily Dickinson (1830–1886).

Dandruff

The patron saint against dandruff and scurf is Genesius of Arles (third century). The saint was deprived of his hair and his head when he refused to sacrifice to pagan gods.

Daniel in the Lion's Den

Courage and faith thrive despite danger. Daniel was a Hebrew who, during the Babylonian captivity, prophesied and interpreted dreams. When the Babylonians threw him into a den of lions (Daniel 6:16), the angel of God miraculously caused the lions' mouths to be shut.

> "The only man who wasn't spoilt by being lionized was Daniel."
> — Sir Herbert Beerbohm Tree (1853–1917), quoted in Heskath Pearson's *Beerbohm Tree*.

Danse Macabre

A French term (*Totentanz* in German) which means "dance of death." In Christian art, Death was portrayed as a skeleton leading people of all ranks to the grave. In the late Middle Ages the *danse macabre* was a popular allegory of death the great leveller. Inspired by the horrors of the plague and the Hundred Years' War (1337–1453), it was based on a legend that skeletons would rise from their graves and lead the living in a deathly dance. The most celebrated images of the *danse macabre* are found in a series of 51 woodcuts published by Hans Holbein the Younger (1497–1543) in 1535.

Dark Night of the Soul

(*see also* Accidie)

A period of spiritual and mental exhaustion. Dark night of the soul is usually thought of as a modern expression but it goes back to St. John of the Cross (1542–1591), who used it as the title of a book.

> "In a real dark night of the soul it is always three o'clock in the morning, day after day."
> — *The Crack Up*, F. Scott Fitzgerald (1896–1940).

Daughter of Eve

(*see also* Eve)

Any woman since Eve, the first woman.

Daughter of the Horseleech

Someone who is always taking but never giving back. A horseleech is a bloodsucker with a propensity for adhering to the nostrils and tongue of horses as they stoop to drink from marshy ponds.

> "The horseleech hath two daughters crying Give, Give"
> (Proverbs 30:15).

Davy Jones' Locker

The sea as the grave of drowned sailors. The term has been in use since the 18th century. The origin is obscure but Davy may be a corruption of the West Indian *duppy* (devil), and Jones a corruption of Jonah. Jonah, of course, was swallowed by a great fish or whale.

Day of Judgment *see* Doomsday

Day of Reckoning
(*see also* Doomsday)

The time when everyone will be held to account for his or her actions. It stems from the Day of Judgment when Christ returns to judge mankind. The term is sometimes used in a jocular manner to mean the date that debts come due.

> "God will not look you over for medals, degrees or diplomas, but for scars."
> —*Epigrams*, Elbert Hubbard
> (1856–1915).

Days are Numbered *see* One's Days are Numbered

De Profundis

Latin for "Out of the depths." A heartfelt appeal from the depths of wretchedness and humiliation. Psalm 130 is called by this name because of the opening words in the Latin translation. *De Profundis* (1905) was the title of a posthumously published book by Oscar Wilde (1854–1900) written during the author's imprisonment.

Dead Bury their Dead *see* Let the Dead Bury their Dead

Dead Dog, A
(*see also* Dog; Is Thy Servant a Dog, That He Should Do This Thing; Living Dog Is Better Than a Dead Lion)

Something completely worthless.

> "After whom do you pursue? After a dead dog! After a flea!"
> (1 Samuel 24:14).

Dead Sea Apple *see* Dead Sea Fruit

Dead Sea Fruit

Something which is strived for but when obtained turns out to be a bitter disappointment. It is a metaphor for superficial pleasures. Fruit from the shores of the Dead Sea looked attractive but when picked crumbled to ashes (Deuteronomy 32:32–33). The fruit is also called the Dead Sea apple or vine of Sodom.

> Like to apples on the Dead Sea's shore, All ashes to taste.
> —*Childe Harold's Pilgrimage*,
> Lord Byron (1788–1824).

Death, Euphemisms for

"Slept with his fathers" occurs 35 times in the Old Testament. "To fall asleep" and "To fall on sleep" are commonly used in the New Testament. Others are "To depart and be with Christ" (Philippians 1:23); "The putting off of my body" (2 Peter 1:14); "Gave up the ghost" (John 19:30); "Like the flower of the grass he will pass away" (James 1:10); "Before I depart and be no more" (Psalms 39:13); "Go down into silence" (Psalms 115:17); "I shall go the way whence I shall not return" (Job 16:22); "And now I am about to go the way of all the earth" (Joshua 23:14); "Because man goes to his eternal home" (Ecclesiastes 12:5); and "I am to be gathered to my people" (Genesis 49:29). Cemetery is a euphemism created by early Christian writers from the Greek word for dormitory.

> Death, so call'd, is a thing which makes men weep,
> And yet a third of life is pass's in sleep.
> —*Don Juan*, Lord Byron (1788–1824).

Death by Artillery

Those in danger from artillery barrages can pray to their own patron saint, Barbara, who was martyred c. 235. Her killer was struck down by lightning and from this comes Barbara's association with artillery.

Death in the Pot

During a famine in Gilgal a stew was made from wild vines and herbs which turned out to be poisonous. When the sons of the prophets tasted the stew, they cried, "O man of God, there is death in the pot!" (2 Kings 4:40). Elisha added meal to the pot and the food became fit to eat.

Death Warrant of Jesus Christ
(*see also* Jesus Christ)

In 1810 some workers near Naples found a marble vase which contained what was purported to be the death warrant of Jesus:

> Sentence rendered by Pontius Pilate, acting Governor of Lower Galilee, stating that Jesus of Nazareth shall suffer death on the cross.
> In the year seventeen of the Emperor Tiberius Caesar, and the 27th day of March, the city of the holy Jerusalem,—Annas and Caiaphas being priests, sacrificators of the people of God,— Pontius Pilate, Governor of Lower Galilee, sitting in the presidential chair of the praetory, condemns Jesus of Nazareth to die on the cross between two thieves, the great and notorious evidence of the people saying:
> 1. Jesus is a seducer.
> 2. He is seditious.
> 3. He is the enemy of the law.
> 4. He calls himself falsely the Son of God.
> 5. He calls himself falsely the King of Israel.
> 6. He entered into the temple, followed by a multitude bearing palm-branches in their hands.
> Order the first centurion, Quilius Cornelius, to lead him to the place of execution. Forbids any person whomsoever, either poor or rich, to oppose

> the death of Jesus Christ.
> The witnesses who signed the condemnation of Jesus are:
> 1. Daniel Robani, a Pharisee.
> 2. Joannus Robani.
> 3. Raphael Robani.
> 4. Capet, a citizen.
> Jesus shall go out of the city of Jerusalem by the gate of Struenus.

Death Where Is thy Sting?

Death is not to be feared. The expression comes from 1 Corinthians 16:54–55:

> "When the perishable puts on the imperishable, and the mortal puts on immortality, then shall come to pass the saying that is written: 'Death is swallowed up in victory.' 'O death, where is thy victory? O death, where is they sting?'"

Decollation

Beheading, especially, of a saint, who was thus martyred. The Feast of the Decollation of St. John the Baptist is observed on August 29.

Dei Gratia
(*see also* Godless Florins)

"By the grace of God." A Latin phrase which has appeared on British coins since 1106. It is usually abbreviated as D.G.

Dei Judicium
(*see also* Ordeals)

"The judgment of God." A Latin phrase used to describe the judgment by ordeals.

Delilah
(*see also* Samson)

Any treacherous female is a Delilah. Delilah, as is usually believed, tricked the mighty Samson into allowing her to cut his hair and thus lose his strength (Judges 16:1–21). In fact Delilah called for a man to shave the head of the sleeping Samson rather than do the deed herself. Her name comes from the Hebrew "to enfeeble."

> "I have a lot of respect for that dame.
> There's one lady barber that made good."
> — Mae West (1892–1980),
> *Going to Town* (film).

Delivery of the Law

An image which appears in art from the fourth century, even though there is no biblical authority for it. Jesus is depicted fulfilling the old law, by handing a scroll of his new law to St. Peter. It is known as *Traditio Legis*.

Delta

Δ The fifth letter of the Greek alphabet. Because it is a figure with three equal sides, it represents the Trinity and the equality of the Father, the Son and the Holy Spirit. An eye within a delta symbolizes God the all-seeing.

Deluge *see* Flood

Den of Thieves

(*see also* Cast the Moneychangers Out of the Temple)

A sordid place frequented by dishonest persons. When Jesus threw the money changers out of the temple, he accused them by saying,

> "It is written, My house shall be called
> the house of prayer; but ye have made it
> a den of thieves" (Matthew 21:13).

Denial Bible

A Bible of 1792 in which a misprint occurred. In Luke 22:34 Philip, instead of Peter, is stated to be the apostle who will deny Jesus.

Dentists

St. Appollonia (d. 249), was a pious virgin of Alexandria. Attacked by a mob, she suffered to have her teeth torn out rather than recant her faith. As the patron saint of dentists, she can be invoked against toothache. Appolonia is depicted holding a tooth in a set of pincers.

> "For years I have let dentists ride
> roughshod over my teeth; I have been
> sawed, hacked, chopped, whittled, be-
> witched, bewildered, tattooed, and
> signed in again; but this is cuspid's
> last stand."
> — *Crazy Like a Fox*, S. J. Perelman
> (1904–1979).

Deo Optimo Maximo *see* D.O.M.

Deodand

Something given to God. If a person was killed because of a personal chattel, then that possession would be sold and the proceeds given to the church as an expiatory offering. For example, if a person died in a riding accident then the horse would be sold. Since the person had died without extreme unction, the money would pay for a Mass for the repose of his soul. The practice was abolished in 1846.

> "If a man falls from a boat or ship in
> fresh water, and is drowned, it hath been
> said, that the vessel and cargo are in
> strictness of law a deodand."
> — *Commentaries on the Laws of England*,
> William Blackstone (1723–1780).

Desert Shall Bloom, The

A common allusion to desert reclamation projects, especially those in Israel.

Originally it was a prediction that the exiled Hebrews would return to their homeland.

> "The wilderness and the dry land shall be glad, the desert shall rejoice and blossom abundantly, and rejoice with joy and singing"
> (Isaiah 35:1–2).

Devil *see* Satan

Devil and the Deep Blue Sea
see Between the Devil and the Deep Blue Sea

Devil-dodgers

According to the *Oxford English Dictionary* this is an amusing term for ranting preachers and evangelists, and those who listen to them. It has been in use since at least 1791.

Devil's Advocate

When a person or thing is generally considered praiseworthy someone who argues against that position is said to be a devil's advocate. The devil's advocate may not necessarily believe the argument he puts forth. When someone is proposed for beatification or canonization in the Roman Catholic Church, an *advocatus diaboli* (official title: *promotor fidei*–defender of the faith) is appointed to bring forth all possible reasons why the person should not proceed to sainthood. The first mention of a devil's advocate occurred during the canonization of St. Lorenzo Guistiniani (1381–1455) in the 16th century.

Devil's Bible

A Bible inscribed on the skins of 30 asses and taken to Sweden after the Thirty Years' War (1618–1648). Legend says that a poor monk was condemned to death unless he could copy the entire Bible on asses' skins in a single night. The monk made a deal with the devil, offering his soul in return for the manuscript.

Devil's Bones

Dice which were once made from bone and lead the unwary to ruin.

Devil's Books

Also, the devil's picture book. Playing cards were so called by the Puritans.

> "What hours, what nights, what health did he waste over the devil's books!"
> —*Four Georges*, William Makepeace Thackeray (1811–1863).

Devil's Door

A small doorway in the north wall of churches. The north was the domain of Satan and the door was opened at baptisms and communion services to let the devil out.

Devil's Dozen

Thirteen. Twelve plus one for the devil.

Devil's Four Poster

A hand of whist containing four clubs. It was believed that such a hand could never be a winner. The four of clubs was called the devil's bedpost.

Devil's Luck

Luck that is too good to be true probably isn't. Lucky people were thought to be in league with the devil. This expression was in use in the 19th century.

Devil's Mass

Loud and indiscriminate cursing.

Devil's Picture Book *see*
Devil's Books

Devilshine

Demonic power.

Dextera Domini

The "right hand of God," which was the sign of power and energy with which God judged and created. It was one of the earliest symbols of God the Father.

D.G. see Dei Gratia

Dickens

A euphemism for the devil, as in "Raising the Dickens." Dickens, which has nothing to do with Charles Dickens (1812–1870), is probably derived from Nick or Old Nick, other names for the devil. Dickens is also an exclamation of irritation, exasperation, or surprise, as in, "What the Dickens!"

> "I cannot tell what the dickens his name is."
> —*Merry Wives of Windsor*, William Shakespeare (1564–1616).

Dies Irae

The title and opening words of a 13th century Latin hymn used in the mass for the repose of the dead, or Requiem. The words mean "day of wrath," and came to be used for the day of reckoning or judgment.

Discalced

A word which comes from the Latin for "without shoes." It describes members of religious orders who go barefoot or wear sandals instead of shoes. The custom derives from Luke 10:4.

> Carry no purse, no bag, no sandals.

Discharge Bible

A Bible of 1806 that confused the word *discharge* for *charge* in 1 Timothy 5:21. "I *discharge* thee before God …" appears instead of "I *charge* thee before God …."

Discipline, A
(*see also* Flagellants)

A scourge or whip used to mortify the flesh for religious penance.

> "Before the cross and altar a lamp was still burning … and on the floor lay a small discipline or penitential scourge of small cord and wire, the lashes of which were stained with recent blood."
> — *The Talisman*, Sir Walter Scott (1771–1832).

Diseases and Misfortunes, Patron Saints of
(*see also* Patron Saints)

Abandoned Children Ivo of Kermartin, Jerome Emiliani; *Ague* Pernel, Petronella; *AIDS Sufferers* Therese of Lisieux; *Alcoholism* Martin, Urban; *Animals, Danger from* Vitus; *Arm Pain* Amalburga; *Backward Children* Hilary of Poitiers; *Bad Weather* Medard; *Barrenness* Margaret, Anthony of Padua; *Bleary Eyes* Otilic, Clare; *Blindness* Thomas à Becket, Lucy, Agathocles, Dunstan; *Bodily Afflictions* Our Lady of Lourdes, Roque, Sebastian; *Boils and Swellings* Roque, Cosme; *Breast Cancer* Agatha; *Brigandage* Leonard of Noblac; *Broken Bones* Drogo, Stanislaus Kostka; *Bruises* Amalburga; *Burns* John the Apostle; *Caterpillars* Magnus of Fussen; *Cattle Diseases* Blaise; *Children in Danger* Cunegund; *Children Who Cannot Walk* Sabina; *Children's Diseases* Blaise; *Civil Disorder and Riot* Andrew Corsini; *Cold Weather* Sebald; *Colic* Erasmus; *Convulsions* John the Baptist, *Willibrord; Cramps* Pancras; *Deafness* Francis de Sales; *Death by Artillery* Barbara; *Demonic*

Possession Dymphna; *Despairing Prostitutes* Margaret of Cortona; *Desperate Cases* Jude; *Diseases in General* Roque, Sebastian; *Dizziness or Vertigo* Ulric; *Dogbites* Vitus; *Doubts* Catherine, Joseph, Thomas the Apostle; *Drought* Scholastica; *Dying* Barbara, Joseph; *Earaches* Cornelius, Polycarp of Smyrna; *Earthquakes* Emygdius; *Epilepsy* Valentine, Cornelius, Vitus; *Escape from Devils* Margaret of Antioch; *False Accusations* Mennas, Pancratius, Raymond Nonnatus; *Fire* Agatha, Florian, Catherine of Siena; *Flood, Fire and Earthquake* Christopher; *Gallstones* Benedict; *Gout* Wolfgang, Maurice, Andrew; *Handicaps* Giles; *Hanged Men* Colman, Dismas; *Hangovers* Bibiana; *Hoarseness* Bernadine of Siena, Maurus; *Hydrophobia* Hubert; *Idiocy* Gildas; *Infamy* Susan; *Infection* Roque; *Insects* Gratus of Aosta; *Jealousy* Elizabeth of Portugal; *Leprosy* Lazarus, Giles; *Lightening* Apollonia; *Losing Keys* Zita; *Lost Property* Ethelbert, Elian, Anthony of Padua; *Mad Dogs* Sithney; *Madness* Dymphna, Fillan; *Migraines* Gereon; *Mine Collapses* Barbara; *Miscarriages* Catherine of Siena, Catherine of Sweden; *Moles, Danger from* Ulric; *Nettle Rash* Benedict; *Nightmares* Christopher, Raphael the Archangel; *Orphans* Jerome Emiliani; *Oversleeping* Vitus; *Pain* Madron; *Palsy* Cornelius; *Perjury* Felix of Nola, Pancras; *Pestilence* Cosmas, Damian; *Plague* Roque; *Poison* Benedict, John the Apostle; *Poor* Anthony of Padua, Giles, Lawrence; *Rats* Gertrude, Huldrick; *Recently Dead* Gertrude of Nivelles; *Repentant Prostitutes* Mary Magdalene, Mary of Egypt, Margaret of Cortona; *Respiratory Disease* Blaise; *St. Vitus's Dance* Vitus; *Shipwreck* Anthony of Padua, Jodocus; *Sick* Camillus de Lellis, John of God, Michael; *Skin Disease* Roque; *Sick Animals* Beuno; *Sick Children* Aldegondes; *Sleepwalkers* Dymphna; *Smallpox* Martin of Tours; *Snakebite* Paul; *Sore Throat* Blaise, Ignatius of Antioch; *Spinsters* Andrew, Catherine of Alexandria; *Spousal Abuse* Rita of Cascia; *Stammering* Notker Balbulus; *Starvation* Anthony of Padua; *Storms* Barbara; *Sudden Death* Martin; *Syphilis* Fiacre, George; *Tonsillitis* Blaise; *Toothaches* Apollonia, Blaise; *Twitching* Bartholomew the Apostle, Cornelius; *Virginity, Loss of* Susan; *Wasps* Friard; *Witchcraft* Benedict.

Dismas

The name traditionally given to the penitent thief or good thief who was crucified alongside Jesus. Dismas is depicted carrying a cross and as having been released by Christ from Limbo. Because of his faith Jesus made him a promise.

"Truly, I say to you, today you will be with me in Paradise" (Luke 23:43).

Distaff Side
(*see also* St. Distaff's Day)

The female line of a person's ancestry. A distaff is a cleft stick that was used to hold flax or wool. It is an attribute of Eve, who was condemned to spin wool, as well as to "raise Cain," after being expelled from Eden.

Dittography
(*see also* Haplography; Homeoteleuton)

An inaccuracy that sometimes occurred when Bibles were copied by hand. A weary scribe would accidentally repeat the same letter or word.

Dives and Lazarus

In Luke 16:19–31 we are told the story of an unnamed rich man who lived in luxury while Lazarus the beggar, covered with sores, lay at his doorstep. The rich man came to be called *Dives*, Latin for "rich man." Both men died. Lazarus went to heaven and the rich man to hell. Dives seeing the lowly Lazarus in paradise begs for a drop of water to cool his torment but is told that he is receiving what he deserves. Dives is the personification of the sin of gluttony.

Divide and Conquer
(*see also* House Divided)

To sow discord among enemies allowing you to pick them off one by one. The expression was inspired by Matthew 12:25:

> "Every kingdom divided against itself is laid waste, and no city or house divided against itself will stand."

Divide the Sheep from the Goats

A prophecy of the Last Judgment. The sheep are the righteous and the goats are the wicked. This common expression comes from Matthew 25:33 and means to separate the good from the bad:

> "He will place the sheep at his right hand, but the goats at the left."

Divination *see* Clidomancy; Dowsing; Epatoscomancy; Key and Bible; Rhabdomancy; Scrying; Urim and Thummim; Urimancy

Divine Cuckold
(*see also* Betrothal and Marriage of the Virgin Mary)

St. Joseph was the husband of the Virgin Mary and the earthly father of Jesus Christ. He is seen as a supremely virtuous man, the perfect father and artisan. In scenes of Christ's nativity Joseph is depicted as a strong laboring man in his early 30s. But this conception of Joseph dates only from the 16th century. Before that he was not highly regarded. He was depicted as a divine cuckold, an almost irrelevant ob-server of great events in which he played no part. To explain why he did not conceive his son, he was shown as an impotent old man. According to legend, Joseph was 89 years of age when he was divinely chosen to be Mary's bridegroom. He was also a widower, which meant that the brothers and sisters of Jesus were children of an earlier marriage.

Divine Right of Kings

The ancient doctrine that kings rule by a direct ordinance from God, apart from the will of the people. In the Old Testament, kings are frequently called "God's anointed." The king was considered to be God's representative on earth.

> "The right divine of kings to govern wrong."
> —*Dunciad*, Alexander Pope (1688–1744).

Diving Rod *see* Dowsing

Do Not Suffer Fools Gladly

A refusal to put up with stupid people. Today this expression is used in a literal sense, but in 2 Corinthians 11:19, from which it comes, Paul was probably being sarcastic. He meant that those who put up with fools are fools themselves.

> "For ye suffer fools gladly, seeing ye *yourselves* are wise."

Do Unto Others as You Would Have Others Do Unto You
(*see also* Sermon on the Mount)

Not a quotation but a popular paraphrase of Matthew 7:12. Since the 17th century it has been called the Golden Law and since the 19th, the Golden Rule. The phrase comes from the Sermon on the Mount.

> "So whatever you wish that men would do to you, do so to them; for this is the law and the prophets."

Doffing the Hat
(*see also* Quaker)

It is the custom, even now, for a man to remove his hat as a sign of respect in the presence of superiors, especially royals. The Quakers objected to this on the grounds that Jesus Christ was their only master and steadfastly remained hatted. When the Quaker leader, William Penn (1644–1718), stood before Charles II (1630–1685) he kept his hat firmly on his head. The king removed his. "Friend Charles," asked the Quaker, "why dost thou uncover thy head?" Charles smiled as he replied, "Friend Penn, it is the custom here that only one person wears his hat in the king's presence."

Dog
(*see also* Dead Dog; Is thy Servant a Dog, That He Should Do This Thing; Living Dog Is Better Than a Dead Lion)

The first animal to be domesticated, the dog usually symbolized fidelity, courage and devotion (Job 30:1; Isaiah 56:10). However, the dog could also represent evil (Revelation 22:15; Philippians 3:2). In art black and white dogs represented the colors in the habit of the Dominican Order. A pun, *Domini canes*, was used to indicate that the Dominicans were the dogs of the Lord. St. Hubert of Liege (c. 569–727), a passionate hunter, has become the patron saint of dogs, dog owners, and the patron saint against dog bites and mad dogs.

> "For a living dog is better than a dead lion" (Ecclesiastes 9:4)

Doggone
(*see also* G.D.; Goddamn)

A mild curse. It is a euphemism for Goddamn. Dog, of course, is God spelled backwards.

Dog-whipper

An ecclesiastical official whose duty was to whip stray dogs out of church during times of worship. The dog-whipper was equipped with a long ash stick at the end of which was fastened a strip of leather three feet long.

Dolphin
(*see also* Anchor)

Because dolphins were reputed to rescue shipwrecked sailors, they became a symbol of salvation. Because some thought the dolphin to be the fish that swallowed Jonah, it was a symbol of the resurrection. In art the dolphin represents Christ as the savior of souls from the waters of death. A dolphin with a ship or anchor suggests Christ as the guide of the church. A dolphin on an anchor represents Christ on the cross.

D.O.M.
(*see also* Bénédictine)

Initials of *Deo optimo maximo*, "To God the best and greatest," a formula originally applied to the pagan god Jupiter but adopted by Christians for use over church doors and on monuments. It is also inscribed on bottles of Bénédictine liqueur.

Donation of Constantine

A document purportedly issued by Emperor Constantine of Rome which gave legal status and temporal authority to the Church and wealth and privileges to Pope Sylvester I (reigned 314 to 335) and his successors. It was reported that the pope cured Constantine of leprosy, converted him to Christianity and inspired him to close all the pagan temples in Rome. The Donation was proven to be a forgery composed in France or Italy c. 750–850.

Donkey *see* Ass

Doomsday
(*see also* Day of Reckoning; Millennium; Second Coming)

Any cataclysmic ending. In modern times it has come to be associated with nuclear devastation. Originally a doom was a legal judgment or decree and doomsday was the day of judgment. It was also called Day of Judgment, Judgment Day or Last Judgment.

> "Flee from the wrath to come" (Matthew 3:7).

Dorcas Society

A women's charitable organization, which distributes clothing to the poor. Its name comes from Dorcas in Acts 9:39, who made tunics and other garments for widows.

Dormition of the Blessed Virgin Mary *see* Assumption of the Virgin

Double-edged Sword

Both good and bad can result from what one says or does. The reference is to Revelation 1:16 and the double-edged sword from the mouth of the Son of Man, which can save or condemn. The double-edged sword, or "two-edged sword" is also mentioned in Hebrews 4:12.

> "For the word of God is living and active, sharper than any two-edged sword, piercing to the division of soul and spirit, of joints and marrow, and discerning the thoughts and intentions of the heart."

Doubting Thomas

Someone who is difficult to convince. The original Doubting Thomas was St. Thomas, the apostle who refused to believe that Jesus had been resurrected until he touched the wounds (John 20:24–29). Thomas had questioned Jesus earlier (John 14:5).

Dove of Peace

The universal symbol of peace and harmony. It may have originated with the account of Noah sending out a dove to find dry land after the Flood. When the bird returned with an olive branch, it indicated that the waters had receded and that God had forgiven mankind. The dove often symbolizes the Holy Spirit, divine inspiration, purity and the human soul. The holy spirit descended upon Christ "in bodily form, as a dove" (Luke 3:22). Experiments have shown that caged doves are not as peaceful as we thought. They will sometimes kill each other.

> "Oh that I had wings like a dove! For then I would fly away and be at rest" (Psalms 4:6).

Dove's Dung and Ass's Head

In a famine in Samaria, "an ass's head sold for eighty shekels of silver, and the fourth part of a kab of dove's dung for five shekels of silver" (2 Kings 6:25). This is probably a mistranslation of lentils and carob.

Dowsing
(*see also* Rhabdomancy)

Searching for underground deposits of water or minerals by means of a forked stick or divining rod, which bends downward when the deposit is located. Sometimes a dowser uses a pendulum suspended from a chain or a thread. A biblical example of dowsing may occur in Exodus 17:6, when God tells Moses,

> "You shall strike the rock, and water shall come out of it, that the people may drink."

Dragon

A huge mythical winged monster of ferocious disposition, often capable of breathing out smoke and fire. In the Bible the dragon, often confused with the serpent, symbolizes the devil or the spirit of evil. Satan is called "the great dragon" (Revelation 12:9). Defeating a dragon symbolizes victory over sin. A pregnant woman, probably representing humanity, is threatened by "a great red dragon, with seven heads, and ten horns" (Revelation 12:1–6). Many legends of saints killing dragons were inspired by, "The dragon shalt thou trample under feet" (Psalms 91:13). St. George is the most famous dragon slayer. St. Margaret of Antioch was swallowed by a dragon, but after making the sign of the cross burst from its belly. Saints Andrew, Martha, Donatus, Samson, Florent, Cado, Maudet, Pol, Clement of Metz, Philip the Apostle, Romain of Rouen and Keyne have all been pictured with dragons. The dispatch of a dragon by the archangel Michael comes from, "Now war arose in heaven, Michael and his angels fighting against the dragon" (Revelation 12:7–9).

Drat

(*see also* Od's)

A mild oath. It is a variant of *'Od rot* or God rot.

Drivers *see* Bad Drivers

Drop in the Bucket, A

Any insignificant amount is so called.

Since the mid–20th century "A drop in the ocean" has become popular. The original expression, slightly misquoted, comes from Isaiah 40:15:

> "Behold, the nations are like a drop from a bucket, and are accounted as the dust on the scales."

Dropsy

A disease characterized by the accumulation of fluid in the tissues of the body, especially the legs. Dropsy is mentioned in the Bible only in Luke 14:2–4 where a sufferer was healed by Jesus.

Drunkard

(*see also* Creature; Hangover; Martin Drunk)

According to Genesis 9:21, Noah was the first drunkard. "And he drank of the wine, and became drunk, and lay uncovered in his tent." Drunkenness is considered a sin and is frequently condemned in the Bible. The patron saint of hangover sufferers is St. Bibiana (fourth century) and of alcoholics, John of God (1495–1556), a reformed wastrel.

> Not drunk is he who from the floor
> Can rise alone, and still drink more,
> But drunk is he who prostrate lies,
> Without the power to drink or rise.
> —*Misfortune of Elphin*, Thomas Love Peacock (1785–1866).

Dry as a Bone

Anything extremely dry. The expression goes back to Ezekiel's vision of the Valley of the Dry Bones:

> "Prophecy to these bones, and say to them, O dry bones, hear the word of the Lord" (Ezekiel 37:4).

Dulcimer

A trapezoidal instrument with metal

strings played with spoon-shaped beaters held in each hand. In Daniel 3:5 of the King James Bible (1611) the word is used for bagpipe.

Dulia
(*see also* Hyperdulia; Latria)

In the Roman Catholic Church, dulia was worship directed to saints and angels; in the Orthodox Church, it entailed veneration of icons as the representatives of saints. Dulia is less than the homage paid to God and Mary, the Mother of God.

Dumb Ox
(*see also* Ox; Quodlibet)

Nickname given to St. Thomas Aquinas (c. 1225–1274) by his fellow monks. Other names were Sicilian Ox and Great Dumb Sicilian Ox. His teacher, Albertus Magnus (c. 1193–1280), said of him, "You may call him a dumb ox, but he will give such a bellow in learning that will astonish the whole world." The "dumb ox" was truly a leviathan of learning, but some of the problems he wrestled with seem decidedly odd by modern standards–Whether Christ was a hermaphrodite? Whether many angels can be in the same space? Whether the pious at the resurrection will rise with their bowels? Whether there are excrements in Paradise?

> "Three things are necessary for the salvation of man: to know what he ought to believe, to know what he ought to desire, and to know what he ought to do."
> — *Two Precepts of Charity*, St. Thomas Aquinas (c. 1225–1274).

Dunce

John Duns Scotus (c. 1266–c. 1308) was a brilliant scholastic philosopher and theologian. It is ironic that his name has given rise to dunce. Two centuries after his time, his followers, *Dunsmen*, preached against the new learning of the Renaissance. The humanists scorned them as ignorant blockheads. *Dunsman* became *dunse* and eventually *dunce*.

> How much a dunce that has been
> sent to roam
> Excels a dunce that has been kept
> at home!
> — *The Progress of Error*, William Cowper (1731–1800).

Dust and Ashes

An expression of repentance and humility.

> "Behold, I have taken upon myself to speak to the Lord, I who am but dust and ashes" (Genesis 18:27).

Dust to Dust *see* Ashes to Ashes, Dust to Dust

E

Eagle *see* Phoenix

Earn the Wages of Sin, To
(*see also* Wages of Sin)

Until recently, those who earned the wages of sin had been given the death penalty, usually by hanging, as a punishment for a serious crime. However, when Paul spoke of the wages of sin he was talking about spiritual death rather than physical extinction, a worse fate, in his view. The wages of righteousness, by the way, is eternal life.

> "The wages of sin is death"
> (Romans 6:23).

Ears to Ear Bible

A Bible printed in 1810 which lacked an all-important *h*. Matthew 13:43 reads, "Who hath ears to *ear* let him hear." It should read, "Who hath ears to *hear* let him hear."

Earthly Paradise
(*see also* Brendan the Navigator)

Since the expulsion of Adam and Eve from the Garden of Eden, there is no longer any paradise on the earth for humanity. Human beings must aspire to a heavenly paradise after death. Nonetheless, people still have a longing for an earthly paradise, be it Arcadia, Avalon, Camelot, Utopia, or Shangri-la.

> "Of Paradise I cannot speak properly, for I have not been there."
> — *Book of John Mandeville*, John Mandeville (14th Century).

Ease

A euphemism in the King James Bible (1611) for a bowel movement. "When thou wilt ease thyself abroad, thou shalt dig therewith, and shalt turn back and cover that which comes from thee" (Deuteronomy 23:13). The Revised Standard Version (1952) is equally fastidious. "When you sit down outside," is the approved translation.

East

Because Jesus is the Sun of Righteousness and the Dayspring, it became customary to place altars at the east side of churches and for the congregation to face eastward, the direction of the rising sun, when reciting the creed. The dead were buried with their feet to the east in the hope of resurrection.

> I only know that creeds to me
> Are but new names for mystery,
> That good is good from east to east,

> And more I do not know or need
> To know, to love my neighbor well.
> — *The Tale of Tall Alexander*, Joaquin Miller (c. 1841–1913).

East of Eden

After Cain slew his brother Abel he was exiled east of Eden (Genesis 4:16). John Steinbeck (1902–1968) called his famous novel about brothers in conflict *East of Eden* (1952).

Easter
(*see also* Easter Egg)

The Christian Paschal celebration commemorating Christ's resurrection. It supplanted a festival for the Teutonic goddess of fertility, *Eostre*, that took place around the vernal equinox, March 21. Easter occurs on a Sunday between March 22 and April 25, the first Sunday after the first full moon that occurs between those dates. Despite a proposal that Easter be held on a fixed date and despite there being no canonical objection to the change, the dating of Easter remains as it always has been. Both the Easter egg and the Easter rabbit, a symbol of fertility, are connected to the pagan festival. Eggs were colored red as a symbol of the blood of redemption. In the King James Bible (1611), the word Easter is only used in Acts 12:4. The Revised Standard Version (1952) uses "Passover."

> "God expects from men that their Easter devotions would in some measure come up to their Easter clothes."
> — *Sermons*, Robert South (1634–1716).

Easter Egg
(*see also* Easter; Egg)

The egg is a symbol of creation and rebirth. The Easter egg may have arisen from the custom of bringing eggs, a food forbidden during Lent, to church to be blessed on Easter

Sunday, after which they could be eaten. Easter Eggs were introduced into England from Germany in the 19th century. Brightly colored eggs represent the sunlight of spring.

> "An egg is dear on Easter day."
> —*Russian Proverb.*

Eat, Drink and Be Merry, For Tomorrow We Die
(*see also* Belshazzar's Feast)

Short-sighted pleasures. A slight paraphrase of Isaiah 22:13. "Let us eat and drink for tomorrow we die." Jesus told a parable of a rich man who wanted to "eat, drink, and be merry." The man did not realize that he would die that very night (Luke 12:16–20).

Ecce Homo!

"Behold the Man!" In the Latin translation of the Bible, Pilate spoke these words (John 19:5) when he declared that he found no fault in Jesus. The term is used for images of Jesus wearing the crown of thorns and bound by ropes as he is shown to the people by Pilate.

Ecclesiastes
(*see also* All Is Vanity)

A book of the Old Testament characterized by a cynical and pessimistic condemnation of worldly attachments and pleasures. The word "vanity" in the singular or plural occurs 38 times. Happiness is equated with fearing God.

> Paraphrase of Ecclesiastes: Objective consideration of contemporary phenomena compels the conclusion that success or failure in competitive activities exhibits no tendency to be commensurate with innate capacity, but that a considerable element of the unpredictable must invariably be taken into account.
> —*Selected Essays*, George Orwell (1903–1950).

Education of St. Mary the Virgin
(*see also* Virgin Mary)

Since the Virgin Mary was chosen by God before time, there was some theological dispute about whether or not she needed instruction. She must have innately possessed all knowledge. Legends arose that she had spent her girlhood in the temple and that Anne, her mother, taught her to read and sew. When Mary pricked her finger, it foreshadowed the suffering she would endure at the death of her son. She wove the veil in the temple that was torn at the time of the crucifixion.

Egad
(*see also* Gad)

A mild oath. Gad is a euphemism for God.

Egg
(*see also* Easter Egg; Ostrich)

Because the ostrich leaves its eggs in the dust to hatch by themselves, the egg symbolizes the virgin birth of Jesus. It is also a symbol of the resurrection.

> "The wings of the ostrich wave proudly; but are they the pinions and plumage of love? For she leaves her eggs to the earth, and lets them be warmed on the ground" (Job 39:13–14).

Eight
(*see also* Numbers)

A number with many associations of regeneration and rebirth. Christ rose from the tomb eight days after entering Jerusalem; eight people were saved in the ark and therefore baptismal fonts are sometimes octagonal; there are eight beatitudes; Jesus was named and circumcised eight days after his birth; there are eight canonical hours; early Christian basilicas were often eight-sided. Eight is a mystical number that suggests completion.

Elder

(*see also* Judas)

A tree of the honeysuckle family on which, legend says, Judas Iscariot hanged himself. It was considered to be a disgrace to be crowned with elder. In *Cymbaline*, William Shakespeare (1564–1616) uses "the stinking elder" as a token of grief. Eruptions on its bark are called Judas's ears.

Elephant and Castle

The elephant was an animal supposedly modest and chaste. It was faithful to its spouse and mated only to reproduce, as Christians were supposed to do. Alexander the Great (357–323 B.C.) encountered enemy archers in howdahs on the backs of elephants. This gave rise to the image of the elephant and castle, the unassailable church supported by an impregnable foundation of faith. Elephants are not mentioned in the Bible, although ivory is. Elephants are mentioned in the Apocrypha.

> "And upon the elephants were wooden towers strong and covered"
> (I Maccabees 6:37)

Eleven

(*see also* Numbers)

St. Augustine (354–430) considered the number 11 to be evil, a transgression of 10, the number of the law.

Eleventh Commandment

A jocular addition to the Ten Commandments. "Thou shalt not be caught." Miguel de Cervantes (1547–1616) wrote an 11th commandment of his own in *Don Quixote*: "Mind your own business."

Eleventh Hour

At the last moment. The idea comes from Matthew 20:1–16, in which the vineyard owner hires workers for a 12-hour work day. He continues to hire workers until the 11th hour, a parable of God's boundless grace. The 11th hour, the last hour of work, was not the last hour before midnight but the hour before sunset.

Eli, Eli Lamma Sabacthani

"My God, my God, why hast thou forsaken me?" Jesus uttered this moving cry of human suffering as he hung on the cross. The words, spoken in Aramaic, are found in Matthew 27:46 and Mark 15:34, quoting Psalms 23:1.

Eligius, St. *see* Seize the Devil by the Nose

Elijah's Melons

Stones on Mount Carmel. Because a landowner refused to give Elijah some melons to eat, his crop was turned to stones.

Elmo, St. *see* St. Elmo's Fire

Emblematic Poetry

Poetry which is shaped to form a figure or illustration. It is also called shaped or figurative poetry. A Christian example is shown on the facing page, a poem titled simply "The Cross," author unknown. Other emblematic poems were written in the forms of eggs, altars and wings.

Blest they who seek,
While in their youth,
With spirit meek,
The way of truth;
To them the sacred Scriptures now display
Christ as the only true and living way.
His precious blood on Calvary was given
To make them heirs of endless bliss in heaven;
And e'en on earth the child of God can trace
The glorious blessings of his Savior's grace.
For them He bore
His Father's frown;
For them He wore
The thorny Crown;
Nailed to the Cross,
Endured its pain,
That His life's loss
Might be their gain.
Then haste to choose
That better part,
Nor dare refuse
The Lord thy heart
Lest He declare,
"I know you not,"
And deep despair
Should be your lot.
Now look to Jesus, who on Calvary died,
And trust on Him alone who there was crucified.

Ends of the Earth, To the
(*see also* Four Corners
of the Earth)

To go to the most remote place imaginable. The expression, based on the notion of a flat earth, has survived the discovery that the earth is spherical.

"All the ends of the earth have
seen the victory of our God"
(Psalms 98:3).

Enemies *see* Love Your Enemies

Engagement *see* Betrothal

English Pope

A name given to Adrian IV (c. 1100–1159), the only English pope. Born as Nicholas Breakspear, he became the pope in 1154. The doctrine of transubstantiation was established during his pontificate, as was the use of the title, Vicar of Christ.

Enoch, Book of
(*see also* Jashar; Lost Books)

An apocryphal work mentioned in Jude 14, 15. It vanished, apart from excerpts, about A.D. 800. An Ethiopian manuscript was discovered in 1773 and published in English in 1838. The book claims to provide the revelations God gave to Enoch, the origin of the laws of nature, and the history of the kingdom of God.

Epatoscomancy
(*see also* Hepatoscopy)

Divining the future by means of inspecting the entrails of sacrificial animals. In Ezekiel 21:21 there is an example of the liver being used for divination:

"For the king of Babylon stands at the
two ways, to use divination; he shakes
the arrows, he consults the teraphim,
he looks at the liver."

Epiphany
(*see also* Befana, St.;
Tiffany; Tiphany)

A momentous revelation is an epiphany. It is also a festival celebrating the manifestation of Christ to the Gentiles, as revealed by his appearance to the shepherds and the Magi, his baptism by John the Baptist, and his first miracle at Cana. It is observed 12 days after Christmas, January 6, and is sometimes called the Twelfth Day, or Christmas of the Gentiles. It has been observed since at least 194 and is older than Christmas.

Equidistant Letter Sequences (E.L.S.)
(*see also* Gematria)

A statistical phenomenon in which sequences of letters can be discovered which spell out allegedly secret messages. E.L.S. appeals to people who believe the Bible is a book within a book and contains esoteric messages. For example, searching the Hebrew letters of Genesis for patterns, about 300 related pairs of words can be found. Believers in E.L.S. have claimed to predict all manners of current events. The only problem is that the E.L.S. phenomenon can work with any lengthy text. Similar results have been obtained using *War and Peace*, by Leo Tolstoy (1828–1910), and *Moby Dick*, by Herman Melville (1819–1891).

Ermine

A weasel known for its thick, soft fur. In Christian tradition the animal is a symbol of purity because it was reputed to surrender to its pursuers rather than dirty its immaculate white winter coat attempting to escape. It symbolizes the Virgin Mary and the Incarnation of Christ. The animal became associated with the motto, "better death than dishonor." The animal's fur is now considered to be the height of luxury.

Ethelreda, St. *see* Tawdry

Evangelist

From the Greek, meaning "one who announces good news." The men known as the four evangelists, the writers of the Gospels, were Matthew, Mark, Luke and John. An evangelist has come to mean any preacher of the Gospel, especially itinerant Protestant revivalists, and television preachers.

> "Evangelist, n. A bearer of good tidings, particularly (in a religious sense) such as assure us of our own salvation and the damnation of our neighbors."
> — *The Devil's Dictionary*, Ambrose Bierce (1842–1914).

Eve
(*see also* Adam; Adam's Rib; Bone of My Bones; Daughter of Eve; Tree of Knowledge of Good and Evil; Would You Adam and Eve It?)

The first woman, Adam's wife and named by him, "because she was the mother of all living" (Genesis 3:20). In Hebrew her name is related to live. Eve brought sin into the world by eating of the fruit of the Tree of Good and Evil. Her punishment was the pain of childbirth: "In pain you shall bring forth children" (Genesis 3:16). Eve was created from Adam's rib, which signified her closeness and equality with him: "This at last is bone of my bones and flesh of my flesh" (Genesis 2:23). A controversial theory based on mitochondrial DNA, genetic material passed from mother to child, speculates that a common maternal ancestor of us all lived in Africa 200,000 years ago.

> "When Eve ate this particular apple, she became aware of her own womanhood, mentally. And mentally she began to experiment with it. She has been experimenting ever since. So has man. To the rage and horror of both of them."
> — *Fantasia of the Unconscious*, D. H. Lawrence (1885–1930).

Even-Christian

A fellow Christian or neighbor.

> "...the more pity that great folk should have countenance in this world to drown or hang themselves, more than their even Christian."
> — *Hamlet*, William Shakespeare (1564–1616).

Evil Eye

The belief that someone has the power to bewitch, kill and do evil merely by a glance of the eyes. A legend arose that Pope Pius IX (1792–1878) had the evil eye. During a procession the pope happened to glance up at an open window. At that moment a nurse standing at the window lost hold of an infant which tumbled to the ground and was killed. In Galatians 3:1 the notion of the evil eye is used metaphorically to illustrate the spiritual weakness of the people. Other possible biblical references are in Deuteronomy 28:34, where the power is involuntary and not maliciously cultivated, and in Judges 8:21, where the ornaments on the necks of camels may be charms to ward off the evil eye.

Ex Cathedra
(*see also* Papal Infallibility)

A Latin phrase which means "from the chair." Someone who speaks with knowledge and authority is said to speak *ex cathedra*. The phrase is sometimes used ironically. When the pope speaks, from the throne of the pontiff, on matters of morals, faith and doctrine he is speaking *ex cathedra* and is infallible. The doctrine of infallibility was promulgated in 1870.

Exaltation of the Holy
Cross *see* Holy Cross Day

Excommunication *see* Anathema

Extreme Unction

One of the seven sacraments of the Roman Catholic Church. A priest, while praying, dips his thumb into holy oil and anoints a dying person upon the eyes, ears, nose, mouth, hands and feet in the form of a cross. The sacrament imparts strength and grace during the final hours of life. The oil is blessed once a year on Maundy-Thursday.

> "Is any among you sick? Let him call for the elders of the church, and let them pray over him, anointing him with oil in the name of the Lord" (James 5:14).

Eye

The idea of the all-seeing eye of God is based on Proverbs 15:3: "The eyes of the Lord are in every place, keeping watch on the evil and the good." Within a triangle the eye symbolizes the Trinity. Eyes on a platter are an attribute of St. Lucy (d. 304), who plucked the eyes out of her head and sent them to an unwanted suitor who had admired them. Her eyes were miraculously restored and Lucy became the patron saint of those with eye trouble.

Eye for an Eye
(*see also* Turn the Other Cheek)

The principle of retaliation, *lex talionis*, in Mosaic law. By today's standards this is considered vindictive and harsh punishment, but in Old Testament times it was seen as a limit on vengeance. The principle is countermanded in Matthew 5:38–39, where we are urged to turn the other cheek.

> "If any harm follows, then you shall give life for life, eye for eye, tooth for a tooth, hand for hand, foot for foot, burn for burn, wound for wound, stripe for stripe" (Exodus 21:23–24).

Eye of a Needle
(*see also* Camel; Rich Man's Comfort)

Anything impossible or extremely difficult to achieve.

> "For it is easier for a camel to go through the eye of a needle than for a rich man to enter the kingdom of God" (Luke 18:25).

Eye to Eye

To be eye to eye or to see eye to eye is to be in complete agreement with someone else. It stems from Isaiah 52:8:

> "Hark, your watchmen lift up their voice, together they sing for joy; for eye to eye they see the return of the Lord to Zion."

F

Faggot

Heretics were burned at a stake surrounded by bundles of sticks called faggots. Heretics who gave up their false doctrines were compelled to wear embroidered representations of faggots on their arms as a demonstration of the fate they had so narrowly avoided.

> I think that friars and their hoods,
> Their doctrines and their maggots,
> Have lighted up too many feuds,
> And far too many faggots.
> —*Chant of Brazen Head*, Winthrop Mackworth Praed (1802–1839).

Faith That Moves Mountains

There is nothing more powerful than faith.

> "Truly, I say to you, if you have faith and never doubt … if you say to this mountain, 'Be taken up and cast into the sea,' it will be done" (Matthew 21:21).

Falcon

A bird of prey which, in its wild state, symbolizes unregenerate prideful humankind. Once tamed, the falcon symbolizes the converted pagan. The falcon

is not mentioned in the King James Bible (1611).

> "A falcon, towering in her pride of place …"
> —*Macbeth*, William Shakespeare (1564–1616).

Fall, The

A lapse from a privileged position. Adam and Eve fell from God's grace because they ate of the fruit of the Tree of Knowledge of Good and Evil (Genesis 3).

> "The desire of power in excess caused the angels to fall; the desire of knowledge in excess caused man to fall."
> —*Of Goodness*, Francis Bacon (1561–1616).

Fall by the Wayside

To be left behind or forgotten is the meaning of this phrase today. The expression is derived from Matthew 13, the Parable of the Sower, where it means something different. The seed that fell by the wayside was not forgotten. It failed to take root.

Fall from Grace

To lose a privileged position or fall into sinfulness.

> "Christ is become of no effect unto you, whosoever of you are justified by the law; ye are fallen from grace" (Galatians 5:4).

Fall on Your Sword

This saying refers to committing suicide or self-sacrifice when all is lost. It comes from 1 Samuel 31:4–5 and 1 Chronicles 10:4–5.

Fallen Angel
(*see also* Angels; Lucifer)

Anyone who has fallen from grace or a

position of power and privilege. The fallen angels were those angels who joined Lucifer in his rebellion against God and were cast into hell.

> "Depart from me, you cursed, into the eternal fire prepared for the devil and his angels" (Matthew 25:41).

False Prophets *see* Wolf in Sheep's Clothing

Fat of the Land

To live in luxury. Other than in this phrase the word *fat* has lost the meaning of *the best*. Now fat is an undesirable, referring to waste or excessive girth.

> "... and you shall eat the fat of the land" (Genesis 45:18).

Faun
(*see also* Satyr)

A lascivious hairy man of the forest with horns and the tail of a goat. In Christian art the faun is symbolic of lust.

Fear of God

A common biblical expression, often misunderstood. It means to hold God in reverence and awe.

> "I fear God, yet am not afraid of him." —*Religio Medici*, Sir Thomas Browne (1605–1682).

Feast of Fools
(*see also* Boy Bishop)

An expression which means a time of unrestrained jollity. Beginning in the 12th century, the Feast of Fools or Feast of the Ass was a good-natured burlesque of church rituals. Held on the day of the Feast of the Circumcision (January 1) or the Feast of the Epiphany (January 6), it purported to honor the ass upon which Jesus entered Jerusalem. There was a pope of fools, an archbishop of dolts, a boy bishop and an abbot of unreason supported by "priests" dressed as women. Participants wore masks, or had their faces smeared with ashes. They brayed instead of saying "Amen," and conducted mock masses, played dice on the altar, burned old shoes in the censer and generally behaved as irreligiously as possible. At first the Feast of Fools was held in cathedrals and churches, but eventually it escaped ecclesiastical control and moved into the streets where the parody became harsher. Public nudity, obscene songs and gestures, and the pelting of onlookers with dung were featured. The Feast of Fools was suppressed in the 16th century.

Feet of Clay

Someone who is admired but turns out to have a fatal weakness is said to have feet of clay. In Daniel 2:33 a huge idol with "legs of iron, its feet partly of iron and partly of clay" was erected. In the prophecy of Daniel the legs represented the dynasties that ruled Asia Minor and Egypt in the fourth century B.C. In the literal sense the feet of clay made the idol vulnerable to destruction.

Fifteen
(*see also* Numbers)

A symbol of progress because of the 15 steps of the temple, which the Virgin Mary climbed when she left her mother and father.

Fig Leaves
(*see also* Adam's Needle)

The leaves of a common Mediterranean plant of suitable size and shape for Adam and Eve to employ as a covering for their genitals after their fall from innocence.

Fig 92

Much later, stonecutters were kept busy carving fig leaves to cover the male genitalia of the Vatican's vast collection of Greek and Roman statuary.

> "Then the eyes of both were opened, and they knew that they were naked; and they sewed fig leaves together and made themselves aprons"
> (Genesis 3:7).

Fig Sunday
(*see also* Palm Sunday)

An old name for Palm Sunday. Figs used to be eaten on that day in commemoration of the barren fig tree mentioned in Mark 11:12–14.

Fight the Good Fight

Nowadays this has become a vaguely humorous expression for trying one's best, but when Paul used the expression he was talking about the fight for eternal salvation. It comes from 1 Timothy 6:12:

> "Fight the good fight of faith."

Figs *see* Naughty Figs

Figurative Poetry *see*
Emblematic Poetry

Filoque Controversy

A dispute between the Western and Eastern Churches that has festered since the sixth century. The Western Church maintains that the Holy Spirit proceeds from the Father and the Son, *Filoque*, while the Eastern Church maintains that the Spirit comes from the Father only. According to the Western Church, if the Father and Son are one, then whatever proceeds from the Father must proceed from the Son as well. This is known as the Procession of the Holy Spirit.

For the Eastern Church, such a doctrine compromises the primacy of the Father, the source of all divinity. The *Filoque* controversy is one of the main points of difference between the churches.

Filthy Lucre

A contemptuous reference to ill-gotten money. It is found in the King James Bible (1611). "Whose mouths must be stopped, who subvert whole houses, teaching things which they ought not, for filthy lucre's sake" (Titus 1:11). Today the expression is often humorously applied to riches no matter how acquired.

> "Money is welcome tho' it be in a dirty clout, but 'tis far more acceptable if it come in a clean handkerchief."
> —*Familiar Letters*, James Howell (c. 1594–1666).

Fire and Brimstone

To threaten the sinful with damnation in hell is the meaning of fire and brimstone. Brimstone is another name for sulphur and its suffocating smell. Fire and brimstone is a common biblical image of divine punishment. Genesis 19:24; Deuteronomy 29:23; Job 18:15; Psalm 11:6; Isaiah 30:33, 34:9 and Revelations 21:8 are examples of its use.

> The minister gave out his text and droned along monotonously through an argument that was so prosy that many a head by and by began to nod — and yet it was an argument that dealt in limitless fire and brimstone and thinned the predestined elect down to a company so small as to be hardly worth saving.
> — *The Adventures of Tom Sawyer*, Mark Twain (1835–1910).

First Born of Egypt
(*see also* Plagues of Egypt)

The tenth and the most horrible of the plagues visited upon Egypt. The first-born of the Israelites escaped death because the Israelites had been instructed by Moses to sprinkle lamb's blood over the lintels of their doors.

> "Thus says the Lord: About midnight I will go forth in the midst of Egypt; and all the first-born in the land of Egypt shall die, from the first-born of Pharaoh who sits upon his throne, even to the first-born of the cattle" (Exodus 11:4–5).

Fish *see* Ichthus

Fish Days
(*see also* He Eats No Fish;
Holy Mackerel)

Days on which Roman Catholics were forbidden to eat meat: Fridays, Ash Wednesday and Wednesdays in Lent.

Fisherman's Ring
(*see also* Pope)

A ring depicting St. Peter as a fisherman. A fisherman's ring is given to each pope, as heir to St. Peter, for use as a seal. Upon the death of a pope it is destroyed. "Fishers of men" is a metaphor for winning souls.

> "As he walked by the Sea of Galilee, he saw two brothers, Simon who is called Peter and Andrew his brother, casting a net into the sea; for they were fishermen. And he said to them, 'Follow me, and we will make you fishers of men.' Immediately they left their nets and followed him" (Matthew 4:18–20).

Five
(*see also* Numbers)

Five symbolizes humanity after the fall. There are five senses, five wounds of Christ, five books of Moses and five fishes and five loaves that fed the multitude.

> If from his home the lad that day
> His five small loaves had failed to take,
> Would Christ have wrought —
> can any say —
> The miracle beside the lake?
> —*A Store of Loaves*, Margaret Junkin Preston (1820–1897).

Flagellants
(*see also* Discipline, A)

Fanatical groups, active in the 13th and 14th centuries, who believed that they could appease divine wrath and atone for the sins of the world by publicly whipping and scourging themselves about the shoulders with leather thongs. Sometimes the thongs were capped with iron points. The flagellants arose as a reaction to outbreaks of the plague and were declared heretics in 1349. Flagellants traveled in organized bands vowing to endure self-torture for 33 days in honor of Christ's 33 years of life on earth. Isolated revivals of the movement appeared as late as the 19th century. To lash oneself one thousand times was equivalent to chanting 10 psalms; 15 thousand times was equivalent to the entire book of Psalms. St. Dominic Loricatus (1170–1221) whipped himself 300,000 times in six days. In some monasteries collective flagellation took place every Friday after confession.

> "Flog your enemies with the Name of Jesus, for there is no weapon more powerful in heaven or on earth."
> —*Ladder of Divine Ascent*, St. John Climacus (c.579–649).

Flagellum Dei *see* Scourge of God

Flags *see* Christian Imagery
on Flags; Crosses on Flags; St.
Andrew's Cross; Union Jack

Flaming Sword

After Adam and Eve ate of the forbidden fruit, God drove them from the Garden of Eden with "a flaming sword which turned every way" (Genesis 3:24).

Fleet Marriages

Clandestine Christian marriage ceremonies, without banns or licenses, performed by corrupt and poverty-stricken clerics in the Fleet Prison, London. Thirty marriages a day were common. In the four months prior to February 12, 1705, there were 2,954 marriages. Such marriages were declared null and void in 1774.

Flesh and Blood *see* I'm Only
Flesh and Blood

Flesh of My Flesh *see* Bone
of My Bones

Fleshpot

Literally a pot where meat is cooked. From its earliest usage *fleshpot* has been associated with luxury but the emphasis was always on *pot*. Now the emphasis is on *flesh* and the word means a place offering every variety of sensuality imaginable, especially carnal. It comes from Exodus 16:3:

> "Would that we had died by the hand of the Lord in the land of Egypt. When we sat by the fleshpots and ate bread to the full; for you have brought us out into this wilderness to kill the whole assembly with hunger."

Flood
(*see also* Noah; Noah's Ark)

A deluge which according to Genesis 6–9 covered the entire world. The only survivors of this catastrophe were Noah and his family and the mated pairs of animals brought on board the ark, a huge wooden vessel built by Noah at God's order. According to Hebrew reckoning, the flood occurred in 2348 B.C. In the Greek Septuagint chronology it occurred in 3155 B.C. If taken literally, the earth was covered with 20,000 feet of water, the equivalent of 500,000,000 cubic miles of water, all of which fell in 960 hours, 40 days and 40 nights. Where did all the water come from? One theory had it that the earth once had rings like Saturn but composed of water. Another suggestion was that vast quantities of underground water welled up through cracks in the earth's surface. Others have attempted to prove that the story of the Flood represents the ancient memory of a catastrophe that covered only the Middle East.

> "The only thing that stops God sending a second Flood is that the first one was useless."
> — *Characters and Anecdotes*, Nicolas Chamfort (1741–1794).

Florida

The state of Florida received its name because it was discovered on Palm Sunday, 1512, by Juan Ponce de Léon (c. 1460–1521). In Spanish the day was called *Pascua Florida* (flowering Easter). *La Florida* was originally the Spanish name for the entire eastern seaboard of North America as far north as Newfoundland.

> "... The very name Florida carried the message of warmth and ease and comfort. It was irresistible."
> — *Travels With Charley*, John Steinbeck (1902–1968).

Fly
(*see also* Beelzebub)

Because it spreads disease, the fly is a symbol of sin. It is also the symbol of the devil because Satan is Beelzebub, the Lord of the Flies. Flies constituted one of the plagues of Egypt.

Fly in the Ointment

Some trifling defect which can spoil even the best things in life.

"Dead flies make the perfumer's ointment give off an evil odor; so a little folly outweighs wisdom and honor" (Ecclesiastes 10:1).

Flying Scroll of Zechariah

Predictions of misfortune. A parchment (Zechariah 5:1–5) 20 cubits long by 10 cubits wide which fluttered in the air when unfurled. It foretold the calamities about to be visited upon the Hebrews.

Follow in the Footsteps of, To

To follow behind an esteemed leader or innovator.

"For to this you have been called, because Christ also suffered for you, leaving you an example, that you should follow in his steps" (1 Peter 2:21).

Fool Bible

A 17th century Bible printed Psalms 14:1 as, "The fool hath said in his heart there is *a* God," instead of, "*no* God." The printer was fined heavily.

Fool's Paradise *see* Limbo:

Limbus Fatuorum

For Better or Worse

Stoically accepting of the good and the bad. Its present use comes from the marriage service in the *Book of Common Prayer* (1579):

"For better or worse, for richer, for poorer, in sickness or in health."

For Everything There Is a Season

A famous Bible passage (Ecclesiastes 3:1–8), which describes the balance and order of human existence. "For everything there is a season, and a time for every matter under heaven: a time to be born, and a time to die," etc. The Byrds, a rock and roll band of the 1960s, famously performed the passage in the song "Turn, Turn, Turn," with music composed by Pete Seeger.

For God's Sake

An expression of surprise or annoyance. A sake was an official privilege.

"For God's sake, let us sit upon the ground and tell sad stories of the death of kings."
—*Richard II*, William Shakespeare (1564–1616).

For Pete's Sake

A mild expression of surprise or outrage. Pete is a euphemism for God or St. Peter.

Forbidden Fruit
(*see also* Apple)

Anything desired but forbidden. God commanded Adam and Eve not to eat the fruit of the Tree of Knowledge of Good and Evil in the Garden of Eden. When Adam and Eve gave in to temptation they were driven out of Eden (Genesis 3:1–16). The words "forbidden fruit" do not appear in the biblical narrative.

Of man's first disobedience, and the fruit
Of that forbidden tree whose mortal taste
Brought death into the World, and all over woe,
With loss of Eden ...
—*Paradise Lost*, John Milton (1608–1674).

Forbidding the Banns

From the ninth century it has been

customary to announce in church on three successive Sundays the intention of a couple to marry. This is called publishing the banns. If anyone had a formal objection to the marriage taking place it is called forbidding the banns.

Foreskin of Christ

(*see also* Circumcision of Jesus)

There is a tradition that after the circumcision of Jesus, Mary preserved the foreskin, giving it to St. John the Evangelist. Another story says that an old woman preserved the foreskin in a vase of oil. It was this oil that Mary Magdalene had used to anoint Jesus. Over the centuries a number of churches have claimed to possess, as a relic, the foreskin of Christ.

Forgotten Sins Bible

A Bible of 1638 in which Luke 7:47 is rendered as "Her sins, which are many, are *forgotten*," instead of "*forgiven*."

Forty

(*see also* Numbers)

A number with many biblical associations: 40 days and 40 nights brought the Flood; Moses, Elijah and Christ fasted for 40 days; The Children of Israel spent 40 years wandering in the desert; Spies spent 40 days investigating Canaan; 40 days was the time devoted to burying the dead; Jonah gave Ninevah 40 days to repent; Isaac married Rebecca when he was 40 years of age; Esau was 40 when he married two Hittite women; Joseph and his kinsmen fasted 40 days for Jacob, their father; Eli was a judge of Israel for 40 years; Goliath defied Saul's army for 40 days; Kings David and Solomon reigned for 40 years each; Ezekial bore the iniquities of the house of Judah for 40 days; After his resurrection Christ remained on the earth for 40 days; Tradi-

tion has it that Christ was 40 hours in his tomb.

Forty Stripes Save One

In Deuteronomy 25:2–3 it says that a wicked man may only be beaten 40 times. In order to avoid exceeding the punishment, it was customary to stop at 39. A scourge with 13 thongs was devised and with this a guilty man would be struck three times. Irreverent theological students have sometimes referred to the Thirty-nine Articles of the Anglican Church as 40 stripes save one. The ship's articles of pirate captain John Phillips (?–1724) decreed that the punishment for being careless with a lit candle or for striking a crewmate was "forty stripes lacking one on the bare back."

Fountain

A symbol of the Virgin Mary. "A fountain sealed" (Song of Solomon 4:12), is interpreted as Mary's perpetual virginity. "For with thee is the fountain of life" (Psalms 36:9). Jesus is called the fountain of life.

Four

(*see also* Numbers)

The earth has four corners, there are four Rivers of Paradise, there are Four Horsemen of the Apocalypse, four Gospels, four evangelists and four cardinal virtues (prudence, fortitude, justice and temperance). Four is a mystical number that represents the created world and the human body.

> Matthew, Mark, Luke and John,
> Bless the bed that I lie on.
> Four corners to my bed,
> Four angels round my head.
> One to watch, and one to pray,
> And two to bear my soul away.
> —*A Candle in the Dark*,
> Thomas Adey (fl. 1655).

Four Corners of the Earth
(*see also* Ends of the Earth)

Stemming from a time when the earth was thought to be flat, the expression survives to mean the entire earth: "... gather the dispersed of Judah from the four corners of the earth" (Isaiah 11:12). Scientists in 1965 determined that there may be four "corners" of the earth — in Ireland, near the Cape of Good Hope, off the Peruvian coast and in the Pacific Ocean between Japan and New Guinea. Each of these locations, several thousand square miles, is about 120 feet higher than the geodetic mean and has a stronger gravitational pull than the surrounding area.

Four Horsemen of the Apocalypse
(*see also* Apocalypse)

A euphemism for the end of time or a cataclysm. In Revelation 6:2–8 John opens the Book of Seven Seals and sees a vision of riders on red, black, pale and white horses. The red horse symbolizes bloodshed and war, the black represents famine, the pale horse is death and the white horse symbolizes civil strife.

Four–leaved Clover
(*see also* Calvary Clover)

A talisman of good luck, if not given away, because of its rarity and resemblance to a cross. A two-leaved clover enables a maiden to see her future husband. A three-leaved clover represents the trinity and a five-leaved clover is a sign of bad luck, unless given away.

Fourteen
(*see also* Numbers; Seven)

A number signifying goodness and mercy, since it is composed of a double seven, the mystical number of completeness and perfection.

Fourteen Stations of the Catholic Church *see* Stations of the Cross

Fox

Because it is considered to be crafty and sly, the fox symbolizes trickery and the devil. The animal denotes heretics and was used in anticlerical burlesques.

> "And Jesus said to him, 'Foxes have holes, and birds of the air have nests; but the Son of man has nowhere to lay his head'" (Matthew 8:20).

Francis, St. *see* St. Francis's Distemper

Frankincense and Myrrh

Frankincense and myrrh were among the rare and valued gifts presented to the infant Jesus by the wise men (Matthew 2:11). Frankincense symbolized divinity, and myrrh was a funerary spice foretelling the crucifixion and resurrection. They are both fragrant resins obtained from trees native to Arabia and East Africa. Frankincense and myrrh are used as incense because they give off a sweet, spicy aroma when burned. The wisps of white smoke represent the offering of prayers and petitions to heaven. The product known today as frankincense is not the same as that of biblical times. It is obtained from the Norway spruce fir.

Friday

Fridays are often considered unlucky because the crucifixion took place on that day. Sailors, in particular, considered it unlucky to commence a voyage on Friday. A story is told of someone anxious to prove the superstition wrong who had a ship's keel layed on a Friday, launched on a Friday, masts erected on a Friday, cargo shipped on a Friday and commanded by a Captain Friday. She sailed on Friday and was, of course, never heard from again.

> "On Friday, too! The day I dread."
> —*Fables*, John Gay (1685–1732).

Frog

Because frogs were one of the plagues of Egypt, they are symbols of evil and uncleanliness. But because it hibernated in winter and reappeared in spring the frog can also be a symbol of the resurrection.

> "Frogs in the marsh mud drone
> their old lament."
> —*Ecologues*, Virgil (70–19 B.C.).

G

Gabriel
(*see also* Archangels; Gabriel's Hounds)

Although he is not called such in the Bible, Gabriel is an archangel. As the messenger of God he interpreted Daniel's vision of the future (Daniel 8:16–26) and announced the births of John the Baptist (Luke 1:11–20) and Jesus (Luke 1:26–38). The trumpet of Gabriel will announce the day of judgment.

> "When the last trumpet sounds the *Times* will want to check with Gabriel himself, and for the next edition will try to get it confirmed by an even Higher Authority."
> —*Gambit*, Rex Stout (1886–1975).

Gabriel's Hounds
(*see also* Gabriel; Goose)

Wild geese, because the cries and wing beats of a flock of geese have been likened to that of a spectral pack of hounds. The birds were supposed to be the souls of unbaptized children fated to wander until the day of judgment. Gabriel is, of course, the archangel Gabriel.

Gad
(*see also* Egad)

A euphemism for God and an expression of mild surprise or exasperation. Gad was also the name of a tribe of Israel and of two minor Old Testament figures. Gad occurs in the form of *by gad*, *egad* and *gadzooks*. *Zooks* is probably connected to *hooks*, or the nails used in Christ's crucifixion.

Galilean *see* Thou Hast Conquered Galilean

Gall of Bitterness
(*see also* Wormwood and Gall)

Bitter and extreme affliction. Grief and joy were thought to be governed by the gallbladder.

> "For I see that you are in the gall of bitterness and in the bond of iniquity" (Acts 8:23).

Garden of Gethsemane *see* Gethsemane

Gargoyle

Any extremely ugly person. A gargoyle is also a grotesque animal or human figure, usually made of stone. They were used as rain spouts on the roofs of medieval churches and other buildings. They symbolize the evils of the world when compared to the spiritual security found within the church. Gargoyles depicted evil spirits fleeing the sacred confines of a church.

G.D.

(*see also* Doggone; Goddamn)

A euphemism for the G-word, Goddamn. Presumably, the abbreviation makes the swearing acceptable in polite company. G.D. is often employed in a lighthearted fashion.

Gee

A mild oath, which is a euphemism for Jesus. It is related to *geewhillikers* and *gee whiz*.

Gematria

(*see also* Equidistant Letter Sequences; 666)

Gematria are numerical relationships and equivalents of letters and words in the Bible which purport to reveal secret or esoteric messages. The system operates on the theory that every letter in Hebrew possesses a numerical value. Thus Abraham's steward Eliezar (Genesis 15:2) is worth all of Abraham's 318 servants because the numerical value of Eliezar is 318.

Genealogy

Genealogy, sometimes called the science of snobs, has concocted some fantastical, even blasphemous, family trees for people who wished to demonstrate a connection with Old Testament prophets, Noah, the Three Wise Men or Christ himself. The Anglo-Saxon and Swedish kings were content to trace their descent from Adam as did James I of England and Charles I of Spain. They were eager to prove that their royal houses were the oldest in Europe. Of course Adam, as the first man, is everyone's ancestor. The key biblical connection was with Abraham. Once that relationship was established, it was not too difficult to show kinship with St. Joseph and Jesus. The Lévis family in France hired a genealogist to "prove" that they were descended from the tribe of Levi in the Old Testament. When riding to church the Duc de Lévis was in the habit of shouting, "To my cousin, coachman!" Another family, by the name of Pons, claimed descent from Pontius Pilate. When members of the two families met, the head of the Lévis clan said, "Your relatives have treated mine rather shabbily!"

Geneva *see* Protestant Rome

Geneva Bible *see* Breeches Bible

Gentiles

A word used by Jews to denote non–Jews. The early Christians used the word for those who were neither Jews nor Christians. Mormons call all non–Mormons Gentiles. This creates an unusual problem in classification.

> "Jews in Utah, being non–Mormons, are theoretically subject to classification as Gentiles, which gives rise to the well-known remark that 'Utah is the only place in the world where Jews are Gentiles.'"
> — *Inside U.S.A.*, John Gunther (1901–1970).

Gesmas

The unrepentant thief crucified with Jesus. The name is traditional but does not occur in the Bible.

Get Thee Behind Me Satan

Spoken when renouncing temptation. The biblical meaning is different. Jesus spoke these harsh words to Peter, who had suggested that Jesus need not be crucified and thus not fulfill God's plan:

> "Get thee behind me, Satan: thou art an

offence unto me: for thou savorest not the things that be of God, but those that be of men" (Matthew 16:23).

Gethsemane

Any scene of suffering or a lonely ordeal. The Garden of Gethsemane was near Jerusalem, at the foot of the Mount of Olives. It was the place to which Jesus retired to pray on the night of his betrayal and arrest. "Then Jesus went with them to a place called Gethsemane, and he said to his disciples, 'Sit here, while I go yonder and pray…. My soul is very sorrowful, even to death; remain here, and watch with me'" (Matthew 26: 36, 38). Though he asked his disciples to keep watch, they fell asleep and Jesus was alone. The event has been called "The Agony in the Garden."

Giants

(*see also* Goliath)

"There were giants in the earth in those days" (Genesis 6:4), is a fragment of an ancient myth about a race of giants, Nephilim, who mated with women. Their wickedness was so great that God was provoked into sending the great flood. The pre–Israelite tribes of Anakim and Rephaim were also described as giants. In Christian art Goliath is depicted as a giant, as is St. Christopher carrying the infant Jesus on his shoulders.

> Strong were our sires, and as they
> fought they writ;
> Conquering with force of arms, and
> dint of wit:
> Theirs was a giant race before the flood.
> —*Epistle to Mr. Congreve*, John
> Dryden (1631–1700).

Gibeonite

(*see also* Hewers of Wood
and Drawers of Water)

The slave of a slave, a menial or drudge. Because of their trickery the Israelites made

the people of Gibeon "hewers of wood and drawers of water" (Joshua 9:27).

Gideon Society

A nondenominational Christian organization which places Bibles in hotel rooms, prisons, hospitals, schools, etc. To date more than 70 million Bibles have been distributed by the Gideons free of charge. Founded in 1899, the society is named after Gideon, who was chosen by God to deliver Israel from its enemies.

> "Why do they put the Gideon Bibles
> only in the bedrooms,
> where its usually too late, and not in
> the barroom downstairs?"
> —*Contribution to a Contribution*,
> Christopher Morley (1890–1957).

Giles, St. *see* Handicapped

Giotto's O

Pope Boniface VIII (c. 1235–1303), seeking the best artists in Italy to adorn churches and cathedrals, so the story goes, sent for samples of their work. Giotto di Bondone (c. 1266–1337), while still a shepherd boy, hurriedly drew a single O on a piece of paper and sent that to the pope. The pope marveled at the perfect O and immediately engaged Giotto. Something that is as round as Giotto's O is perfect but took little effort. Giotto became the most important artist of his day producing many religious images.

> " … the practical teaching of the masters
> of Art was summed up by the
> O of Giotto."
> —*The Queen of the Air*, John
> Ruskin (1819–1900).

Gird Up Your Loins

To prepare oneself for difficult action or hard work either physical or mental. In biblical times people would tuck up the ends of long garments into their belts so they could move more freely and not soil their clothes.

> "Gird up your loins, and take my staff in your hand, and go" (2 Kings 4:29).

Girl

The word girl occurs only twice in the King James Bible (1611), in Joel 3:3 and Zechariah 8:5. The word originally applied to a child of either sex. A boy could be called a knave-girl. One of the patron saints of girls is Maria Goretti, who was stabbed to death in 1902 at the age of 12. She was canonized for her purity in 1950, in the presence of her killer who had transformed his life after experiencing a vision of Maria.

Gis

Corruption of JHS, or Jesus.

> By Gis, and by Saint Charity,
> Alack, and fie for shame!
> —*Hamlet*, William Shakespeare
> (1564–1616).

Give the Devil His Due

To give a wicked man credit for some talent or skill.

Give Up the Ghost *see* Death, Euphemisms for

Glastonbury Thorn
(*see also* Joseph of Arimathea)

A hawthorn tree in Glastonbury, England, said always to bloom on Christmas Eve. Joseph of Arimathea is supposed to have visited the spot and planted his staff, brought with him from the Holy Land, which then took root. It was a sign to build the first Christian church in Britain on the spot. Glastonbury thorn is the name of a variety of hawthorn which blossoms at Christmas.

Glory
(*see also* Aureole, Halo)

A large aureole or halo that surrounds the entire body and seems to radiate light. Moses, Elijah and Christ are shown this way in depictions of the Transfiguration. The glory was white, gold or yellow.

Gnash One's Teeth
(*see also* Weeping and Gnashing of Teeth)

Anger or frustration. "Men will weep and gnash their teeth" (Matthew 8:12). The dictionary defines gnash as grinding the teeth together, so the expression is redundant.

> "Bung him out ... Cast him into the outer darkness, where there is wailing and gnashing of teeth."
> —*Jeeves in the Offing*, P. G. Wodehouse (1881–1975).

Go and Sin No More

A rebuke to hypocrites. In John 8:9–11 Jesus shows forgiveness to a woman caught in adultery and instructs her accusers that they are not without sin either.

Go to the Devil

To go to rack and ruin. An expression which, contrary to popular belief, has no direct Christian or biblical origin. In the 17th century it referred to the Devil Tavern in London, a popular watering hole for lawyers and writers. Frequent references to the tavern occur in the literature of the period.

Goat

(*see also* Scapegoat)

The domestic variety of goat was considered to be a symbol of lust, because of the size of its phallus. The devil took the form of a cloven-hoofed he-goat. Mountain goats, however, because of their sharp sight, represented the all-seeing eye of God. The wild goat only ate health-giving grass and symbolized those who chose virtue and rejected vice.

> If poisonous minerals, and if that tree,
> Whose fruit threw death on else
> immortal us,
> If lecherous goats, if serpents envious
> Cannot be damned; alas; why
> should I be?
> —*Holy Sonnets*, John
> Donne (1572–1631).

God Bless You

The custom of saying this phrase when someone sneezes probably goes back to St. Gregory the Great (c. 540–604) who said it to victims of the plague.

God Finally Caught His Eye

The writer George S. Kaufman (1889–1961) had a particularly strong dislike of waiters. His epitaph for a deceased waiter was "God finally caught his eye."

God Rest You Merry, Gentlemen

The punctuation for this Christian carol should have a comma after "merry." In other words, God keep you happy and cheerful, gentlemen. A common punctuation error puts the comma after "you."

Goddamn

(*see also* Doggone; G.D.)

The G-word, a strong blasphemous curse. The English said this curse so often that in the Middle Ages the French called them *Les Goddamns*.

God's Acre

A cemetery or churchyard. The idea is that the dead will be sown there in hope of resurrection (1 Corinthians 15:36–44).

> I like that ancient Saxon phrase,
> which calls
> The burial-ground God's-Acre!
> —*God's-Acre*, Henry Wadsworth
> Longfellow (1807–1882).

God's Truce *see* Truce of God

God-spell *see* Gospel

God Ye Good Den

An abbreviation of "God give you good evening."

> Nurse: God ye good morrow,
> gentlemen.
> Mer: God ye good den,
> fair gentlewoman.
> —*Romeo and Juliet*, William
> Shakespeare (1564–1616).

Godless Books

The only two books of the Bible that do not mention God are Song of Solomon and Esther.

Godless Florins

A name given to English florins minted in 1849, from which the initial F.D., *Fidei Defensor*, "defender of the faith," was omitted. The coins were also called Graceless Florins because D.G., *Dei Gratia*, "By the grace of God," was also omitted.

Godspell *see* Gospel

Gog and Magog

Sometimes used to refer to any pair of important people in fields such as literature or politics. In Revelation 20:8 Gog and Magog are two nations allied with Satan who will wage war against God's people. They will usher in the great war at the end of time. Gog was also used in oaths as an archaic corruption of God: "By Gog!" "By Gog's blood!" "By Gog's bones!"

Golden Bowl

The allusion in Ecclesiastes is to death and the impermanence of all earthly things. Henry James used the symbolism of the broken golden bowl in his novel *The Golden Bowl* (1904) for fleeting and imperfect relationships.

> "Remember also your Creator in the days of your youth, before the evil days come ... before the silver cord is snapped, or the golden bowl is broken" (Ecclesiastes 12:1,6).

Golden Calf

Wealth, or other false ideals, too highly esteemed. When Moses climbed Mt. Sinai to be given the Ten Commandments, the Israelites under the leadership of Aaron melted golden jewelry to make an idol of a calf (Exodus 32:1–4).

Golden Number
(*see also* Numbers)

The number of the 19-year lunar or metonic cycle. It was written on some calendars in gold and is used to determine the date of Easter and other moveable feasts. At the end of the cycle of 235 lunar months the full moon always appears on the same calendar date as it did at the beginning. To discover a year's golden number, add one to it and divide by 19. The remainder will be the golden number. If there is no remainder the golden number is 19.

Golden Rule *see* Do Unto Others as You Would Have Others Do Unto You

Goldfinch

Because it was thought to eat thorns and thistles, this songbird came to symbolize Christ's suffering. In art, when held in the hand of the infant Jesus, the goldfinch foretells the Passion. When held in the hand of Mary the bird suggests Mary's sorrowful foreknowledge.

Golgotha *see* Calvary and Golgotha

Goliath
(*see also* Giants)

David, when a mere shepherd boy, slew this Philistine champion with a well-placed stone from a slingshot (1 Samuel 17:23–54). Goliath's height was "six cubits and a span" (1 Samuel 17:4). If we assume a cubit to be 21 inches, then Goliath was about 10½ feet tall. Less well known is the fact that 2 Samuel 21:19 records a second giant named Goliath the Gittite, "the shaft of whose spear was like a weaver's beam." He was slain by Elhanan in an unspecified manner. "Goliath" has come to refer to any very big, extremely strong man.

Golly

A mild oath of surprise. The word is a euphemism for God. Related terms include *golly gee, goldang* and *goldarn. Gee* is itself a euphemism for Jesus while *dang* and *darn* are euphemisms for damn.

Good Grief

A popular expression of regret which

comes from "God's grief," Christ's suffering on the cross. Related expressions include *good gosh*, *good gracious* and *good gravy*.

Good Samaritan
(*see also* Good Samaritan in Officialese)

A person who does a good deed or makes a donation to charity with no thought of personal gain. In Luke 10:30–37, Jesus tells the parable of a traveler who was left for dead by thieves. Passers-by ignored the man. It took a Samaritan to bind the man's wounds and care for him. The Samaritans, reviled by most Jews, were a schismatic Jewish sect who only accepted the first five books of the Old Testament as canonical. For Jesus to construct a parable around a Samaritan must have been startling to his hearers. A small community of Samaritans still exists in Israel. The term *Good Samaritan* does not appear in the Bible story. He is simply a Samaritan.

Good Samaritan in Officialese
(*see also* Good Samaritan)

After World War II, Philip Fothergill, a British politician, retold the familiar story in the following way:

> The Samaritan, on finding the injured man by the roadside, telephoned the Jerusalem and Jericho Joint Hospital Board. Owing to an unfortunate misunderstanding between the two depots, there was a delay of five hours in sending an ambulance and by the time it arrived the victim had died.
> No possible blame can be attached to the Samaritan for doing so little. It must be remembered that he was a citizen of a suspect power. Moreover, the visa on his passport was probably out of date, and if he had fallen into the hands of the local police he would have been thrown into jail or deported by the Jewish authorities as an undesirable alien.

Good Shepherd

Someone responsible for the religious guidance and care of others. There is a plethora of images of the shepherd and his sheep, God and his people, pastor and congregation, in the Bible.

> "I am the good shepherd. The good shepherd lays down his life for the sheep" (John 10:11).

Good Thief *see* Dismas

Goodbye

A contraction of "God be with ye." The word does not appear in the King James Bible (1611).

Goodman, St.

St. Omobuono, *Good Man*, (d. 1197), was a prosperous merchant from Cremona, Italy. He was the epitome of generosity. No matter how much he gave to the poor, it was always miraculously replenished by angels.

Goose
(*see also* Barnacle Geese; Gabriel's Hounds; Misericord)

On a misericord the image of a goose listening to a fox was a way of warning the congregation to watch out for false preachers. The goose is an attribute of St. Martin of Tours (c. 316–397) because when hiding to avoid being made a bishop he was given away by a goose.

Gopher Wood

Genesis 6:14 records how Noah constructed his ark from gopher wood. No one knows what gopher wood, is so the King James Bible (1611) left the Hebrew word "gopher" untranslated. Modern Bible translations use "cypress," but the accuracy of this is far from certain. Gopher wood has nothing to do with the rodent of the same name. Other suggestions for gopher wood are juniper, reed bundles, fir, acacia, ebony, cedar or pine. Gopher could also refer to a construction method and not to a type of wood at all.

Gosh

An exclamation of surprise or dismay. It is used by people who want to avoid saying God. Related words include *gosh-almighty, gosh-dang, gosh-darn* and *ohmigosh. Dang* and *darn* are euphemisms for damn.

Goshen *see* Land O' Goshen

Gospel

Commonly believed to have been derived from *God-spell*, Anglo-Saxon for good news. More likely the meaning was *God-story*, a narrative about God.

> "It was a common saying among the Puritans, 'Brown bread and the Gospel is good fare'"
> —*Commentary Isaiah XXX*, Matthew Henry (1662–1714).

Gospel Truth, The

Incontrovertible truth. Gospel truth is something that is as true and unfailing as the Gospels.

Gossip

Trivial talk spoken behind a person's back. Also the person who engages in such talk. Originally the word referred to the sponsor of a baptism; *God-sibb*, a kinsman with God. William Shakespeare (1564–1616) used the word in this fashion in *Two Gentlemen of Verona*:

> "'Tis not a maid, for she hath had gossips; yet 'tis a maid, for she is her master's maid, and serves for wages."

Gourd
(*see also* Prophet's Gourd)

A symbol of the resurrection because God caused a gourd to spring up and shade Job from his grief. Job 4:6 is its only mention in the Bible. As a symbol of redemption the gourd contrasted with the apple, the instrument of the Fall. Because gourds were hollowed out to carry water, they are attributes of pilgrims and pilgrim saints.

Grail *see* Holy Grail

Grandparents of Jesus
(*see also* Holy Family; Jesus Christ; Jesus, Family of)

According to the Book of James, an apocryphal work, Joachim and Anne became the father and mother of the Virgin Mary and the grandparents of Jesus. A rich man of Nazareth, who gave generously to the poor and the Temple, Joachim had fathered no children. After Joachim retired by himself to the wilderness for a 40-day fast, the angel Gabriel told him to return home. Upon seeing his wife Anne, Joachim kissed her and at that moment Mary was conceived, free of original sin. Anne was perceived as the personification of perfect motherhood because of the saintliness she imparted to Mary.

Greater Love Hath No Man

Self sacrifice and unconditional love. Nowadays the expression is often ironically.

"Greater love hath no man than this, that a man lay down his life for his friends" (John 15:13).

Green

Because of its obvious association with growing things, the color green came to represent immortality, hope and the growth of the Holy Spirit in man.

Green Pastures

Any pleasant environment. Probably one of the most famous biblical passages, these lines are often spoken at funerals:

"The Lord is my shepherd, I shall not want; he makes me lie down in green pastures. He leads me beside still waters; he restores my soul" (Psalms 23:1–3).

Greeting Card Manufacturers

The makers of greeting cards have their own patron saint, the aptly named St. Valentine (d. c. 264).

Grey

Symbolizing the immortality of the soul and the death of the body, grey is the color worn by members of some religious orders.

Griffin

A mythical beast with the body and tail of a lion, and the head and wings of an eagle. It was believed to be one of the unclean beasts forbidden in Leviticus 11:20. When it wasn't carrying men to its nest in its fearsome talons, the griffin hoarded gold. It symbolizes both knowledge and usury.

H

Haddock *see* Peter's Fish

Hagioscope
(*see also* Lepers)

A low oblique window placed in the walls of medieval churches. Through these openings those suffering from leprosy and other loathsome skin diseases could see the Mass. A hagioscope was sometimes called a squint.

Hail Mary *see* Ave Maria

Hair of Absalom *see* Absalom's Hair

Hair Shirt
(*see also* Sackcloth and Ashes)

A purposefully uncomfortable garment worn, fur side next to the skin, for mortification or penance. It was an undershirt made from stubbly goatskin or coarse horse hair. To wear a hair shirt is to patiently endure tribulations.

Hallelujah

Also allelujah. From the Hebrew for "praise Yahweh." Hallelujah is used as an exclamation of praise in the Psalms and in the liturgies of many Christian churches. St. Jerome introduced it into Christian worship in the fourth century. An Italian folktale has it that the word is derived from three soldiers — a Roman, a Piedmontese from Northern Italy and a German — who were guarding Christ's body after the crucifixion. When Christ rose from the dead, the Roman shouted *Ha!*, the Piedmontese *Lè lu!* (It's him) and the German *Ja!*

"Do not abandon yourselves to despair.... We are the Easter people and hallelujah is our song."
—*Address in Harlem*, Pope John Paul II (1920–2005).

Hallelujah Lass

A jocular term formerly applied to women in the Salvation Army.

Hallucinogens *see* L.S.D.

Halo
(*see also* Glory; Mandorla)

Also called a nimbus. In art, a radiant disk of light surrounding the head of a holy person. A triangular halo was used for God the father, a cross-shaped halo for Christ resurrected. Persons who were still alive when depicted in an artwork received a square halo. Mary, angels and saints were given round halos. Legendary or allegorical figures received hexagonal halos. Often a halo, especially in a depiction of Christ, will be combined with sacred monograms, stars or a cross. Beginning in the third century, halos were used in images of Christ, and from the fifth century in depictions of the Virgin Mary, saints and angels. Originally halos were blue, but by the fifth century yellow, gold and rainbow colors became common. Halo also refers to the glamour or glory surrounding a famous person or idealized thing.

What after all
Is a halo?
It's only one more thing to keep clean.
— *The Lady's Not for Burning*, Christopher Fry (1907–2005).

Hand of God

A hand coming out of a cloud, while bestowing a blessing, was the usual way of depicting the first person of the Trinity, God the Father. This came from the two meanings of *yad*, a Hebrew word which can mean hand or power. Thus, God's hand expresses his power. The souls of the righteous were sometimes portrayed as small figures in God's hand.

"The righteous ... are in the hands of God" (Ecclesiastes 9:1).

Handicapped

St. Giles (c. 712) is the patron saint of the disabled. Legend says that he received an arrow in the knee as a result of a hunting accident. Refusing to be healed he remained crippled for life, the better to mortify his flesh. Churches dedicated to him were usually located beyond the walls of medieval towns to better receive the handicapped, people who would not be permitted within the city gates.

Hanged as High as Haman

To be destroyed by one's own plotting, or hoist on one's own petard. In Esther 3–7, Haman plotted against the Jews, especially Mordecai, for whom he had prepared a gallows, "of fifty cubits high." But Esther saved the day and Haman went to the gallows himself.

Hangover
(*see also* Drunkard)

Those suffering the horrors of a hangover can turn to Bibiana (d. c. 361), their own patron saint. A garden near the saint's grave grew a miraculous herb which cured headaches.

Haplography
(*see also* Dittography; Homeoteluton)

An inaccuracy which sometimes occurred when Bibles were copied by hand. A weary scribe would accidentally omit a letter or an entire word.

Hard Shell — Soft Shell

These terms have been applied to the conservative and liberal wings of the Baptist Church, taken from the different stages of development in crabs.

> "You're a Christian?"
> "Church of England," said Mr. Polly.
> "H'm," said the employer, a little checked. "For good all round business work I should have preferred a Baptist."
> — *The History of Mr. Polly*,
> H. G. Wells (1866–1946).

Hare

(*see also* Rabbit)

A creature related to the rabbit but usually larger and having longer legs and ears. Because it was an animal believed to reproduce by parthenogenesis, it symbolizes Christ's virgin birth. The hare also symbolized timidness and, because of its supposed power to change its sex at will, lust.

> ...the hare of whom the proverb goes,
> Whose valor plucks dead lions by the beard.
> — *King John II*, William Shakespeare (1564–1616).

Haroot and Maroot

(*see also* Angels)

Angels of medieval legend who, because of a lack of compassion, became prone to human passions. They were exiled to earth and its temptations, where they became kings of Babel and teachers of black magic.

Hart

An adult male deer, the symbol of the Christian searching for the water of eternal life. It was believed that the hart could sniff out snakes in their den and stomp them to death. This symbolizes Christ, who can discover the devil and defeat him.

> "As a hart longs for flowing streams, so longs my soul for thee, O God" (Psalm 42:1).

Harwood, Rev. Edward *see* Bowdlerized Bible

He Bible

In the earliest edition of the King James Bible, published in 1611, there is confusion about Ruth 3:15. In the so-called *He Bible* the verse appears as " ... and *he* went into the city." Another version, the *She Bible*, says " ... and *she* went into the city." The *he* version is correct but most later editions continue to use "*she*."

He Eats No Fish

(*see also* Fish Days; Holy Mackerel)

In 16th and 17th century England this expression meant that a person could be trusted because he was not a Roman Catholic. Catholics were required to eat fish on Fridays; Protestants were not.

He That Runs May Read

A popular abbreviation of Habakkuk 2:2. Something so obvious and easy to understand that it can be read on the run.

> "Write the vision; make it plain upon tablets, so he may run who reads it."

Head Carriers

Certain saints — Alban (d. 304), Denis (d. c. 258), Lucian (d. 312), and others — who met martyrdom by beheading, are depicted carrying their heads in their hands.

St. Denis was supposed to have carried his severed head six miles before laying it down on the spot where a cathedral would be built in his memory.

Headaches

The patron saint of headaches is St. Acacius, who is depicted with a crown of thorns.

Hear! Hear!

A formal expression of approval that has been used in parliament since the 17th century. Disapproval was signified by humming, which earned the response, "Hear him," which by 1689 had become, "Hear, hear!" Its occurrence in the Bible (2 Samuel 20:16) is probably a coincidence:

> "Then a wise woman called from the city, 'Hear! Hear!'"

Heathen

(*see also* Pagan)

Originally someone who dwelt on the heath. After Christianity became the religion of the towns, the pagans on the heath opposed the new faith. The word now means a person who is neither Christian, Jew nor Muslim. It is sometimes used as an insult for the unenlightened or the uncultured. Some have felt that Luke 14:23 permits the use of force to covert a heathen:

> "Go out to the highways and hedges, and *compel* people to come in, that my house may be filled."

Heaven's Dimensions

"The city lies foursquare, its length the same as its breadth; and he measured the city with his rod, twelve thousand stadia; its length and breadth and height are equal" (Revelation 22:16). We can assume that 12,000 stadia equal 1,500 miles. Therefore, Heaven will be 1,500 × 1,500 × 1,500, or 3,375,000,000 cubic miles.

Heaven's Gate

Jacob, awakening from his dream of a ladder to heaven, spoke,

> "How awesome is this place! This is none other than the house of God, and this is the gate of heaven" (Genesis 28:17).

Heavens to Betsy

An oath of surprise or outrage. Betsy is a euphemism for God.

Heavy Heart

Someone with a heavy heart is very sad indeed.

> "Heaviness in the heart of man maketh it stop: but a good word maketh it glad" (Proverbs 12:25).

Hell

The place or state of eternal punishment for the souls of sinners. The word is used 21 times in the King James Bible (1611). Nine times the word is a translation of *Hades* (home of the dead in Greek mythology), eight times of *Gehenna* (the Hebrew place of torment and abomination), and once of *Tartarus* (a place worse than Hades).

Hell's Angels

Fiends from hell; the messengers of Satan. Now the name of a notorious motorcycle gang.

Hen and Chickens

A common artistic subject suggesting the providence of God.

"O Jerusalem, Jerusalem, killing the prophets and stoning those who are sent to you! How often would I have gathered your children together as a hen gathers her brood under her wings, and you would not!" (Matthew 23:37).

Henotheism

The belief that while other gods may exist only one god is important for a particular people or tribe. The Israelites passed through this stage of belief, which is midway between polytheism and monotheism.

"God has taken his place in the divine council, in the midst of the gods he holds judgment" (Psalms 82:1).

Hepatoscopy
(*see also* Epatoscomancy)

Divination by means of inspecting the livers of sacrificial animals.

"To use divination ... he looks at the liver" (Ezekiel 21:21).

Herod

The family name of rulers of Judea mentioned in the New Testament. They are often confused and thought of as a single brutal tyrant. In fact there were at least five Herods. The two most important are:

Herod Antipas (21 B.C.–A.D. 39) (*see also* Salome) Not to be confused with his father, Herod the Great (73–4 B.C.). Herod Antipas was a tetrarch, the ruler of a quarter of a Roman province, from 4 B.C. to A.D. 39. Pontius Pilate sent Jesus to Herod Antipas who "treated him with contempt and mocked him" (Luke 23:11). At the behest of Salome, Herod Antipas had John the Baptist beheaded.

Herod the Great (73–4 B.C.) (*see also* Massacre of the Innocents; Out-Herod Herod) Not to be confused with his son,

Herod Antipas (21 B.C.–A.D. 39). Herod the Great was king of Judea at the time of the birth of Jesus. Fearful that a great king had been born to challenge him, Herod ordered all boys two years of age and under to be killed. This horrible crime is called the Massacre of the Innocents. Herod the Great's name has become synonymous with extreme tyranny.

Hewers of Wood and Drawers of Water
(*see also* Gibeonite)

Hard and menial work for low pay. Because of their trickery, Joshua passed a harsh judgment on the Gibeonites when he said,

"Now therefore you are cursed, and some of you shall always be slaves, hewers of wood and drawers of water for the house of my God" (Joshua 9:23).

Hexameron

A period of six days, the time of the Creation as recorded in Genesis 1.

Hide Your Light Under a Bushel

Hiding your abilities with excessive modesty. The expression is a paraphrase of Matthew 5:15. The bushel was a wooden or earthenware container that was difficult for light to penetrate:

"Nor do men light a lamp and put it under a bushel, but on a stand, and it gives light to all in the house."

His Days Are Numbered

Said when someone has limited time or is near death; from Daniel 5:26:

"God has numbered the days of your kingdom and brought it to an end."

His Martinmas Will Come as It Does to Every Hog

November 11 is Martinmas, the feast of St. Martin. It was traditionally the time when hogs and other livestock were slaughtered and salted. The proverb means that a man's death is as certain to come as that of a hog's at Martinmas.

Hocus-pocus

(*see also* Abracadabra)

A mock Latin phrase, sometimes rendered as hokey-pokey, beloved by magicians and conjurers since the 17th century. It is possibly a parody of *hoc est corpus*, "This is the Body," in the Latin communion service.

> "The law is a sort of hocus-pocus science."
> —*Love a la Mode*, Charles Macklin (c. 1697–1797).

Hokey-pokey *see* Hocus-pocus

Hold a Candle to the Devil

To assist that which is evil. The reference is to the custom of burning candles before the images of saints.

Holiday

A corruption of Holy Day. Originally holy days were festival days in the Roman Catholic Church.

> The holiest of all holidays are those
> Kept by ourselves in silence and apart;
> The secret anniversaries of the heart.
> —*Holidays*, Henry Wadsworth Longfellow (1807–1882).

Holidays *see* All Souls' Day; Ash Wednesday; Assumption of the Virgin; Boxing Day; Candlemas

Day; Childermas; Christmas; Easter; Epiphany; Feast of Fools; Fig Sunday; His Martinmas Will Come as It Does to Every Hog; Holy Cross Day; Lent; New Year's Day; Palm Sunday; St. Agnes's Eve; St. Grouse's Day; St. Monday; St. Patridge Day; St. Swithin's Day; Whitsunday

Holly

(*see also* Christmas)

A family of plants with prickly leaves and thus symbolic of the crown of thorns worn by Christ at the crucifixion. Holly is now synonymous with Christmas. Legend says that when the holy family fled into Egypt they sheltered under a holly tree. God caused the tree to spread its branches so they could hide from Herod's troops. Blessed by Mary, the tree became an evergreen and a symbol of immortality. The Romans gave each other holly branches as an expression of good fortune at the new year.

Holy Bingo

In the 19th century Christian missionaries in Africa introduced the game of bingo along with the Bible. Many Africans began to associate the Christian heaven with the game, specifically a winner's joyous shout of "Bingo." As a result, bingo became the word for Heaven in many languages.

Holy Coat

The garment worn by Christ which Roman soldiers gambled over at the crucifixion. This seamless coat was supposed to have been woven by Mary, the mother of Jesus. According to legend the coat was worn by Jesus and grew as he did. The relic was believed to have been discovered by St. Helena (c. 250–c. 330).

Holy Cross Day

September 14 is Holy Cross Day, a feast which commemorates the return of the relic of the holy cross of Jesus to Jerusalem in 630. After St. Helena (c. 250–c. 330) discovered the true cross, a piece of it remained in Jerusalem at the Church of the Holy Sepulchre until 615, when it was carried off by the king of Persia. It was retrieved by the Emperor Heraclius (c. 575–641) in 630 and returned to Jerusalem. As the emperor began to enter the city by the way Jesus had used on his way to Calvary, parapet stones fell and blocked the emperor's way. An angel appeared holding a cross, saying that Jesus had come to Jerusalem humbly riding on an ass. Heraclius removed his finery and humbly entered the city, carrying the relic of the cross. Jews in Rome were forced to attend church on Holy Cross Day and listen to a sermon, a practice which endured until 1840.

Holy Face *see* Volto Santo

Holy Family

(*see also* Grandparents of Jesus; Jesus, Family of)

Mary, Joseph and the infant Jesus. Sometimes Elizabeth, Anne (the mother of Mary), and John the Baptist are included.

Holy Fish

Fish that lived only in wells near churches were called holy fish. Considered sacred, they lived two in each well and ate hazelnuts which fell from nearby trees. The fish were supposed to have magical and oracular properties.

Holy Grail

Any noble ideal or spiritual quest. The Holy Grail was a legendary emerald chalice or dish used by Jesus at the Last Supper. After passing to Pilate, who used it to wash his hands, the Grail came into the possession of Joseph of Arimathea. In it Joseph caught drops of Christ's blood as he hung on the cross. Joseph then carried the Grail to England, where it was subsequently buried and the location lost. Only a knight absolutely pure in thought and deed could find it. The search for the Holy Grail was the inspiration for many of the tales surrounding King Arthur and the Knights of the Round Table. The Holy Grail had the power of prolonging life and preserving chastity. Also called *Sangrail.*

> "One thing I know. If living isn't a seeking for the grail it may be a damned amusing game."
> — *This Side of Paradise*, F. Scott Fitzgerald (1896–1940).

Holy Handkerchief *see* Mandylion

Holy Innocents' Day *see* Childermas

Holy Mackerel

(*see also* Fish Days; He Eats No Fish)

A common expression of surprise or amazement. It stems from a contemptuous reference to Roman Catholics as mackerel snatchers, people obliged to eat fish on Fridays.

Holy Nails

The nails by which Christ was fastened to the cross at the crucifixion. There were either three nails (one for each palm and one through the crossed feet), or four (one for each limb). Whatever their number, it was believed that they were saved by Nicodemus, a Pharisee who took part in the burial of Jesus. St. Helena (c. 250–c. 330), according to legend, had one nail incorporated in the crown of the Emperor Constantine (c. 280–337) and another in his horse's bridle, so that he would be victorious in battle. More than 30 churches have claimed to possess one of the Holy Nails.

Holy of Holies

Also *Sanctum Sanctorum*. A private sanctuary or a place which only the most privileged are permitted to enter. It was the most sacred precinct in the Jewish Temple.

Holy Oil

Oil brought to Europe from Jerusalem in the fourth century and oil blessed at the tombs of saints. Its reputation was such that when Marco Polo journeyed to China in the 13th century, Kublai Khan (1216–1294) requested that holy oil be brought to him from Jerusalem.

Holy Roman Empire

The name applied to a changing group of territories in Germany, Holland, Austria, Bohemia, Italy and parts of France — 300 principalities and about 1,500 semi-independent states. It grew out of a desire to unite Western Christendom under a single political ruler and revive the glories of the ancient Roman Empire. The Holy Roman Empire was founded in 962 by Otto I of Germany who revived the earlier empire founded by Charlemagne in 800. It was never a unified political entity, although in its early centuries a feudal suzerainty was established over many of its constituent states. Inevitably, there were disputes between emperors and popes. By the 14th century the Empire had gone into steep decline and had become essentially a German institution; a loose federation of states under the House of Hapsburg.

But faced with the Protestant Reformation, nationalism and the notions of liberty and enlightenment unleashed by the French Revolution, the Holy Roman Empire became an anachronistic shell. Nevertheless, it survived until 1806. Its detractors declared that it was neither holy, nor Roman, nor an empire.

Holy Rood

The cross of the crucifixion, or a representation of it. The Feast of the Exaltation of the Cross, or Rood-mass-day, commemorates the finding of a piece of the true cross by St. Helena, c. 326.

Holy Shroud *see* Shroud of Turin

Holy Smoke

A common expression of surprise or amazement. It is a profane reference to the Holy Ghost.

Holy Toledo

An expression of mild surprise or vexation. Toledo, a city in Spain, was holy to both Christians and Moslems.

Holy Water *see* As the Devil Loves Holy Water; Court Holy Water; Holy Water Sprinkler

Holy Water Sprinkler
(*see also* Asperges; Court Holy Water)

A wry name for a gruesome club studded with spikes. In the hands of a medieval knight skilled in its use, the weapon could cause blood to flow like sprinkled holy water.

Holy Writ

Specifically the Bible, the Scriptures.

But anything considered to be authoritative can be called Holy Writ.

> And thus I clothe my naked villany
> With odd old ends, stolen forth
> of holy writ;
> And seem a saint, when most I
> play the devil.
> — *King Richard III*, William
> Shakespeare (1564–1616).

Holystone

A Bible-shaped piece of sandstone, or coarse pumice, used to clean the decks of wooden ships. Sailors had to kneel to perform this task, as if at prayer.

The word was originally spelled *holeystone*. It supposedly lost its *e* because the sailors who used it knew no ease (*e's*).

> "Six days shalt thou labor and all thou art able, and on the seventh — holystone the decks and scrape the cable."
> — *Two Years Before the Mast*,
> R. H. Dana (1815–1882).

Homeoteleuton

(*see also* Dittography; Haplography)

An inaccuracy that sometimes occurred when Bibles were written by hand. An overworked scribe was likely to confuse words which had the same ending.

Horns of Moses

Art depicting Moses, especially from the Middle Ages, frequently shows him with horns on his forehead. This comes from a curious misunderstanding of Exodus 34: 29–30. When Moses came down from Mount Sinai, "the skin of his face shone...." The Hebrew word for shining can be translated as "sending forth beams" or "sending forth horns." The Latin Vulgate chose the second possibility and translated the passage as, "his face was horned." Horns are associated with cuckoldry. A man who accepted paternity for another's bastard was said "to stand Moses."

Horse

Symbolic of lust and virility. The animal was believed to lose its sexual vitality when its mane was cut. The patron saints of horses are Eligius (c. 590–c. 660), Martin of Tours (c. 316–397), and Hippolytus (d. c. 235).

> "God forbid that I should go to any heaven in which there are no horses."
> — *Letter to Teddy Roosevelt*, R. B. Cunninghame-Graham (1852–1936).

Horseshoe

Why is the horseshoe lucky? One theory says that a horseshoe turned on its side resembles a C, the first letter of Christ. Metal horseshoes, a Roman invention, have been used since the second century B.C. Leather horseshoes were in use even earlier. Makers of horseshoes can call upon their patron saints of Eligius (c. 590–660) and John the Baptist (first century).

Host

Bread or wafer used in celebration of the Eucharist. The host is unleavened in the West and leavened in the East. The name comes from the Latin *hostia*, "hostage." After consecration the bread is the body of Christ, the hostage for our sins.

Hot Cross Bun

A spicy bun traditionally eaten on Good Friday. It was originally made from dough kneaded for the host and then marked with a cross. A tradition has it that the bun can keep for 12 months without going moldy. Some people hang one up in their homes as a charm against evil.

One a penny, two a penny,
hot cross buns;
If you have no daughters, give
them to your sons.
— *Hot Cross Buns*, Anon.

House Divided
(*see also* Divide and Conquer)

Internal dissension.

"And if a house is divided against itself,
that house will not be able to stand"
(Mark 3:25; Matthew 12:25).

House of Many Mansions

In a theological sense the House of
Many Mansions is a place of salvation for all
followers of Jesus. In a literal sense, "mansions" is used here for "rooms."

"Let not your heart be troubled: ye believe in God, believe also in me. In my
Father's house are many mansions: if it
were not so, I would have told you. I go
to prepare a place for you" (John 14:2).

How Are the Mighty Fallen

Said, often with a sense of grim satisfaction, when any powerful person is humbled.

"Thy glory, O Israel, is slain upon they
high places! How the mighty
are fallen!" (2 Samuel 1:19).

Hugh of Grenoble, St. *see* Chickens Into Turtles

Humanitarian

Someone devoted to humanity's wel-
fare. Originally the term referred to heretical sects who believed that Jesus was human
and not divine.

"Unfortunately humanitarianism has
been the mark of an inhuman time."
— *All I Survey*, G. K. Chesterton
(1874–1936).

Hyperdulia
(*see also* Dulia; Latria)

Veneration paid to the Virgin Mary as
Mother of God. It is less than the homage
paid to God, *latria*, but more than that paid
to a saint, *dulia*.

Hyssop

Of the mint family, a perennial herb
with a sweet smell. Because of its diuretic
properties, this plant came to symbolize forgiveness, penitence and spiritual cleansing.
Holy water could be sprinkled with it.

"Purge me with hyssop, and I shall
be clean; wash me, and I shall be
whiter than snow" (Psalms 51:7).

I

IΣ

The first and last letters of the Greek
word for Jesus, IHΣOΥΣ. It is a sacred
monogram.

IΣ ΞΣ NIKA

A sacred Greek monogram meaning,
"Jesus Christ, conqueror." IΣ are the first and
last letters of IHΣOΥΣ, the word for Jesus.
ΞΣ are the first and last letters for ΞPIΣTOΣ,
Christ. NIKA means conqueror.

Ichthus

The Greek word for fish which forms
the initials of a sentence meaning, "Jesus
Christ, the son of God, the savior" (*Iēsous,
CHristos, THeou, Uios, Sōtēr*). Subsequently,
the fish became a symbol of Christ, appearing on seals, rings, urns and tombstones.
Today it is commonly seen as a bumper
sticker on cars. Christ was the fisher of men's

souls and performed the miracle of the loaves and fishes. When the inhabitants of Rimini refused to listen to St. Anthony (1195–1231), the saint went to the shore and preached to the fish. The fish, it was reported, lifted their heads above the water and listened attentively to the sermon. In the time of Roman persecution a Christian would draw an arc in the dirt —(— when meeting a stranger. If the stranger made a reverse arc —)— forming a crude fish outline —( )— they knew they were both Christians.

Iconoclasm

Opposition to the established order or to cherished beliefs. Iconoclasm was a reform movement in the Eastern Church in the eighth and ninth centuries. Icons and other images in churches were destroyed by those who opposed idolatry. In 843 the veneration of icons was officially sanctioned, but was distinguished from the worship offered to God.

Identical Bible Chapters

(*see also* Chapters in the Bible; Longest Chapter in Bible; Middle Chapter of Bible; Shortest Chapter in Bible)

2 Kings 19 and Isaiah 37 are identical. Ezra 2 and Nehemiah 7 are the same.

Identical Bible Verses

(*see also* Longest Verse in Bible; Middle Verse of Bible; Shortest Verse in Bible; Verses in the Bible)

In Psalm 107, verses 8, 15, 21 and 35 are the same. The verses of Psalm 136 end the same. 2 Chronicles 36:22–23 and Ezra 1:1–3a are the same.

Idle Bible

In the Bible edition of 1809, Zechariah

11:17 is rendered, "the idle shepherd." In the Revised Standard Version (1952) this has become, "my worthless shepherd."

Idle Rich *see* At Ease in Zion

If Thy Right Eye Offend Thee

A very harsh insistence on righteousness. It has been used as a justification for the expulsion of unfit church members.

> "If your right eye causes you to sin, pluck it out and throw it away" (Matthew 5:29).

Ignatius of Antioch, St. *see* Child Blessed by Jesus

I.H.S.

(*see also* Jesus Paper; Labarum)

Originally a symbol of Dionysos, with an unknown meaning, I.H.S. became a common Christian monogram appearing on vestments, chalices and other ceremonial objects. It is the transliteration of a Greek abbreviation for Jesus. The Greek New Testament was always written in capital letters and well-known names were abbreviated. When Latin scribes made copies of the scriptures, they adopted the Greek abbreviation for Jesus, *IH*, transliterating it into I.H.S. Forgetting that the Greek H is a long E, they read, *Iesus Hominum Salvator*, "Jesus savior of men" into the abbreviation. When the Jesuits were founded in 1540, I.H.S. was interpreted as *In hoc salus*, "In this safety." It was also interpreted as *In hoc signo*, "In this sign," which miraculously appeared in the sky before Constantine's army. The most incorrect reading of I.H.S is "I have suffered."

Illuminati

A name given to members of certain sects and secret societies who claim to have special knowledge or enlightenment. It now has a vaguely sinister connotation. The word was originally quite innocent, being applied to the newly baptized because they were given lighted candles as a sign that they had been illuminated by the Holy Spirit.

I'm Only Flesh and Blood

A plea that a person is only a fallible human and cannot possibly accomplish everything. It probably comes from Matthew 16: 17, "For flesh and blood has not revealed this to you," and Ephesians 6:12, "For we are not contending against flesh and blood."

O God! That bread should be so dear,
And flesh and blood so cheap!
— *The Song of the Shirt*, Thomas
Hood (1799–1845).

Imprimatur
(*see also* Nihil Obstat)

Sanction or approval. In the Roman Catholic Church it is the official permission required by canon law before a religious or theological work can be published. The publication which receives an imprimatur has been approved by a censor appointed by a diocesan bishop. The word means in Latin, "let it be printed." An imprimatur is not an endorsement but simply an indication that the book contains nothing harmful to faith and morals.

In Hoc Signo *see* I.H.S.

In One's Right Mind

To be sane, often after a period of extreme excitement. The expression is commonly used in the negative sense as in, "no one in his right mind would do such a thing." The original reference is to Mark 5:5:

"And they came to Jesus, and saw the demoniac sitting there, clothed and in his right mind, the man who had the legion and they were afraid."

In the Beginning Was the Word

Word was a Greek philosophical concept, the principle of rationality in the midst of chaos, or divine reason. John wants to make clear that the Word has become incarnate in Christ. This is not to be confused with "the word of God," scripture or divine revelation.

"In the beginning was the Word, and the Word was with God, and the Word was God.... In him was life, and the life was the light of men" (John 1:1,4).

In the Fullness of Time

At the proper time. The expression has now become a notorious expression of bureaucratic obfuscation and lethargy. The origin of the term can be found in Galatians 4:4:

"But when the fullness of the time was come, God sent forth his Son, made of a woman, made under the law."

In the Last of Matthew

An old expression which means "the last gasp." A Roman Catholic priest, so the story goes, preached that Protestantism was in the last of Matthew. He meant the last five words of Matthew, which in Latin are "The end of the dispensation." Modern versions of the Bible translate the phrase as, "The end of the world," or "the close of the age."

In the Sweat of thy Face
(*see also* Adam's Curse)

Adam was punished for disobeying God by having to work to survive.

"In the sweat of thy face you shall eat bread" (Genesis 3:19).

In the Twinkling of an Eye

Something that happens almost instantaneously. The expression comes from 1 Corinthians 15:51–52:

> "Lo! I tell you a mystery. We shall not all sleep, but we shall all be changed, in a moment, in the twinkling of an eye at the last trumpet."

Incest *see* Cain's Wife

Incorrupt
(*see also* Odor of Sanctity)

A phenomenon associated with saints. It has been reported that after death the bodies, or body parts, of saints can appear lifelike and free of decay for centuries. The body of St. Francis de Sales (1567–1622) remained incorrupt for a decade after his death. The body of St. Francis of Paola (c. 1416–1507) was said to have remained intact 55 years after death, and that of Antoninius of Florence (1389–1459) 130 years.

Incunabula Bible

Incunabula are books printed before 1501. A Bible of 1594 in which the date on the title page incorrectly reads 1495 is known as the Incunabula Bible.

Index Librorum Prohibitorum

A catalogue of books that were forbidden for any Catholic to read because, in the judgment of papal authorities, they contained heresies. It was introduced in the 16th century and endured until 1966. The punishment for reading any of the banned books was excommunication. The *Index Expurgatorius* was a list of books that could be read after offending passages had been removed. Among those who have appeared in the *Index* were Joseph Addison (1672–1719), Francis

Bacon (1561–1626), Geoffrey Chaucer (c. 1340–1400), Nicholas Copernicus (1473–1543), Dante Alighieri (1265–1321), Alexandre Dumas (1803–1870), Edward Gibbon (1737–1794), Oliver Goldsmith (1730–1774), Victor Hugo (1802–1885), John Locke (1632–1704), John Milton (1608–1674), Michel de Montaigne (1533–1592), Blaise Pascal (1623–1662), and Voltaire (1694–1778).

Indulgence
(*see also* Pardoners; Treasury of the Church)

Contrary to popular opinion, an indulgence is not a permission to commit sin or the purchase of forgiveness. It is not supposed to be the pardon of a sin but the remission of ecclesiastical penalties for an already penitent sinner. Grants of absolution were first issued by Pope Leo III c. 800. They were sold for the first time in 1313 and the practice was greatly abused. It was the sale of indulgences in Germany in 1517 that angered Martin Luther (1483–1546) and helped spark the Reformation. The sale of indulgences was condemned by the Council of Trent in 1563. Indulgences are still granted and can be either plenary (a full remission of penalties) or partial. In modern usage the word "indulgence" means to give in to self-gratification.

Inherit the Wind

To create a storm of trouble. "He who troubles his household will inherit the wind" (Proverbs 11:29). A famous play about the Scopes Trial, a courtroom battle over the teaching of evolution, has this title. The trial occurred in Tennessee in 1925. Clarence Darrow (1857–1938) defended a teacher, John Scopes (1901–1970), who was charged with violating the state law against teaching evolution in public schools. William Jennings Bryan (1860–1925) led the prosecution, winning the case. Scopes was fined $100 but the conviction was overturned by the Tennessee supreme court. The famous play, by Jerome Lawrence (1915–2004) and Robert Lee (1918–1994), was made into an equally famous movie in 1960.

Inner Man

An expression that means the soul or spirit. Since the 11th century it has also been humorously used as a euphemism for the stomach. The original meaning comes from Ephesians 3:16:

> "He may grant you to be strengthened with might through his Spirit in the inner man."

Innocents *see* Massacre of the Innocents

Inquisition see Auto-Da-Fé

I.N.R.I.

The initial letters of the Latin inscription, *IESUS NAZARENUS REX IUDAEORUM,* "Jesus of Nazareth, King of the Jews." This mocking title, also in Greek and Hebrew, was placed on the cross of Jesus (John 19:19).

Intermonastery Loans
(see also Librarian Pope; Librarians; Libraries)

In the Middle Ages monastery libraries as far apart as England and Greece could borrow from each other. A deposit of money, equal in value to the book, was required. On at least one occasion the deposit was lost on account of the book being eaten by a bear! No word about the borrower. Since monk-librarians were held personally responsible for the loss of any books, very little borrowing occurred.

Internet Saint

The patron saint of the Internet is St. Isidore of Seville (c. 560–636). Isidore was a prolific scholar, the author of histories, a dictionary and encyclopedia.

Is Saul Among the Prophets?

Said of someone who supports what he had formerly opposed. The reference is to 1 Samuel 10:12: "Is Saul also among the prophets?"

Is Thy Servant a Dog, That He Should Do This Thing?
(see also Dead Dog; Dog; Living Dog Is Better Than a Dead Lion)

A complaint by someone ordered to do something demeaning. It is a paraphrase of 2 Kings 8:13:

> "What is your servant, who is but a dog, that he should do this great thing?"

Ishmael *see* Call Me Ishmael

Israel *see* Lost Tribes of Israel

Italics

Type, said to be based on the handwriting of the poet Plutarch (1304–1374), in which the letters slope from left to right. They were first used by Aldo Manuzzio (1450–1515) and dedicated to Italy, hence the name. Italics are used to give a word emphasis. Italics in the Bible are not part of the original text but have been added by translators for clarity.

Ite Missa Est

The origin of the word "Mass." The

phrase means "Go you are dismissed," in Latin. The words are the dismissal at the conclusion of a Mass.

Ivory

Ivory has long been a symbol of fortitude and moral purity. Its hardness and dazzling whiteness suggested the incorruptible body of Christ in the tomb. An ivory tower symbolized beauty. "Your neck is like an ivory tower" (Song of Solomon 7:4). In 1837 Charles Augustin Sainte-Buive (1804–1869) used the expression to describe the poet Alfred de Vigny (1797–1863) living in privileged, ascetic separation from the harsh realities of the world. This is the meaning, often applied to academia, which has endured.

J

J

For centuries *J* was a mere calligraphic variation of *I*. The 10th letter of the alphabet does not appear in the original King James Bible (1611) because *J* was not differentiated from *I* until the middle of the 17th century. Prior to that time *I* was both a consonant and a vowel. After that time *J* took over the consonantal function.

Jacob's Ladder
(*see also* Stone of Scone)

In a dream (Genesis 28:10–22), Jacob he saw a ladder reaching to heaven, with angels ascending and descending. Symbolizing the human communion with God, Jacob's ladder was supposed to have 15 rungs, each corresponding to a different virtue. But was Jacob's ladder really a ladder? The Hebrew word that is used is closer in meaning to "stairway." A stairway would

make it possible for angels to simultaneously ascend and descend. Jacob's ladder was the name for a hanging ladder of chain or rope with rungs of wood or iron. A steep flight of steps or a run in a stocking can also have this name. It is also the name of a perennial plant with white or blue flowers and ladder-like leaves.

> "Talk to him of Jacob's ladder, and he would ask the number of steps."
> —*A Matter-of-fact Man*, Douglas Jerrold (1803–1857).

Jacob's Stone *see* Stone of Scone

Jactitation of Marriage

An expression from old Canon law meaning to falsely claim to be married.

Januarius, St. *see* Blood of St. Januarius

Jashar
(*see also* Lost Books; Sun and Moon Stand Still)

A lost Hebrew book quoted in Joshua 10:13 and 2 Samuel 1:17. The word means "upright" or "just," so it is assumed that the Book of Jashar recounted the deeds of the upright. Forgeries purporting to be the Book of Jashar have appeared.

Jehosaphat *see* Jumpin' Jehosaphat

Jehovah
(*see also* Tetragrammaton, Yahweh)

An erroneous transliteration of the Hebrew word for God in the Old Testament. Jewish scholars, in order to protect the unutterable name of God, took the word's consonants, *YHWH*, and combined them with the vowels from *Elohim*, "God" and *Adonai*,

"My Lord," to make *YeHoW (or V) aH*. In the King James Bible (1611), Jehovah occurs 6,855 times.

> Tell them I am, Jehova said
> To Moses, while earth heard in dread,
> And smitten to the heart
> At once above, beneath, around,
> All nature, without voice or sound,
> Replied, O' Lord, Thou art.
> —*Song to David*, Christopher
> Smart (1722–1771).

Jehu *see* Bad Drivers

Jeremiad and Jeremiah

A jeremiad is a lengthy lamentation or mournful complaint. The word comes from the prophet Jeremiah who, in the book named after him and in Lamentations, lamented the fall of Jerusalem and predicted the ruin of Israel at the hands of her enemies. A Jeremiah is someone who is incurably pessimistic.

> "I have seen your abominations, your adulteries and neighings, your lewd harlotries, on the hills in the field. Woe to you, O Jerusalem" (Jeremiah 13:27).

Jericho *see* Walls Came Tumbling Down

Jeroboam

Any large goblet or huge bottle of wine; specifically, a bottle holding three liters. It comes from the name of the first king of Israel. King Jeroboam's rebellion against Rehoboam led to the separate kingdoms of Israel and Judah. Why King Jeroboam's name was attached to a wine bottle remains obscure, but it probably has something to do with his description in the King James Bible (1611) as "a mighty man of valor" (1 Kings 11:28). Jeroboam was sinful but was not portrayed as a drunkard. Wine

makers were then inspired to name even larger bottles after other biblical figures, with even less reason. Rehoboam (son of Solomon, king of Israel) 4.5 liters; Methuselah (longest living man in the Bible) 6 liters; Salmanazar (Assyrian king) 9 liters; Balthazar (Babylonian king) 12 liters; Nebuchadnezzar (Babylonian king) 15 liters.

> "Visions of Dionysiac revels danced in our heads, bachelor suppers whereat naked actresses erupted from pies as we reeled around quaffing jeroboams of champagne."
> —*Chicken Inspector no. 23*,
> S. J. Perelman (1904–1975).

Jesus Bug

The common, and slightly blasphemous, name for the water strider, a family of insects able to walk on water as did Jesus in Matthew 14:25. The insects have long slender legs fringed with hairs which give them this unusual ability.

Jesus Christ

(*see also* Baptism of Jesus; Birthdate of Jesus; Boyhood of Jesus; Brothers and Sisters of Jesus; Christ; Christ of the Trades; Circumcision of Jesus; Death Warrant of Jesus; Foreskin of Christ; Grandparents of Jesus; Jesus, Family of; Languages of Jesus; Light of the World; Man of Sorrows; Messiah; Nativity of Jesus)

"Jesus Christ" is frequently thought of as the Messiah's first and last names but this is not correct. Jesus was his given name, but Christ is a title derived from the Hebrew for *the anointed one*. Strictly speaking the name should be Jesus *the* Christ.

> How sweet the name of Jesus sounds
> In a believer's ear!

It soothes his sorrows, heals his wounds,
And drives away his fears.
—*Olney Hymns*, John Newton
(1725–1807).

Jesus, Family of
(*see also* Brothers and Sisters
of Jesus; Grandparents of Jesus;
Holy Family; Jesus Christ)

Jesus came from a large family. He had sisters unnamed and four brothers — Joseph, Judas, Simon and James. James became a disciple and martyr. Traditions about the perpetual virginity of Mary claimed that the siblings of Jesus were fathered by Joseph during an earlier marriage. According to the apocryphal *Book of James*, Joachim and Anne were the parents of Mary and the grandparents of Jesus. John the Baptist was a cousin.

Jesus, Languages of *see*
Languages of Jesus

Jesus Paper
(*see also* I.H.S.)

Large sheets of paper, 28½ by 21½ inches stamped with the watermark I.H.S.

Jew's Myrtle
(*see also* Crown of Thorns)

The butcher's broom, a family of dark green shrubs native to Eurasia. Jesus's crown of thorns was believed to have been made from it.

Jezebel
(*see also* Naboth's Vineyard)

Any shameless and immoral woman, often in the context of "a painted Jezebel." Jezebel was the wicked wife of King Ahab who encouraged the worship of false gods and arranged for the judicial murder of Naboth. Her end was gruesome. She was thrown from a window, trampled by horses and eaten by dogs (2 Kings 9:30–37).

> "Who was Jezebel, by the way? The name seems familiar, but I can't place her."
> "A character in the Old Testament, sir. A queen of Israel."
> "Of course, yes. Be forgetting my own name next. Eaten by dogs, wasn't she?"
> "Yes, sir."
> "Can't have been pleasant for her."
> "No, sir."
> —*Jeeves in the Offing*, P. G. Wodehouse (1881–1975).

Jiminy Cricket

Apart from being the name of a Disney cartoon character, the friend of Pinocchio, Jiminy Cricket is a euphemism for Jesus Christ. Jiminy comes from *Gemini*, which is derived from the Latin *Jesu domine*.

Jingo *see* By Jingo

Joachim, St. *see* Grandparents
of Jesus

Job's Comforter
(*see also* Patience of Job;
Poor as Job's Turkey)

Someone who appears to be sympathetic during a time of trouble but actually makes matters worse. He often advises a sufferer that his troubles are self-inflicted. After suffering trials and tribulations and receiving scant help from his friends, Job is bound to say,

> "I have heard many such things; miserable comforters are you all" (Job 16:2).

Job's Turkey *see* Poor as Job's Turkey

Jobation

A long tiresome scolding like those inflicted on Job by his friends.

Jonah

(*see also* Prophet's Gourd; Whale)

Someone who brings bad luck to himself and others is a Jonah. The reference is to Jonah, who had the bad luck to be thrown overboard during a storm at sea and then swallowed by a whale.

> "And the lord appointed a great fish to swallow up Jonah; and Jonah was in the belly of the fish three days and three nights" (Jonah 1:17).

Jordan

An old name for a chamber pot. The derivation is unclear but it may come from *Jordan-bottle*, a receptacle that pilgrims and crusaders would fill with water from the river Jordan prior to a homeward journey.

> "Why, they will allow us ne'er a jordan, and then we leak in the chimney, and your chamber-lie breeds fleas like a loach."
> —*Henry IV, Part I*, William Shakespeare (1564–1616).

Joseph, St. *see* Divine Cuckold

Joseph and Potiphar's Wife

Joseph became an overseer in the home of Potiphar, a high-ranking official of the Egyptian pharaoh. When Potiphar's wife attempted to seduce him, Joseph resisted. Falsely accused of rape, Joseph was imprisoned (Genesis 39). Joseph is an allusion to a man of sexual virtue.

Joseph of Arimathea

(*see also* Glastonbury Thorn)

A rich Jew, a member of the Sanhedrin, the Jewish court in Jerusalem, and secret follower of Jesus. After the crucifixion Joseph placed the body of Christ in his own family tomb. Legend has it that Joseph of Arimathea founded a monastery at Glastonbury, thus establishing Christianity in England. A late medieval legend has Joseph bringing the Holy Grail to England. From his staff grew the Holy Thorn of Glastonbury.

Joshua Tree

(*see also* Adam's Needle)

A treelike species of the yucca native to arid regions. Mormons crossing the desert are said to have named it because the plant's outstretched branches resembled the arms of Joshua leading them out of the wilderness.

Jubal

Brother of Tubal-cain, Jubal was the originator of music and singing.

> "He was the father of all those who play the lyre and pipe" (Genesis 4:21).

Jubilee

(*see also* Sabbatical Year)

A time of rejoicing or a celebration of an important anniversary. In the law of Leviticus 25:8–17, 29–31, every 50 years there was to be a celebration of the deliverance from Egyptian captivity. Each jubilee was separated by seven Sabbaths of years: $7 \times 7 = 49$. All farming was to stop, slaves to be liberated and lands returned to their original owners. The Jubilee was probably more of an ideal than an actual practice. In Roman Catholic tradition a jubilee year, which usually occurs every 25 years, is a time of plenary indulgence. Pope Boniface VIII (c. 1235–1303) celebrated the first Jubilee or Holy Year in 1300 and decreed that it be repeated every one hundred years. Clement VI (1291–1352) reduced the time to 50 years and Paul II in 1470 to 25 years.

> Rise and shine and give God the glory
> For the year of Jubilee.
> —*Rise and Shine*, Anon.

Judas

(*see also* Elder; Judas Bible; Judas-colored Hair; Judas Kiss; Judas Slit; Judas Tree; Thirty Pieces of Silver)

Any great betrayer or hypocrite. Judas Iscariot was the disciple who betrayed Christ for 30 pieces of silver and later hanged himself in remorse. According to legend Judas is released from the torments of hell every Christmas Eve and allowed to cool himself for a day on an iceberg.

> "If we had not been taught how to interpret the story of the Passion, would we have been able to say from their actions alone whether it was the jealous Judas or the cowardly Peter who loved Christ?"
> —*The End of the Affair*, Graham Greene (1904–1991).

Judas Bible

(*see also* Judas)

A Bible of 1611 in which Matthew 26:36 inadvertently and startlingly substitutes "*Judas*" for "*Jesus*," rendering the verse,

> "Then Judas went with them to a place called Gethsemane, and he said to his disciples, 'Sit here, while I go yonder and pray.'"

Judas-colored Hair

(*see also* Judas)

Although there is nothing in the Bible to support it, there has long been a popular belief that Judas had red hair and a red beard.

> Rosalind: His hair is of the dissembling color.

> Celia: Something browner than Judas's...
> —*As You Like It*, William Shakespeare (1564–1616).

Judas Hole *see* Judas Slit

Judas Kiss

(*see also* Judas; Kiss of Death)

An act of simulated courtesy or deceitful affection.

> "And he came up to Jesus at once and said, 'Hail, Master!' and he kissed him" (Matthew 26:49).

Judas Slit

(*see also* Judas)

The peephole in a prison door. Also called the Judas hole.

Judas Tree

(*see also* Judas)

Common name for a family of leguminous trees of southern Europe and Eurasia. Legend says that it is the tree upon which Judas Iscariot hanged himself.

Judge Not Lest You Be Judged

An abbreviation of Matthew 7:1–2, which cautions against assuming superiority:

> "Judge not, that you be not judged. For the judgment you pronounce you will be judged, and the measure you give will be the measure you get."

Judgment Day *see* Doomsday

Julian the Apostate

(*see also* Thou Hast Conquered Galilean)

The name given to Flavius Claudius Julianus (c. 331–363), a nephew of Constantine (c. 280–337). On becoming emperor of Rome, Julian renounced his Christian faith and reinstated the worship of the Greco-Roman gods. After he died fighting the Persians in Mesopotamia, a legend arose that St. Mercurius, whom Julian had put to death for refusing to give up Christianity, was raised from the tomb to kill the apostate. A pale soldier on a white horse stabbed Julian in the liver and then vanished. As the dying emperor was carried to his tent, he shouted *Vicisti Galilaee!* "Thou hast conquered Galilean!"

Jumpin' Jehosaphat

Jehosaphat was king of Judah from 873 to 849 B.C. With the addition of the alliterative word "jumpin'" his name has, for unknown reasons, become a mild oath or expression of surprise. There are five lesser Jehosaphats mentioned in the Bible. Jehosaphat has been a euphemism for Jesus since the 19th century.

K

Kedar's Tents

To live in the wilderness. Kedar was a nomad and a son of Ishmael.

> "Woe is to me, that I sojourn in Meshech, that I dwell among the tents of Kedar!" (Psalm 120:5).

Keep the Faith

Don't lose hope and don't give up. An expression commonly used during the civil rights movement of the 1960s. It comes from 2 Timothy 4:7:

> "I have fought the good fight, I have finished the race, I have kept the faith."

Kenelm, St. *see* Seven-Year-Old Saint

Kentish Fire

Thunderous applause, applause given three times, then three more times and once more after that. The expression comes from meetings held in Kent in 1828–1829 in opposition to the Catholic Relief Bill.

Key and Bible
(*see also* Clidomancy)

A means for settling disputes. The Bible is opened at Psalm 51 or Ruth 1, passages dealing with cleansing from sin and steadfast loyalty, and a key is placed on the page. The Bible is then tied with a length of twine and held by the fourth finger of the two disputants. The two then read the words indicated by the key. The key will then turn toward the guilty person and the Bible falls to the ground.

Key Shall Be Upon His Shoulder, The

To have complete authority.

> "And I shall place on his shoulder the key of the house of David; he shall open, and none shall shut; and he shall shut, and none shall open" (Isaiah 22:22).

Kick Against the Pricks

To fight against overwhelming odds or to put up resistance that is futile. The prick is an ox-goad. This very unbiblical expression comes from Acts 9:5 in the King James Bible (1611).

> "It is hard for thee to kick against the pricks."

Kill-priest

A rather harsh term for port wine and the clergy's reputed fondness for it.

Kill the Fatted Calf

To welcome with every luxury, especially to prepare an elaborate homecoming. It comes from Luke 15:30:

> "But when this son of yours came, who has devoured your living with harlots, you killed for him the fatted calf!"

King James Bible
(*see also* Revised Standard Version; Vulgate)

Officially the Authorized Version. The English translation of the Bible authorized by James I of England (1566–1625). It was published in 1611 and was based on the Bishop's Bible, published in 1572. The King James Bible remains a standard of English usage. Modern copies of this translation are not identical with the first edition, however. Numerous typographical errors have been corrected, and the punctuation and orthography have been modernized. The use of capitalization and italics has been changed, as well.

King of Kings

A common euphemism for God or a very powerful ruler. One of the many titles given to Jesus.

> "He is Lord of lords, and King of kings" (Revelation 17:14).

King Solomon's Mines

The source of King Solomon's fabulous wealth is described in 1 Kings 9:27–28:

> "And Hiram sent with the fleet his servants, seamen who were familiar with the sea, together with the servants of Solomon, and they went to Ophir, and brought from there gold, to the amount of four hundred and twenty talents; and they brought it to King Solomon."

Someone calculated that 17,892 kilograms of gold were brought to Solomon. The ships of Solomon and his ally, Hiram, visited Ophir every third year and each time they returned loaded with gold. Naturally, speculation arose as to where Ophir was. India, Malaysia, the Persian Gulf, and even Peru have been suggested. One possible location is Sophala in Mozambique. In some Bible translations Ophir is called Zophora. Inland from Sophala is Zimbabwe, where can be found the remains of ancient gold diggings. H. Rider Haggard (1856–1925) was inspired by the legend of Solomon's gold to write his famous adventure novel, *King Solomon's Mines*, in 1886.

Kiss

Romantic kissing between men and women does not seem to have been the custom in biblical times. Kissing was used as a greeting, a farewell and as an expression of reverence. Kissing was done on the cheeks, forehead, feet, hands, and beard but never on the lips. Proverbs 24:26 seems to suggest otherwise when it says, "He who gives a right answer kisses the lips." But this is probably a mistranslation. The custom of kissing the bride at a wedding comes from the kiss of peace at High Mass.

> "The anatomical juxtaposition of two orbicularis oris muscles in a state of contraction."
> —*Definition of a Kiss*, Austin Dobson (1840–1921).

Kiss of Death
(*see also* Judas Kiss)

This expression comes from Matthew 26:47–49, where Judas Iscariot betrayed

Jesus by a kiss, thus identifying him to the waiting Roman soldiers. It now has the meaning of good intentions that lead to dire consequences.

Kiss the Book

Kissing the Bible or the New Testament to indicate a public promise or to fulfill the words of an oath.

Kiss the Dust

Also lick the dust. To be killed, humiliated or overcome by enemies.

> "May his foes bow down before him, and his enemies lick the dust!" (Psalms 72:9).

Kiss the Pope's Toe

According to an eighth century story, it was the custom to kiss the pope's hand. But when a woman kissed and squeezed the pope's hand the scandal was so great that henceforth the papal hand was withdrawn and the toe offered instead. In fact it is the pope's shoe, inscribed with a cross, which is kissed by supplicants.

Know Them by Their Fruits

A warning to beware of false prophets and phony preachers.

> "You will know them by their fruits. Are grapes gathered from thorns, or figs from thistles?" (Matthew 7:16).

Kriss Kringle
(*see also* Santa Claus)

Although it is commonly used for Santa Claus, this name originally had nothing to do with him. It is a corruption of the German *Christkindl*, the Christ child.

L

Labarum
(*see also* I.H.S.; ΞP)

A military emblem based on the calvary standard of imperial Rome. It was created by Emperor Constantine in 312 after he had a miraculous vision of the cross. The words *In hoc signo vinces*, "By this sign shall thou conquer" and the Chi-Rho monogram, the first two letters of *Christos* in Greek, Ξ and P intersecting, were inscribed on a purple banner affixed to a golden spear. A detachment of 50 soldiers stood guard over it.

Labor of Love

Something not done for gain but for the sheer satisfaction of doing it. The expression comes from Thessalonians 1:3 (and Hebrews 6:10):

> "Remembering before our God and Father your work of faith and labor of love and steadfastness of hope in our Lord Jesus Christ."

Labyrinth

A confusing maze which has only one correct path to the center. It is an obvious symbol of the Christian's one true path to salvation. Many churches of the Middle Ages were decorated with pavement labyrinths. Pilgrims would walk through these, symbolically journeying to the holy city of Jerusalem at the center. Blocked passages represented snares of the devil.

> I fled Him down the nights and down the days,
> I fled Him, down the labyrinth ways
> Of my own mind; and in the midst of tears
> I hid from Him, and under running laughter.
> — *The Hound of Heaven*, Francis Thompson (1859–1907).

Lady's Bedstraw

A wildflower said to have sprung up from the straw Joseph spread on the floor of the stable where Mary gave birth to Jesus.

Lamb of God
(*see also* Agnus Dei; Like a Lamb to the Slaughter)

In the earliest Christian art a depiction of Christ on the cross was considered to be a sacrilege; therefore a lamb was used instead. Christ is frequently identified with the lamb of God. He was the Messiah who permits himself to be "like a lamb that is led to the slaughter" (Isaiah 53:7).

Lance
(*see also* Longinius)

According to John 19:34, when Jesus was dead upon the cross, a soldier pierced his side with a lance. The broken point of the lance became an important relic. It was found by St. Helena (c. 250–c. 330) in Jerusalem, taken to Constantinople in 615, and carried to Paris in 1241, where it remained until lost in the French Revolution. The lance is an emblem of Saints Thomas and Matthew because they were killed with such a weapon.

Land Flowing with Milk and Honey

Originally applied to Canaan, this term came to describe any rich and fertile country. The expression "land of milk and honey" has been in the English language for about a thousand years.

> "I have come down to deliver them ... to a good and broad land, a land flowing with milk and honey; to the place of the Canaanites" (Exodus 3:8).

Land o' Goshen

An expression of dismay or surprise. In Exodus Egypt, a land of great wealth, was named Goshen (Genesis 45–47; Exodus 8–9). Goshen came to mean any land of plenty and comfort.

Land of Beulah   *see* Beulah Land

Land of Nod

In Genesis 4:16, after killing his brother Abel, Cain fled to Nod, an unknown land east of Eden. Possibly because the sound of the word suggests nodding, the land of Nod is now a euphemism for sleepiness, especially when applied to small children. Jonathan Swift in his *Polite Conversation* (1738) was probably the first to use the expression in this way.

Land of the Living

To be alive or to be in the mainstream of events. It comes from Jeremiah 11:19:

> "Let us cut him off from the land of the living."

Language of Eden

"Now the whole earth had one language and few words" (Genesis 11:1). This verse has given rise to much speculation about the first language. Some have said it was Hebrew, Arabic or Chaldean. Celtic scholars claimed that humanity's natural language must be Old Irish. The Persians asserted that Adam and Eve conversed in Persian, the world's most poetic tongue. They also claimed that Arabic, the most persuasive language, was the choice of the serpent, while the angel Gabriel spoke Turkish, the most menacing language, as he drove Adam and Eve from the Garden of Eden. According to legend, King John of

England (c. 1167–1216) was so determined to discover the language of Eden that he had a number of infants locked up and attended by a keeper who, under pain of death, was forbidden to speak to them. After a number of years the king went to see the children and was surprised to hear them chanting,

> King John
> Has many a whim;
> And this is one.

A similar story was told about the king of Egypt by Herodotus in the fifth century B.C.

Languages of Jesus
(*see also* Aramaic; Jesus Christ)

Considering the environment in which he lived, Jesus was probably bilingual and possibly trilingual. Aramaic was the language of the common people of Palestine and there are several examples in the Bible of Jesus speaking it. Jesus was very knowledgeable of the scriptures and they were written in Hebrew. Because of generations of Hellenization, Greek was widely spoken and Jesus may well have been versed in it as well.

Laodicean

A person who is supposedly religious but is, in fact, indifferent. It comes from Revelation 3:14–18, where St. John the Divine castigated the church at Laodicea in Asia Minor. It has come to mean anyone who is timid or indecisive.

Large Family Bible

In a Bible printed in 1820, Isaiah 66:9 says, "Shall I bring to the birth and not *cease* to bring forth," instead of "*cause* to bring forth."

Lark

A member of a family of songbirds common to Eurasia. Because it sings sweetly and flies high toward Heaven, this bird symbolizes the good priest. The lark is not mentioned in the King James Bible (1611).

> Hark! hark! The lark at heaven's gate sings.
> —*Cymbeline*, William Shakespeare (1564–1616).

Lash of Scorpions
(*see also* Scorpion)

A very severe punishment. The expression comes from 1 Kings 12:11. A whip of medieval times with four or five thongs waited with lead was called a scorpion.

> "My father chastise you with whips, but I will chastise you with scorpions."

Last Gasp

The final moment of life. The term appears in the apocryphal book of 2 Maccabees 7:9. It now also has the meaning of exhaustion or last effort.

> "Fight till the last gasp..."
> —*King Henry VI, Part I*, William Shakespeare (1564–1616).

Last Judgment *see* Doomsday

Last Shall Be First and the First Last

An abbreviation that applies to two biblical quotations. The first, "So the last will be first, and the first last" (Matthew 20:16), is a prophesy of the Kingdom of Heaven. The second, "If any one would be first, he must be last of all and servant of all" (Mark 9:35), is a call for humility.

Last Supper

An historical term, not a liturgical one,

for the last meal Jesus shared with his disciples before his arrest and crucifixion. There is some disagreement as to what ceremony was taking place. Matthew 26:17, Mark 14:12 and Luke 22:7 indicate that it was a Seder or Passover meal, but John 13:1 says that it took place before Passover. The solemn re-enactment of the Last Supper, in the form of communion, is central to most branches of Christianity. The painting by Leonardo da Vinci (1452–1519) of the Last Supper is one of the world's most famous works of art.

Latitudinarian

Someone who is largely indifferent to denominational differences and forms of religion. Such a person emphasizes morality over dogma and attempts to reconcile Christian ethics with science and philosophy.

Latria

(*see also* Dulia; Hyperdulia)

Worship offered to God alone, the highest form of veneration.

Laurel

A family of flowering evergreens which symbolize eternity. Because a crown of laurel was awarded to Roman conquerors and champions, it became a symbol of victory for Christians as well.

> The strongest poison ever known
> Came from Caesar's laurel crown.
> —*Auguries of Innocence*, William
> Blake (1757–1827).

Law Unto Themselves

In the bible this is an approving expression, meaning that those outside the Jewish law become part of Christ's law. It now refers to those who are unconventional and make their own rules without regard for others.

> "When Gentiles who have not the law
> do by nature what the law requires, they
> are a law to themselves, even though
> they do not have the law"
> (Romans 2:14).

Lawrence, St. *see* Courteous Spaniard, The

Lawyers

Yves (1253–1303) was a lawyer from Brittany. Because he was incorruptible, he became the patron saint of lawyers. His life gave rise to a Latin rhyme.

> Sanctus Ivo era Brito
> Advocatus et non latro
> Res miranda populo
>
> (St. Ives was a Breton
> a lawyer and not a thief
> which astonished everybody.)

Lazarus *see* Poor as Lazarus

Lazy as Lawrence *see* Courteous Spaniard, The

Lead by the Nose

To control or dominate. The image is that of a large animal being lead by a nose ring.

> "Because you have raged against me and
> your arrogance has come to my ears, I
> will put my hook in your nose and my
> bit in your mouth, and I will turn you
> back on the way by which you came"
> (Isaiah 37:29).

Leda Bible

A bible published in 1572 which caused a storm of protest because of a bizarre choice of illustration. The woodcut in question accompanied the Epistle to the Hebrews. It depicted the Roman god Jupiter, in the form of a swan, visiting Leda, Queen of Sparta, prior to impregnating her with Helen of Troy!

Left

(*see also* Right)

The left side is usually representative of the dark, the evil and the illegitimate. In the last judgment the goats are on the left side while the sheep are on the right. At the crucifixion the bad thief is on Christ's left while the good thief is on the right. People in the Middle Ages had trouble explaining why the Gospel, from the congregation's point of view, was read from the left side of the altar. The reason, which had been forgotten, was that the Gospel, from the priest's point of view, *had* been given the place of honor, the right.

Left Hand Does Not Know What the Right Hand Is Doing, The

Uncoordinated action, ambivalence or secrecy. The Bible meaning is to do good without drawing attention to it.

> "But when you give alms, do not let your left hand know what your right hand is doing" (Matthew 6:3).

Legion *see* Their Name Is Legion

Lent

(*see also* Ash Wednesday)

A pre–Easter fast of 40 days, excluding Sundays. It begins on Ash Wednesday and ends on Holy Saturday. Lent recalls the 40 days of temptation Jesus endured in the wilderness. The custom of giving something up for Lent is an outgrowth of earlier centuries when only one meal a day was permitted. Pope Telesphorus (d. 136) is said to have instituted Lent in 130. In 487 Pope Felix III (d. 492) added four days to Lent, making it 40 days long.

Lentulus, Publius

The supposed governor of Judea before Pontius Pilate. A 13th century forgery was claimed to be the letter Lentulus wrote to the Senate of Rome in which he gives a physical description of Jesus.

> Lentulus, the governor of the Jerusalemites, the Roman Senate and People, greetings. There has appeared in our times, and there still lives, a man of great power, called Jesus Christ. The people call him prophet of truth; his disciples, son of God. He raises the dead, and heals infirmities. He is a man of medium size; he has a venerable aspect, and his beholders can both fear and love him. His hair is the color of the ripe hazlenut, straight down to the ears, but below the ears wavy and curled, with a bluish and bright reflection, flowing over his shoulders. It is parted in two on the top of the head, after the pattern of the Nazarenes. His brow is smooth and very cheerful with a face without wrinkle or spot, embellished by a slightly reddish complexion. His nose and mouth are faultless. His beard is abundant, of the color of his hair, not long, but divided at the chin. His aspect is simple and mature, his eyes are changeable and bright. He is terrible in his reprimands, sweet and amiable in his admonitions, cheerful without loss of gravity. He was never known to laugh, but often to weep. His stature is straight, his hands and arms beautiful to behold. His conversation is grave, infrequent, and modest. He is the most beautiful among the children of men.

Leopard

(*see also* Can the Leopard
Change His Spots?; Panther)

An animal which received its name because it was thought to be a cross between a lion *leo* and a panther *pard*. Because of Revelation 13:2, "And the beast that I saw was like a leopard," the animal was seen as a symbol of sin and destruction. The inability of the leopard to change its spots has become a proverb. It comes from Jeremiah 13:23:

> "Can the Ethiopian change his skin or
> the leopard his spots?"

Lepers

(*see also* Hagioscope)

In the Bible leprosy was considered a punishment for sin meted out by God. Sufferers were obliged to live apart from everyone else and give warnings of their approach. In medieval times people afflicted with leprosy were confined to leper houses. These were called lazaries after Lazarus, the beggar afflicted with sores. Lepers were compelled to sound wooden clappers as a warning of their approach. Leprosy or Hansen's disease is an infectious disease of the skin and nerves which left untreated causes severe disfigurement and death. Effective drugs have been developed to treat the disease, rendering leper colonies unnecessary.

> "Innocence is like a dumb leper who has
> lost his bell, wandering the world,
> meaning no harm."
> — *The Quiet American*, Graham
> Greene (1904–1991).

Leprosy *see* Lepers

Let My People Go

A clarion call for freedom by Black American slaves in the 19th century. "Thus says the Lord, the God of Israel, 'Let my people go'" (Exodus 5:1). There is no statement by Moses more famous than this one. But did he say it? Moses and Aaron together pleaded with Pharaoh to free the Israelites from bondage. In Exodus 4:10 Moses complains that he is "slow of speech and of tongue." It is more likely that Aaron spoke the words. Aaron was high priest and in order to occupy that position was surely an accomplished orator.

> Go down, Moses,
> Way down in Egypt land,
> Tell old Pharaoh,
> Let my people go.
> — *Go Down, Moses*, Anon.

Let the Dead Bury Their Dead

Nothing is more important than following Jesus. That the kingdom of God was of greater importance than the requirement to bury the dead must have been deeply shocking to the hearers of Jesus. The expression now has the sense of letting bygones be bygones.

> "Another of the disciples said to him,
> 'Lord, let me first go and bury my father.' But Jesus said to him, 'Follow me,
> and leave the dead to bury their own
> dead.'" (Matthew 8:21–22).

Letter Killeth, The

Paul contrasts the letter of the Mosaic law with the spirit of God's law. The latter does not have to be written in tablets of stone but in the hearts of believers. The letter of the law means to zealously apply the exact words of the law.

> "The letter killeth but the spirit
> gives life" (2 Corinthians 3:6).

Letters in the Bible

In the King James Bible (1611) there are 2,728,100 letters in the Old Testament and

838,380 letters in the New Testament, for a total of 3,566,480 letters.

Leviathan
(*see also* Behemoth; Crocodile)

A monstrosity. In the Bible a leviathan was a huge sea monster. There are many references to God's victory over such creatures, probably whales or crocodiles (Job 41:1; Psalms 74:14; 104:26; Isaiah 27:1). The leviathan represented the forces of chaos.

> There Leviathan
> Hugest of living creatures, on the deep
> Stretched like a promontory sleeps
> or swims,
> And seems a moving land, and at
> his gills
> Draws in, and at his trunk spouts
> out a sea.
> —*Paradise Lost*, John Milton
> (1608–1674).

Levitation

The raising of a person or thing without any physical means of support. Saints Teresa of Ávila (1515–1582) and Joseph of Cupertino (1603–1663) were among the saints said to possess this amazing power. The last named was called the Flying Friar. There were 70 examples of Joseph defying gravity, including occasions when he lifted a heavy cross into the air and secured holy images high above an altar. Eventually he was compelled to perform his devotions in private so as not to be a distraction to other worshippers. Reports of religious ecstatics levitating have occurred in our own time.

Lewd

A word whose meaning has changed dramatically over the centuries. It now refers to licentiousness. But when it was used in Acts 17:5 in the King James Bible (1611), the word meant to behave lawlessly and had nothing to do with sexual debauchery.

> "But the Jews which believed not, moved with envy, took unto them certain lewd fellows of the baser sort, and gathered a company, and set all the city on an uproar, and assaulted the house of Jason, and sought to bring them out to the people."

Lex Talionis *see* Eye for an Eye

Libertine

Someone who indulges in debauchery and unrestrained sensuality. However, in the King James Bible (1611), the word is used to mean a slave who had been freed or the child of such a person.

> "Then there arose certain of the synagogue, which is called the synagogue of the Libertines ... disputing with Stephen" (Acts 6:9).

The synagogue mentioned here had been founded by Jewish prisoners of war freed by the Romans in A.D. 19.

Librarian Pope
(*see also* Intermonastery Loans; Librarians; Libraries)

Cosimo de Medici (1389–1464) started the first public library in Europe since the days of the Roman Empire. The Medici bank provided a fanatic book collector with an unlimited overdraft to indulge his passion. Upon the book collector's death, all outstanding debts were cancelled in exchange for his 800-book library, for its time a huge collection. The collection was then donated to the city of Florence. Tomasso Parentucelli (1397–1455), the man hired to catalogue the library, was later to shape the Vatican Library as Pope Nicholas V.

Librarians

(*see also* Intermonastery Loans;
Librarian Pope; Libraries)

The earliest librarians in Europe were monks in monasteries. Because of their general ignorance of safe book handling, they became known for treating valuable charges harshly. There were many satirical references to the monk and his books. St. Jerome (c. 342–420), known for his scholarship, is the patron saint of librarians.

> "The cleanliness of decent hands would be of great benefit to books as well as scholars, if it were not that the itch and pimples are characteristic of the clergy."
> —*Philobiblion*, Richard de Bury (1287–1345).

Libraries

(*see also* Book Borrowers;
Books; Intermonastery Loans;
Librarians; Libraries)

In the monasteries of the Middle Ages books were so treasured that they were kept in a locked cupboard at night. During the day a monk could only use one book at a time. He could not take the volume back to his room and he had to use it, under close supervision, in the library. The heavily used books were chained in place.

> "For I bless God in the libraries of the learned and for all the booksellers in the word"
> —*Jubilate Agno*, Christopher Smart (1722–1771).

Lick the Dust *see* Kiss the Dust

Lie with One's Fathers

(*see also* Death, Euphemisms for)

To be buried in your homeland.

> "Let me lie with my fathers; carry me out of Egypt and bury me in their burying place" (Genesis 47:30).

Light of the World

(*see also* Jesus Christ)

This expression alludes to Jesus Christ as the universal savior.

> "Again Jesus spoke to them, saying, 'I am the light of the world; he who follows me will not walk in darkness, but will have the light of life'" (John 8:12).

Like a Lamb to the Slaughter

(*see also* Lamb of God)

A popular abbreviation of Isaiah 53:7, "Like a lamb that is led to the slaughter, and like a sheep that before its shearers is dumb" (Isaiah 53:7). A prophesy of the suffering servant. Acts 8:32 quotes the passage and applies it to Jesus Christ. It has come to mean anyone who is helpless before impending disaster.

Lilies of the Field

(*see also* Lily)

The things of the spirit are far more important than material concerns.

> "And why are you anxious about clothing? Consider the lilies of the field, how they grow; they neither toil nor spin; yet I tell you, even Solomon in all his glory was not arrayed like one of those" (Matthew 6:28–29).

Lilith

A figure from Jewish folklore. Lilith is a demon who haunts the wilderness and stormy weather preying on pregnant woman and innocent babies. The only reference to Lilith in the Bible is in Isaiah 34:14, where she is described as a demon of the desert and, depending on the translation, as "the screech owl," or "the night hag." Later legends cast her as Adam's first wife who fled Paradise because she refused to submit to him. Lilith vowed to harm boy babies up to the eighth day and girl babies up to the 20th day. Bizarrely, some modern feminists consider this horrible demon, whose name Jewish and Christian women were frightened to utter, to be a role model, a symbol of female strength and emancipation.

Lily
(*see also* Lilies of the Field;
Lily of the Valley)

White lilies were said to have grown in the tears of Eve as she was expelled from Eden. The flower, associated with faith, purity and virtue, is the symbol of the Virgin Mary and her perpetual chastity. Anthony of Padua (c. 1195–1231), Clare (1193–1253), Dominic (1170–1221) and Francis of Assisi (c. 1181–1226), saints who led chaste lives, are also associated with the lily. Lilies are mentioned 15 times in the King James Bible (1611).

"Faith is like a lily lifted high and white"
— *Hope is Like a Harebell*, Christina
Georgina Rossetti (1830–1894).

Lily of the Valley
(*see also* Virgin Mary)

Because of its whiteness and pleasing scent, this flower was associated with the purity and sweet nature of the Virgin Mary. The words, "I am a rose of Sharon, a lily of the valley" (Song of Solomon 2:1), were believed to refer to Mary.

Limbo

Or limbus. A place near paradise where dwell the souls of the praiseless and blameless dead. Limbo had four divisions:

Limbus Fatuorum: Someone who deceives himself as to his hopes or good prospects is said to live in a fool's paradise. *Limbus fatuorum* was the Paradise of Fools, a place for the souls of the dead who had

sinned without intent because in life they lacked the ability to distinguish right from wrong.

Limbus Infantum (Limbus Puerorum): The Limbo of Infants. A place for the souls of babies who had died before they could be baptized.

Limbus Patrium: Limbo of the Fathers. A place for the souls of good people who had died before the time of Christ.

Limbus Purgatorius: Purgatory, as it is known in English, is a temporary abode for souls to be cleansed by suffering before they can enter Heaven. Protestants reject Purgatory, maintaining that it has no scriptural base. The word is also used in a secular sense for any extended period of suffering.

Into a Limbo large and broad,
since call'd
The Paradise of Fools, to few unknown.
— *Paradise Lost*, John Milton
(1608–1674).

Lion

The king of beasts and by extension a symbol of Jesus Christ, king of the world. It also represents St. Mark, who began his gospel with John the Baptist and Jesus in the wilderness. The lion is the symbol of Venice, whose patron saint is Mark. The lion is also associated with many saints who lived in the desert and wilderness. It was also a symbol of the resurrection because it was believed that lion cubs were born dead and only came to life after three days when their father breathed upon them.

"No absolute is going to make the lion
lie down with the lamb unless
the lamb is inside."
— *The Later D. H. Lawrence*, D. H.
Lawrence (1885–1930).

Lion Bible

An error ridden Bible published in 1804. 1 Kings 8:19 is rendered, "but thy son that shall come forth out of thy *lions*" rather than "*loins*." Numbers 35:18 reads, "The murderer shall surely be put *together*," in place of "*to death*." Galatians 5:17 became "For the flesh lusteth *after* the Spirit." The correct reading should be, "*against* the Spirit."

Lion in the Streets

An excuse to avoid doing a difficult task.

> "The sluggard says, 'There is a lion in the road! There is a lion in the streets!'" (Proverbs 26:13).

Lion Lies Down with the Lamb, The

The description of a time of ideal peace and harmony. A popular abbreviation of Isaiah 11:6:

> "The wolf shall dwell with the lamb, and the leopard shall lie down with the kid, and the calf and the lion and the fatling together, and a little child shall lead them."

Lion Sermon

A sermon preached annually on October 16, in St. Katherine Cree Church, Leadenhall Street, London, in memory of Sir John Gayer, Lord Mayor of London, 1646–1647. Gayer was traveling in the east when a "king of the desert," threatened to eat him. Gayer got down on his knees and prayed and the great beast departed, leaving him unharmed. Upon his return home he left a sum of money to the church to provide for the sermon.

Lipogram

A form of literary pretentiousness in which the author excludes some letter or let-

ters. A Christian example is the following, in which all vowels except E have been excluded.

The Fall of Eve

> Eve, Eden's empress, needs defended be;
> The Serpent greets her when she seeks the tree.
> Serene, she sees the speckled tempter creep;
> Gentle he seems, — perverted schemer deep, —
> Yet endless pretexts, ever fresh, prefers,
> Perverts her senses, revels when she errs,
> Sneers when she weeps, regrets, repents she fell,
> Then, deep-revenged, reseeks the nether Hell!
> — Anon.

Lip-service

Uttering the words of devotion with no intention of acting upon them; insincerity.

> "Because this people draw near with their mouth and honor me with their lips, while their hearts are far from me" (Isaiah 29:13).

Little Bird Told Me So, A

Nowadays a humorous way of concealing one's sources. It is a condensed version of Ecclesiastes 10:20:

> "Even in your thought, do not curse the king ... for a bird of the air will carry your voice, or some winged creature tell the matter."

Live by the Sword, Die by the Sword

Retribution. A popular paraphrase of Matthew 26:52:

> "Put your sword back into its place; for all who take the sword will perish by the sword."

Living Dog Is Better Than a Dead Lion, A

(*see also* Dead Dog; Dog; Is Thy Servant a Dog, That He Should Do This Thing?)

No matter how glorious was the past, value the present, however humble.

> "But he who is joined with all the living has hope, for a living dog is better than a dead lion" (Ecclesiastes 9:4).

Loaves and Fishes

Jesus took five loaves and two fishes and miraculously fed a multitude (Matthew 14:15–21, John 6:5–14). In Christian art, a loaf held aloft is a symbol of charity.

Long Cross *see* Dagger

Longest Chapter in Bible

(*see also* Chapters in the Bible; Identical Bible Chapters; Middle Chapter of Bible; Shortest Chapter in Bible)

The longest chapter in the Bible is Psalm 119, which has 176 verses.

Longest Verse in Bible

(*see also* Identical Bible Verses; Middle Verse of Bible; Shortest Verse in Bible; Verses in the Bible)

The longest verse in the Bible is Esther 8:9.

Longevity

(*see also* Methuselah)

The following biblical characters were blessed with very long lives — Adam: 930 years; Seth: 912 years; Enosh: 905 years; Kenan: 910 years; Jared: 962 years; Methuselah: 969 years; Noah: 950 years.

Longinius

(*see also* Lance)

A traditional name, derived from the Greek for lance, of the Roman soldier who wounded Christ in the side at the Crucifixion (John 19:34). He was confused with the soldier in Matthew 27:54 who uttered, "Truly, this was the Son of God." Longinius was also supposed to be part of the guard posted at the tomb of Jesus (Matthew 27:65). Legends about Longinius say that he suffered from eye disease until he rubbed his eyes with the hand bloodied by Christ's wound. Other tales recount that he was blinded at the crucifixion, regained his sight at the resurrection, became a Christian and was martyred because he refused to make pagan sacrifices. Longinius is the patron saint of Mantua because he carried there a pyx, a small box for the bread of the Eucharist, containing drops of Christ's blood.

"Lord," Frequency in Bible

The word "Lord" occurs 1,855 times in the King James Bible (1611).

Lord of Creation

(*see also* Be Fruitful and Multiply)

Man was designated the master of all created things:

> "Be fruitful and multiply, and fill the earth and subdue it; and have dominion over the fish of the sea and over the birds of the air and over every living thing that moves upon the earth" (Genesis 1:28).

Lord of the Flies *see* Beelzebub; Fly

Lord's Prayer *see* Backward Blessing; Lord's Prayer in Rhyme; Paternoster

Lord's Prayer in Rhyme

The Lord's Prayer in English translation is a masterpiece. Unfortunately there have been those who just could not leave well enough alone. Here is an example.

> Father in heaven, hallowed
> be they name;
> Thy kingdom come; thy will be done
> the same
> In earth and heaven. Give us
> daily bread;
> Forgive our sins as others we forgive.
> Into temptation let us not be led;
> Deliver us from evil while we live.
> For kingdom, power, and glory
> must remain
> Forever and forever thine; Amen.
> —Anon.

Loreto

Also Loretto; a town in central Italy which is a famous place of pilgrimage. It is home to the Santa Casa or Holy House. Tradition maintains that the small brick and stone structure was the birthplace of the Virgin Mary in Nazareth and the place where she was visited by the angel Gabriel at the Annunciation of the Incarnation of Christ. To save it from infidels, angels transported the house to Croatia in 1291, and then, with a couple of intermediate stops, to Loreto in 1294. It is now enclosed in a church, the *Santuario della Santa Casa.*

> Enter not here unwashed of any spot,
> For a more holy Church the world
> hath not.
> —*An Itinerary*, Fynes
> Moryson (1566–1630).

Lost Books

(*see also* Enoch, Book of; Jashar)

After hearing the preaching of Paul, the Ephesians burned their books (Acts 19:19). These were probably parchments devoted to sun worship and astrology derived from the Greeks, Persians and Egyptians. Other lost books are Jashar, which is mentioned in Joshua 10:13 and 2 Samuel 1:17, and The Book of the Wars of the Lord, quoted in Numbers 21:14–15. Luke 1:1–3 suggests that other accounts of Jesus were written.

> "Inasmuch as many have undertaken to compile a narrative of the things which have been accomplished among us, just as they were delivered to us by those who from the beginning were eyewitnesses and ministers of the word, it seemed good to me also ... to write an orderly account for you ..."

Lost Tribes of Israel

Ten of the 12 tribes of Israel were conquered by the Assyrians in 721 B.C. and carried into captivity. Many far-fetched theories have arisen to explain the fate of these people. Some claim that they became North American Indians, Afghans, Ethiopians, Mexicans, Peruvians, even British. Most likely the lost tribes merged with the people around them and ceased to be Hebrew.

Lot's Wife

Lot and his wife escaped the wicked city of Sodom just before God destroyed it. They were instructed not to look back. Lot's wife disobeyed. She looked back and was turned into a pillar of salt (Genesis 19:26):

> "... she stiffened in every limb, rather like Lot's wife, who as you probably know, did the wrong thing that time there was all that unpleasantness with the cities of the plain and got turned into a pillar of salt, though what was the thought behind this I've never been able to understand. Salt, I mean. Seems so bizarre somehow and not at all what you would expect."
> —*Jeeves in the Offing*, P. G.
> Wodehouse (1881–1975).

Love Thy Neighbor as Thyself

A maxim for human brotherhood and the spirit of charity:

> "Thou shalt love thy neighbor as thyself" (Matthew 19:19).

Love Your Enemies

Powerful words from the Sermon on the Mount. Jesus has overturned the old law of retaliation with a new morality based on forgiveness:

> "But I say to you, Love your enemies and pray for those who persecute you, so that you may be sons of your Father who is in heaven; for he makes his sun rise on the evil and on the good and sends rain on the just and unjust" (Matthew 5:44–45).

Low Sunday *see* Quasimodo Sunday

L.S.D.

Lysergic acid diethylamide, a synthetic crystalline compound that induces powerful hallucinogenic reactions. St. Anthony (c. 250–350), the father of Christian monasticism, is also remembered for his struggles against multitudes of demons who appeared to him in horrible animal form. It has been suggested that St. Anthony may have eaten bread spoiled by the fungus *Claviceps purpurea*, and thus ingested lysergic acid from which L.S.D. is derived.

Lucifer

(*see also* Fallen Angel; Proud as Lucifer)

Lucifer was a rebellious angel who was flung down from Heaven into Hell. Because of Isaiah 14:12, the name of Lucifer was mis-takenly applied to Satan. "How you are fallen from heaven, O Day Star, son of Dawn! How you are cut down to the ground, you who laid the nations low!" The Lucifer mentioned here may have been the king of Babylon. Day Star, the morning star or Venus, was translated in the King James Bible (1611) as Lucifer, a name given to Satan. The identification of the Lucifer of Isaiah with Satan began with St. Jerome (c. 347–420), who so interpreted Luke 10:18. "I saw Satan fall like lightening from heaven." Matches were once called lucifers.

> And when he falls, he falls like Lucifer,
> Never to hope again.
> —*Henry VIII*, William Shakespeare (1564–1616).

Luke, St.

One of the four evangelists. The Gospel of Luke and Acts of the Apostles, both found in the New Testament, are attributed to him. Luke is believed to have been a doctor because in Colossians 4:14 he is referred to as "the beloved physician," although this may have been meant metaphorically. Legend says that Luke painted a portrait of the Virgin Mary and for that reason he is the patron saint of painters and physicians.

Lynx

The sight of the lynx is so keen it was believed that it could see through solid walls. It symbolizes God's all-seeing eye and vigilance. The animal is not mentioned in the *King James Bible* (1611).

Lysergic Acid Diethylamide *see* L.S.D.

M

M

(*see also* Virgin Mary)

The 13th letter of the alphabet; with a crown over it, the monogram of the Virgin Mary.

MA DI

(*see also* Theotakos; Virgin Mary)

The abbreviation of *Mater Dei*, "Mother of God," a title granted to the Virgin Mary by the Council of Ephesus in 431.

Macedonian Cry

A plea for help or guidance from a long distance. It comes from Acts 16:9:

> "And a vision appeared to Paul in the night; There stood a man of Macedonia, and prayed him, saying, Come over into Macedonia, and help us."

Magdalene

(*see also* Mary Magdalene)

That Mary Magdalene is the patron saint of the penitent may be based on a misidentification. To be sure, she was an important figure who witnessed the crucifixion (Mark 15:10), the burial of Jesus and the empty tomb. Jesus cast seven devils from Mary Magdalene (Mark 16:9; Luke 8:2) and appeared to her alone in an apparition (Matthew 28:9). The repentant sinner who washed the feet of Jesus with her tears and dried them with her hair (Luke 7:36–50) has been assumed to be Mary Magdalene but is not named. It may not be she. In art, Mary Magdalene is usually depicted as weeping. Sometimes she is young and beautiful, holding a container of ointment, sometimes a penitent reading the scriptures before a cross or a skull. The English word maudlin is derived from Magdalene. Any bad woman, especially a prostitute, who has given up her sinful life and is repentant can be called a magdalene. A magdalene is also a home for the refuge and reformation of for such women.

Magi

(*see also* Frankincense and Myrrh)

Wise men from the east. The Three Kings of the Orient were probably Zoroastrian astrologers from Persia. In Matthew 2:1–12 it is recorded that Magi, number unspecified, followed a miraculous star to Bethlehem in order to pay tribute to the infant Jesus with gold (a symbol of kingship), frankincense (representing divinity), and myrrh (a funerary spice foretelling the crucifixion and the resurrection). The evil Herod urged the Magi to tell him where Jesus was. Warned in a dream, the Magi fled from Herod, returning to their own land by another route. There is no mention in the Bible of the Magi being kings. That comes from various Old Testament prophecies of kings bearing gifts. The traditional names of the Magi, Balthasar, Melchior and Caspar or Gaspar, are not found in the Bible, either, and date from the sixth century. The visit of the Magi, the first revelation of Jesus to the Gentiles, is commemorated on January 6. In the earliest depictions of the Magi they varied from two to four. The number became fixed at three to correspond to the three gifts. From the fourth century they were shown as kings. Gradually the Magi came to represent different races (Balthazar was usually a black African), as well as youth, manhood, and old age. The word Magi is related to the English word "magic."

> "Now when Jesus was born in Bethlehem of Judea in the days of Herod the king, behold wise men from the East came to Jerusalem, saying, 'Where is he who has been born king of the Jews? For we have seen his star in the east and have come to worship him'"
> (Matthew 2:1–2).

Magic *see* Abracadabra, Hocus-pocus

Make Orders, To

A grim medieval joke. Someone in holy orders was known by his tonsure, or the shaven crown of his head, which symbolized Christ's crown of thorns. To slice off the top off an enemy's head in battle with a sword stroke was called *to make orders.*

Malachy, St. *see* Prophecies of Malachy

Maltese Cross *see* Crisscross

Mammon

A word that occurs only four times in the New Testament (Matthew 6:24; Luke 16:9, 11, 13), and does not occur in the Old Testament. It means material wealth as an evil, an unholy greed for possessions. "You cannot serve God and mammon" (Matthew 6:24). In medieval times the word was taken as the name of the devil of greediness.

> "Mammon is like fire: the usefulest of all servants, if the frightfulest of all masters."
> —*Past and Present*, Thomas Carlyle (1795–1881).

Man in the Moon

The old legend that the man in the moon is gathering sticks comes from Numbers 15:32–36, the story of a man who was stoned to death for gathering sticks on the Sabbath.

Man of Sin *see* Antichrist

Man of Sorrows
(*see also* Jesus Christ)

The prophecy of the Suffering Servant in Isaiah 53:3–7 is understood by Christians to be a prophecy of Christ, who will suffer for the sins of mankind.

> "He was despised and rejected by men; a man of sorrows, and acquainted with grief" (Isaiah 53:3).

Man of War

A warrior. A large naval warship in the age of sail was a man-of-war. (Also the name of a poisonous jellyfish, the Portuguese man-of-war.)

> "The Lord is a man of war" (Exodus 15:3).

Mandorla
(*see also* Almond; Aureole; Halo; Vesica Piscis)

Italian for almond. An almond-shaped aureole, similar to a halo, surrounding the entire body of Christ, the Virgin Mary and Mary Magdalene in paintings and sculptures. The earliest madorlas in Christian art date from the fifth century.

Mandrake

The root of a Eurasian herb of the nightshade family, mentioned in Genesis 30:14–16 and Song of Solomon 7:13. Long associated with magic, such as inducing forgetfulness or being an aphrodisiac, the mandrake earned the reputation of being the forbidden fruit. Human figures cut from the root were believed to be magical. When unearthed, the mandrake was supposed to emit a scream so terrible that it would be fatal to all those who heard it. The roots were believed to be inhabited by the souls of criminals executed for murder.

> Would curses kill, as doth the
> mandrake's groan...
> —*Henry VI, Part II*, William
> Shakespeare (1564–1616).

Mandylion
(*see also* Abgar's Letter to Jesus
and Christ's Reply; Volto Santo)

The true image of Jesus' face impressed on a napkin and sent to an Armenian king. Other legends claim that the image was in the form of a painting. Several churches claim to possess the image of the Holy Face. A legend arose that St. Veronica lent Jesus, on his way to Calvary, a handkerchief to wipe the blood and sweat from his brow, and on it was imprinted an exact image of His face.

Manna from Heaven

Manna was the miraculously appearing food which sustained the Israelites during their long wandering in the Sinai Desert. In the New Testament manna came to symbolize divine blessing. Nowadays, any unexpected gift, often arriving in the nick of time, can be called manna. The manna of the Israelites could be boiled, ground like meal, and made into cakes. It was probably a sweet, resinous substance secreted from the tamarisk tree.

> "And when the dew that lay was gone
> up, behold, upon the face of the wilder-
> ness there lay a small round thing, as
> small as the hoar frost upon the ground.
> And when the children of Israel
> saw it, they said to one another, it is
> manna: for they wist not what it was"
> (Exodus 16:14–15).

Maranatha *see* Anathema
Maranatha

Margaret of Antioch, St. *see* Childbirth

Marigold
(*see also* Virgin Mary)

A common garden plant with large yellow, orange or red flowers. As its name suggests, it is dedicated to the Virgin Mary. William Shakespeare alluded to this in Cymbeline (1610) when he wrote of "winking Mary-buds." Marigolds are not mentioned in the King James Bible (1611).

Mariolatry
(*see also* Virgin Mary)

Excessive devotion to the Virgin Mary and false attribution to her of divine honors; a charge labeled against Roman Catholics by some Protestants.

Mark, St. *see* St. Mark's Eve

Mark of Cain
(*see also* Cain-colored Beard;
Cain's Wife; Cainites)

After Cain killed his brother Abel, he was condemned to wander as an outcast. The popular supposition is that the mark Cain received, akin to a crimson tattoo on the forehead, was a punishment. Genesis 14:13–15 records the exact opposite. After complaining that his punishment was more than he could bear, the mark that Cain received was a sign of God's compassion. It was meant to identify the murderer but protect him from further punishment. The mark is not described.

Mark of the Beast
(*see also* M.B. Waistcoat; 666)

To put the mark of the beast on something is to denounce it as ungodly and evil.

"Foul and evil sores came upon the men who bore the mark of the beast and worshipped its image" (Revelation 16:2).

Marked with a B
(*see also* Blasphemy)

Under Mosaic law blasphemers were stoned to death (Leviticus 24:16). By the Middle Ages those guilty of blasphemy were branded on the forehead with a *B*. This cruel custom lasted into the 17th century.

Marriage *see* Better to Marry
than to Burn; Fleet Marriages; Forbidding the Banns

Martin, St. *see* Martin Drunk;
St. Martin's Summer

Martin Drunk
(*see also* Drunkard; St. Martin's Summer)

St. Martin is the patron saint of drunkards. To be Martin drunk is to be so intoxicated that one must drink more to sober up, if such a thing is possible.

Martinmas *see* His Martinmas
Will Come as It Does to Every Hog

Martyrs' Paste
(*see also* Agnus Dei)

A gray, consecrated medallion made from wax and the dust of a martyr's bones. The medallions are considered to be relics.

Mary, Mother of Jesus *see* Virgin
Mary

Mary Magdalene *see* Magdalene;
Noli Me Tangere

Massacre of the Innocents
(*see also* Childermas; Herod: Herod the Great)

The murder, ordered by Herod, of all boys in Bethlehem two years and under (Matthew 2: 1–16). By this horrible crime Herod hoped that he would kill Jesus, who he feared would replace him as the king of the Jews. The family of Jesus was warned in a dream and fled to Egypt, where they remained until after Herod's death. The Innocents are unique in that they did not die *for* Jesus, as so many martyrs have done, but *instead* of Him. Innocents' Day is observed on December 28. The author of the *Prisoner of Zenda*, Anthony Hope (1863–1933), was overheard to remark at the opening of James Barrie's children's classic, *Peter Pan* in 1904, "Oh, for an hour of Herod!"

Matthias, St. *see* Thirteenth
Apostle

Maudlin *see* Magdalene

M.B. Waistcoat
(*see also* Mark of the Beast)

An undivided clerical waistcoat of the 19th century, considered far too popish for some. It acquired the nickname M.B. for "Mark of the Beast."

> He wasn't good, despite the air
> An M.B. waistcoat gives,
> Indeed, his dearest friends declare
> No greater humbug lives.
> —*First Love*, W. S. Gilbert
> (1836–1911).

Memory Aids

Artificial rhymes and rhythms which serve to jog the memory. Also called *Memoria Technica*, and mnemonic aids. "Thirty days hath September ..." is the most common one. Here is a Scottish mnemonic aid about Adam and Eve.

> God made a garden and put Adam in;
> Adam lo'ed Eve, and so came sin.
> Eve pu'd an apple for Adam frae a tree;
> God said to Adam, "That belangs
> to me."
> Adam said to God, "My marrow
> stole it."
> God said to Adam, "Baith o' ye shall
> thole it."
> Adam rinned awa', fearing God's wrath;
> God sent an angel to ca' Adam forth.
> The angel told the Deil to punish
> Adam's sin;
> The Deil made Hell and put Adam in.
> God begat Christ, Christ went to hell;
> He heuked Adam out, and a' was well.
> — Anon.

Mene, Mene, Tekel, Upharsin
see Writing on the Wall

Mess of Pottage

Pottage is a thick soup. Selling something of value for a trifling sum is selling it for a mess of pottage. The reference is to Genesis 25:29–34, where Esau sold his birthright to Jacob for "bread and pottage of lentils." The phrase "mess of pottage" does not appear in the Bible.

Messiah
(*see also* Christ; Jesus Christ)

From the Hebrew for anointed. In biblical times oil was a very valuable commodity. For a prophet, priest or king to be anointed with oil was a sign that he had been selected by God for an important leadership role in society. Messiah was originally applied to kings. Cyrus of Persia is so referred to in Isaiah 45:1. After the destruction of Judah, the word began to be used for a promised redeemer who would restore the kingdom. When this prince did not come, messiah was interpreted in a spiritual sense

as a Heavenly savior. The unique claim of Christianity is that the promise of the messiah has been fulfilled in the person of Jesus the Christ. Christ is messiah translated into Greek.

> "If another Messiah was born he could hardly do so much good as the printing press."
> —*Aphorisms*, G. C. Lichtenberg
> (1742–1799).

Methodist

A nickname given to the associates of Charles Wesley (1708–1788) on account of their methodical strictness with regard to religion. The name had been around for a long time before that and was once applied to the Jesuits because of their systematic or methodical ways.

> "One of a new kind of puritans lately arisen, so called from their profession to live by rules and in constant method."
> —*Dictionary of the English Language*,
> Samuel Johnson (1709–1784).

Methuselah
(*see also* Jeroboam; Longevity)

Anyone who lives to be a great age. Methuselah, seventh in the line of descent from Adam, was the oldest man in the Bible. He lived to be 969 years old (Genesis 5:27).

Metropolitan
(*see also* Bishop)

A senior bishop who has suffragan bishops under his authority. It has nothing to do with being the bishop of a metropolis, or large city.

Middle Book of Bible
(*see also* Books of the Bible)

The middle book of the Old Testament

is Proverbs; the middle book of the New Testament is 2 Thessalonians.

Middle Chapter of Bible
(*see also* Chapters in the Bible; Identical Bible Chapters; Longest Chapter in Bible; Middle Chapter in Bible; Most Boring Chapters in the Bible; Shortest Chapter in Bible)

The middle chapter of the Bible, as well as the shortest, is Psalm 117. The middle chapter of the Old Testament is Job 29. The middle of the New Testament is Romans 13 and 14.

Middle Line of Bible

The middle line of the Bible is 2 Chronicles 4:16.

Middle Verse of Bible
(*see also* Identical Bible Verses; Longest Verse in Bible; Shortest Verse in Bible; Verses in the Bible)

The middle verse of the Bible is Psalm 118:8. The middle of the Old Testament is 2 Chronicles 20:17–18. The middle verse of the New Testament is Acts 17:17.

Milk and Honey *see* Land Flowing with Milk and Honey

Milk Grotto

A grotto in Bethlehem hewn out of limestone. It is the reputed spot where Mary and the infant Jesus hid from Herod before they fled to Egypt. Its whiteness is said to have been caused by a few drops of Mary's milk. A fragment of stone from the grotto can, so it is believed, increase the flow of a woman's milk.

Millennium
(*see also* Doomsday; Second Coming)

A thousand-year period of peace and prosperity that marks the earthly reign of Christ (Revelation 20:1–5). Some believe the Second Coming of Christ will occur at the beginning of the Millennium, some at the end. At the end of the Millennium Satan will be unbound and make a final quest for power. He and all the wicked will be defeated and cast into a lake of fire.

> "Millennium, n. The period of a thousand years when the lid is to be screwed down, with all the reformers on the under side."
> — *The Devil's Dictionary*, Ambrose Bierce (1842–1914).

Millstone Around Your Neck

A heavy burden, either physical or figurative. The expression is derived from Matthew 18:6, where the meaning is that of righteous punishment:

> "But whoever causes one of these little ones who believe in me to sin, it would be better for him to have a great millstone fastened round his neck and to be drowned in the depth of the sea."

Mine Ears Hast Thou Bored

If a Hebrew bond-servant did not claim his freedom after six years, his ears would be bored with an awl, as a sign of his voluntary attachment to his master for life (Exodus 21:6).

Minister's Rib Factory
(*see also* Adam's Rib)

A nickname derived from Genesis 2:22 which was given to Mount Holyoke College in South Hadley Massachusetts, the oldest women's college in the United States.

The school had a reputation for providing wives for missionaries and ministers.

Miserere

A cry for mercy; a prayer in which mercy is sought. Psalm 51 is given this name because its opening words in Latin are *Miserere mei, Deus*, "Have mercy on me, O God." Miserere was also the name of a small knife, the so-called "dagger of mercy," which was used to stab through the joints in a suit of armor and dispatch a wounded knight.

> "A dagger which in mediaeval warfare was used by the foot soldier to remind an unhorsed knight that he was mortal."
> — *The Devil's Dictionary*, Ambrose Bierce (1842–1914).

Misericord

A piece of wood projecting from the underside of a choir stall's hinged seat. It would often be carved with symbolic religious images. It was designed to aid those required to stand or kneel during lengthy church services.

Misogyny

St. Antony (251–356), a hermit and founder of monasticism, was so distrustful of women that he refused to look upon them or speak to them. In his view women were more dangerous than lions. There could be no peace on earth or goodwill between men and women unless females were boycotted. Tertullian, a Christian writer of the second century, said of women,

> Do you not know that each of you is also an Eve ... You are the devil's gateway, you are the unsealer of the forbidden tree, you are the first deserter of that divine law, you are the one who persuaded him whom the devil was too weak to attack. How easily you de-

stroyed man, the image of God! Because of the death which you brought upon us, even the son of God had to die ...

Mistletoe

From the early 17th century there has been a harmless Christmas custom of exchanging a kiss under a sprig of mistletoe. But mistletoe was not always viewed so innocently. Because the plant is poisonous and was used by the Druids during human sacrifices, the early Christians banned the use of mistletoe as a decoration.

Mitre
(*see also* Bishop)

A peaked, cleft headdress worn by bishops. It is thought by many to symbolize the tongues of fire which descended upon the apostles on the day of Pentecost (Acts 2:3). The halves of the miter represent the Old and New Testaments.

Mnemonic Aids *see* Memory Aids

Mole

A small burrowing mammal which eats insects. Because it lives underground and was believed to be blind and deaf, it represents those who are blind and deaf to the Gospel. The creature is mentioned in Leviticus 11:30, and Isaiah 2:20.

> If you would keep your soul
> From spotted sight or sound,
> Live like the velvet mole;
> Go burrow underground.
> — *The Eagle and the Mole*, Elinor Hoyt Wylie (1885–1928).

Moloch

A hideous Canaanite idol to which children were burnt alive as human sacrifices.

The word is used for any consuming passion, or ruling vice, to which one will sacrifice everything of value.

> Moloch, sceptred king,
> Stood up, the strongest and the
> fiercest spirit
> That fought in heav'n; now fiercer
> by despair.
> —*Paradise Lost*, John
> Milton (1608–1674).

Money *see* Filthy Lucre; Money is the Root of All Evil; Cast the Moneychangers Out of the Temple

Money Is the Root of All Evil

A popular misquotation of 1 Timothy 6:10:

> "For *the love of* money is the root of all evil."

Month's Mind

A Mass said for a dead person a month after death. Also a great desire for something or someone.

> I see you have a month's mind for them.
> —*Two Gentlemen of Verona*, William
> Shakespeare (1564–1616).

More Sea Bible

A Bible of 1641 in which Revelation 21:1 is written, "and there was *more* sea" rather than "*no* more sea."

Mosaics

Poems composed with lines borrowed from other works; also called centos. A Christian example is a hymn by one E. A. Marsh, sung to the tune of *From Greenland's Icy Mountains.*

> I am a pilgrim stranger.
> Hebrews 11: 13

> And often far from home,
> Hebrews 11: 9
> I pass through toil and danger
> 1 Peter 1: 17
> Wherever I may roam.
> 1 Peter 2: 11
> I meet with opposition1
> 1 Corinthians 2: 8–9
> And trials on each hand
> 1 Peter 1: 7
> While publishing salvation
> Romans 10: 10
> As Jesus gave command.
> Mark 16: 15
> etc.

Moses *see* Horns of Moses

Most Boring Chapters in the Bible
(*see also* Chapters in the Bible)

The begats (Genesis 5, 10 and 11) are notoriously dull genealogies. In the King James Bible (1611) everyone is begetting sons and daughters left and right. In the Revised Standard Version (1952) they simply have sons and daughters. However they are translated, these chapters are tedious.

Mother Carey's Chicken

The storm petrel is a sea bird reputed to fly low when a storm is approaching. Its legs dangle when it flies, giving the bird the appearance of walking on water. In fact, the bird is skimming the water in search of surface swimming food. The Virgin Mary, patroness of sailors, was called *mater cara*, "dear mother," (or "Mother Carey"), and was believed to send her chicken to warn seafarers. The bird's name, petrel, is related to St. Peter, who, in imitation of Christ, attempted to walk on water (Matthew 14:28–31). There is a superstition among sailors that the birds have the souls of dead mariners.

Mount Athos *see* Athos, Mount

Mouse

(*see also* Mouse Tower; Poor
as a Church Mouse)

A small creature with an insatiable appetite, a symbol of female greed and lasciviousness. Because it chews in the dark, the
mouse represents the devil, who corrupts
souls in darkness and secrecy. Mice are mentioned six times in the King James Bible
(1611).

Mouse Tower

(*see also* Mouse)

A watchtower built on an island in the
Rhine near Bingen, in southwestern Germany. It is associated with Hatto, Archbishop of Mainz (d. 970), who reputedly
built the tower to escape his assailants.
Hatto is said to have burned a barn full of
people caught stealing food during a
famine. He said of them, "They are like
mice, only good to devour corn." The
bishop was eaten by an army of mice in his
tower. In fact, the tower was built two centuries after Hatto and used as a toll-house.
The German word for toll, *maut*, is similar
to the word for mouse, *maus*. This and the
unpopularity of the toll on corn are the origins of the legend.

> Bishop Hatto fearfully hastened away,
> And he crossed the Rhine without
> delay,
> And reached his tower, and barred
> with care
> All the windows, and doors, and
> loopholes there.
> — *God's Judgment on a Wicked Bishop*,
> Robert Southey (1774–1843).

Moutardier du Pape

In France a conceited person is described as the Pope's mustard-maker. Pope
John XXII (1249–1334), who resided in Avignon, loved mustard to such an extent that
he appointed his nephew as court mustard-
maker. The nephew began to think that he
was somebody special. When an unassum-
ing monk became Pope Clement XIV
(1705–1774) he said,

> "I sigh for my cloister, cell and books.
> You must not have the impression that I
> think myself the *Moutardier du Pape*."

Muggletonians

Followers of a tailor, Lodovic Muggle-
ton (1609–1698), who believed him to be
one of the two prophets spoken of in Revelation 11:3, who will be given power to
prophesy for 1,266 days. The sect lasted
until 1979. Its founder was fined and sent to
the pillory for blasphemy.

Mugwump

In the Algonquian translation of the
Bible, centurion was rendered as mugwump,
the word for great chief. It has come to be
a jocular term for an important person and
a political renegade who cannot be relied
upon to support any party.

> "Mugwump, n. In politics one afflicted
> with self-respect and addicted to
> the vice of independence. A term
> of contempt."
> — *The Devil's Dictionary*, Ambrose
> Bierce (1842–1914).

Multiple Relics

(*see also* Relics)

St. Felicitas and her seven sons were
martyred for their faith in 173. Mother and
sons left behind a remarkable collection of
relics. Including relics lost in the French
Revolution, there were six sets of bodies and
bones held in various churches. There can
be few saints who have left more relics than
St. Teresa of Ávila (1515–1582). Her left arm

is in Lisbon and her right foot in Rome. The fingers of her right hand are to be found in Seville, Rome, Ávila, Paris and Brussels. Slices of her flesh are to be encountered in Rome, Venice, Naples, Paris and Cracow. Teresa's scapular can be found in Naples. In Rome and Brussels are wooden crosses she used to combat devils. The saint's staff, rosary and slippers are in Naples and her veil is in Sardinia. A napkin stained with her blood is in Piacenza. Teresa's teeth can be found in Milan and Venice and a piece of her heart in Milan.

Murderers' Bible

A Bible of 1801 in which Jude 16 incorrectly reads, "There are *murderers*, complainers, walking after their own lusts ..." Later editions use "*murmerers*" or "*grumblers*" in place of *murderers*.

My Cup Runneth Over
(*see also* Oil)

Good fortune. A cup overflowing with oil was a description of God's great generosity. Jesus has overturned the old law of retaliation with a new morality based on forgiveness. Oil was one of the most valuable commodities in the ancient world.

> "Thou preparest a table before me in the presence of mine enemies: thou anointest my head with oil; my cup runneth over" (Psalm 23:5).

My God Why Hast Thou Forsaken Me? *see* Eli, Eli Lamma Sabacthani

My Hour Is Not Yet Come

The time for action is not now. The time of my death is not now. The hour of a person's death was commonly thought to be preordained.

> "When Jesus knew that his hour had come" (John 13:1).

Myrrh *see* Frankincense and Myrrh

Myrtle

A common family of evergreen shrubs found in the Mediterranean region. In Christian terms the plant symbolizes those whom Jesus came to save. In Zechariah 1:8 we are told of a man riding a red horse through a grove of myrtle. This is interpreted as Jesus leading the people of the world.

Mysterium
(*see also* Mark of the Beast; 666)

A word that was formerly engraved on the pope's tiara. Some numerologists claimed that it made up 666, the number of the beast.

Mystical Marriage of St. Catherine
(*see also* Braid St. Catherine's Tresses; Catherine Wheel, Virgins)

Catherine of Alexandria (d. 307), the patron saint of virgins, considered herself to be the mystical bride of Christ. Art from the 14th century onwards depicts the Christ Child in the Virgin Mary's lap placing a ring on Catherine's finger. This symbolized Catherine's spiritual betrothal.

Mystical Winepress

A symbolic image derived from a literal interpretation of the "real presence" in the Eucharist, which became popular in medieval Christian art. Christ was depicted kneeling under a winepress ready to catch the drops of his holy blood.

N

Naboth's Vineyard
(*see also* Jezebel)

Something of value coveted by another person. King Ahab wanted to own Naboth's vineyard, but Naboth refused to give it up. Jezebel, Ahab's wife, engineered the judicial murder of Naboth so her husband could acquire the land. Ahab was punished by Elijah, and Jezebel was devoured by dogs (1 Kings 21).

Nail

To nail someone is to completely overcome resistance, to pin him down. It comes from Isaiah 22:23: "And I will fasten him as a nail in a sure place." Nails were also symbolic of the passion. Early Christian art shows four holy nails being used in the crucifixion. By medieval times only three nails were depicted to reinforce the notion of the trinity.

Names of the Popes
(*see also* Pontiff; Pope)

The custom of the men elected pope changing their names is a very old one. It was said to have begun with Sergius II (d. 846) because his name was originally *Osporci*, Pig-face or Peter di Porca. These claims have been refuted. The first pope to change his name will probably never be known, but it was probably someone named Peter. For a pope to call himself Peter II would be presumptuous and disrespectful to the memory of St. Peter the first pope.

Narcissus *see* Rose of Sharon

Nativity of Jesus
(*see also* Birthdate of Jesus; Christmas; Jesus Christ)

Modern scholarship doubts that Jesus was born in the year one. The traditional date of Christ's birth was fixed by Dionysius Exiguus in the sixth century. Unfortunately, his calculation was as much as six years too late.

> The Saviour comes, by ancient bards foretold!
> Hear him, ye deaf, and all ye blind behold!
> —*Messiah*, Alexander Pope (1688–1744).

Naughty Figs

Anyone reading Jeremiah 24:2 in the King James Bible (1611) can be excused if he is puzzled by the phrase, "very naughty figs." The Revised Standard Version (1952) clears up the confusion when it labels those figs "bad." Naughty was once used to mean something worthless.

Navy *see* Bolivan Navy

Nazarene
(*see also* Can Anything Good Come out of Nazareth?)

Although born in Bethlehem, Jesus spent most of his life in Nazareth. Therefore, Nazarene is one of his appellations. It is also a Muslim term for a Christian. A resident of Nazareth is a Nazarite. The word was also used for someone who dedicated himself to God with a solemn vow and was forbidden to drink alcohol or cut his hair (Numbers 6:1–24).

> "No place in Palestine satisfied me more entirely than Nazareth. Much as one's associations require, it is all there; and one's first and constant emotion here is

of thankfulness that Jesus was reared amidst such natural beauty."
—*Eastern Life Past and Present*, Harriet Martineau (1802–1876).

Nazareth *see* Can Anything Good Come Out of Nazareth?; Nazarene

Nebuchadnezzar *see* Boanthropy

Neck-verse
(*see also* Benefit of Clergy)

In the Middle Ages if a person guilty of a crime could read Psalm 51:1, "Have mercy on me, O God, according to thy steadfast love, according to thy abundant mercy blot out my transgressions," he could claim benefit of clergy and literally save his neck. If the declaration, *Legit ut clericus*, "He reads like a clerk," was made, the prisoner was merely burned on the hand and released.

Neighbors *see* Love Thy Neighbor as Thyself

Nephilim *see* Giants

Never Dying

According to the Bible, Enoch and Elijah escaped death. Elijah was taken up to heaven in a fiery chariot (2 Kings 2:11–12). In a list of Adam's descendants (Genesis 5), the expression "and he died" is omitted for Enoch.

New Eve
(*see also* Virgin Mary)

Sin was brought into the world by Eve, the first woman. Redemption was brought into the world by another woman, the Virgin Mary, the New Eve.

New Jerusalem
(*see also* Pearly Gates)

Any ideal state newly created. In Revelation 21:2, St. John gives a description of paradise. New Jerusalem, the celestial city, is the equivalent of heaven:

"And I saw the holy city, new Jerusalem, coming down out of heaven from God, prepared as a bride adorned from God, prepared as a bride adorned for her husband."

New Testament Books in Rhyme
(*see also* Old Testament Books in Rhyme)

Matthew, Mark, Luke, and John wrote the life of their Lord;
The Acts, what Apostles accomplished, record;
Rome, Corinth, Galatus, Ephesus, hear
What Philippians, Colossians, Thessalonians revere;
Timotheus, Titus, Philemon, precede
The Epistle which Hebrews most gratefully read;
James, Peter, and John, with the short letter Jude,
The rounds of Divine Revelation conclude.
—Anon.

New Wine Into Old Bottles

A common paraphrase of a parable in which Jesus instructs his disciples that the new spiritual order he is introducing requires new practices and institutions. Old bottles are much the same as new bottles but old wineskins are a different matter:

"And no one puts new wine into old wineskins; if he does, the new wine will burst the skins and it will be spilled, and the skins will be destroyed. But new wine must be put into fresh wineskins" (Luke 5:37–38).

New Year's Day

From the seventh century until the end of the 13th century, the civil, ecclesiastical and legal year began on December 25, Christmas Day. The historical year began on January 1. From the 14th century until 1752, the church in England used March 25, the Incarnation of Christ, to begin the year. Dates between January 1 and March 25 were shown with two years. Thus, April 9, 1615, would be recorded as April 9, 1614/15.

Nicholas V *see* Librarian Pope

Nicodemused Into Nothing

To have your hopes and ambitions dashed because of an outlandish name, such as Nicodemus. Nicodemus was a Pharisee who secretly believed in Jesus (John 3:1 ff.) His name is not considered peculiar in the Bible, but later came to be seen so.

> "How many Caesars and Pompeys ... might have done ... well in the world ... had they not been Nicodemused into nothing?"
> — *Tristram Shandy*, Laurence Sterne (1713–1758).

Nihil Obstat
(*see also* Imprimatur)

Latin for "nothing hinders." In the Roman Catholic Church this statement found at the beginning of an ecclesiastical or religious book indicating that the book is free of doctrinal or moral error. Such a book has been approved by a censor and is ready for publication.

Nimbus *see* Halo

Nimrod

Any daring hunter. Nimrod "was a mighty hunter before the Lord" (Genesis 10:9. Because he wore the skins, which God made for Adam after the latter's expulsion from Eden, animals surrendered to Nimrod. It was believed that Nimrod instigated the building of the Tower of Babel.

Nine
(*see also* Numbers)

Because it is a trinity of trinities, nine is a mystical number. There are nine orders of angels; nine fruits of the Holy Spirit: love, joy, peace, patience, kindness, goodness, faith, gentleness and temperance (Galatians 5:22–23); nine crosses: altar, processional, roods on lofts, reliquary, consecration, marking, pectoral, spire and crosses pendent over altars. Leases sometimes have run for 99 or 999 years, trinities of trinities.

Noah
(*see also* Ark's Floor Plan; Flood; Noah's Ark)

The patriarch who was warned of the coming of a cataclysmic flood. He built a great ark to carry a male and female of each animal species to replenish the world when the waters subsided (Genesis 6–8). Similar stories have been recorded in Babylonia, Greece and India. Noah was also the inventor of viticulture.

Noah's Ark
(*see also* Arkologist; Ark's Floor Plan; Flood; Noah)

The ark built by Noah to save his family and a pair of every species of animal from the Flood. It is also a sailors' name for a white band of cloud that stretches across the sky like a rainbow. It can resemble a ship's hull. The ark built by Noah was a three-decked vessel with a roof and a door in the side. It was 300 cubits long, 50 cubits broad and 30 cubits high; a cubit being 18 to 22 inches. In past centuries considerable effort went into describing the number of animals to be housed in the ark and the amount of space and food they would require. It was reckoned that the ark was at least half an acre in size and had a displacement of 81,062 tons. About 300 species of birds and quadrupeds, the number inhabiting the region of the earth dwelt in by Noah, were assumed to have been brought on board.

Noah's Wife

The unnamed wife of Noah who, according to legend, thought Noah mad, and refused, at first, to go aboard the ark.

> And Noah he often said to his wife
> when he sat down to dine,
> I don't care where the water goes if it
> doesn't get into the wine.
> —*Wine and Water*, G. K.
> Chesterton (1874–1936).

Nod *see* Land of Nod

Noli Me Tangere
(*see also* Mary Magdalene)

"Touch me not," in Latin. When the risen Jesus stood before the weeping Mary Magdalene at the empty tomb, she did not recognize him, mistaking him for the gardener. Jesus is thus sometimes depicted holding gardening tools. When Mary Magdalene finally realized who he was, Jesus said, "Touch me not; for I am not yet ascended to my Father" (John 20:18). It is also the name of a balsam which upon being touched spews forth seeds. Formerly the name for the disfiguring skin disease, lupus.

Nolo Episcopari
(*see also* Bishop)

A Latin phrase meaning, "I am not willing to become a bishop." Upon being offered a bishopric it was considered good manners to twice refuse by saying this phrase. If said three times, then the prospective bishop was serious about his refusal.

North Side of the Altar

In churches the Gospel is read on the north side of the altar. The north is the dark side of the earth and the Gospel is the light of the world shining into the darkness.

Not by Bread Alone

There is more to life than materialism.

> "Man shall not live by bread alone, but by every word that proceeds from the mouth of God" (Matthew 4:4).

Not Peace but a Sword

This is a difficult verse for pacifists if interpreted literally. The sword is a metaphor. Jesus was illustrating the conflict of loyalties that will arise, with the kingdom of heaven demanding even more devotion than the family.

> "Do not think that I have come to bring peace on earth; I have not come to bring peace, but a sword. For I have come to set a man against his father, and a daughter against her mother, and a daughter-in-law against her mother-in-law" (Matthew 10:34–35).

Numbers
(*see also* Eight; Eleven; Fifteen; Five; Forty; Four; Fourteen; Golden Number; Nine; Numbers in Revelation; Seven; 666; Ten; Thirteen; Three; Three Score and Ten; Twelve; Two)

The numbers one to 13 symbolize the following:

1 — The oneness of God

2 — The union of God and man in Christ.

3 — The Trinity.

4 — Matthew, Mark, Luke and John, the four evangelists.

5 — The wounds of Christ: two in his hands, two in his feet and one in his side.

6 — The six days of creation.

7 — The gifts of the Holy Spirit and the number of times Jesus spoke from the cross.

8 — The eight Beatitudes (Matthew 5:3–11).

9 — The nine orders of angels.

10— The Ten Commandments.

11 — The Apostles who remained faithful.

12 — The original number of the Apostles.

13 — The number of Apostles after Paul's conversion.

Numbers in Revelation
(*see also* Numbers; Revelations)

3 — Spirit world, the world of good.

4 — Earth number as in "four corners of the earth."

5 —10: Round numbers, approximations, also multiples thereof.

6 — Falling just short of the complete number (seven); human nature.

7 — 4 + 3 (earth + spirit) = 7, the complete or perfect number.

12 — God's redeemed company, the church, the new Israel.

O

Oak

A genus of hardwood trees containing 450 species. Strength and endurance are symbolized by the oak. Some have main-

tained that the cross was made from its hard, durable wood. The oak is mentioned 21 times in the King James Bible (1611).

Oaths
see By Cock and Pie; By George; By Jingo; Crikey; Cripes; Doggone; Drat; Egad; For God's Sake; For Pete's Sake; Gad; G.D.; Gee; Goddamn; Golly; Gosh; Heavens to Betsy; Holy Mackerel; Holy Smoke; Holy Toledo; Jumpin' Jehosaphat; Od's; Tear God's Body; Zounds

Obadiah

A book consisting of one chapter of 21 verses, the shortest book in the Old Testament. It recounts the prophet Obadiah's vision of Israel's deliverance. There are nine other Obadiahs in the Old Testament. In the Middle Ages the prophet Obadiah was confused with the Obadiah mentioned in 1 Kings 18:4, who hid one hundred priests in a cave where they escaped the wrath of Jezebel. Because *that* Obadiah fed them bread and water, the prophet's attributes were a pitcher of water and a loaf of bread.

Odium Theologicum

The intense hatred that arises between proponents of different theological opinions. It has been said that there are no wars so bloody as wars of religion.

Odor of Sanctity
(*see also* Incorrupt)

To die in the odor of sanctity is to die with the best possible reputation. However, to live with the odor of sanctity is to be sanctimonious. Originally the term was taken literally. It was believed that when saints died, their corpses, even many years after death, were free from the ordinary rules of corruption and gave off a sweet and pleasant smell. The related concept, the odor of iniquity, whereby evil people stank horribly after death, never caught on in popular use:

> "We are the good odor of Christ to God" (2 Corinthians 2:15).

Od's

(*see also* Drat)

An abbreviation of *God's* used in such oaths as Od's bodkins! (God's body), Od's pittikins! (God's pity), Od's blessed will! (God's blessed will), Od rot 'em! (God rot them), and Od's zounds! (God's wounds).

Oil

(*see also* My Cup Runneth Over)

A very valuable commodity used to consecrate priests. It symbolizes prosperity and gladness. The oil that is mentioned many times in the Bible was olive oil.

Old as Methuselah

(*see also* Methuselah)

Anything or any person extremely old. Methuselah lived 969 years (Genesis 5:25–27).

Old as the Hills

Any thing or person incredibly old can be so called. The expression may be derived from Job 15:7:

> "Are you the first man that was born? Or were you brought forth before the hills?"

Old Harry

One of the many names for the devil or Satan. Others are Old Bendy, Old Scratch, Old Ned, Old Nick, Old Gentleman and Lord Harry.

Old Men Dream Dreams

The coming of the day of the Lord.

> "Your sons and your daughters shall prophesy, your old men shall dream dreams" (Acts 2:17).

Old Nick *see* Satan

Old Testament Books in Rhyme

(*see also* New Testament Books in Rhyme)

> The great Jehovah speaks to us
> In Genesis and Exodus;
> Leviticus and Numbers see
> Followed by Deuteronomy.
> Joshua and Judges sway the land,
> Ruth gleans a sheaf with trembling hand;
> Samuel and numerous Kings appear
> Whose Chronicles we wondering hear.
> Ezra and Nehemiah, now,
> Esther the beauteous mourner show,
> Job speaks in sighs, David in Psalms,
> The Proverbs teach to scatter alms;
> Ecclesiastes then comes on,
> And the sweet Song of Solomon.
> Isaiah, Jeremiah then
> With Lamentations takes his pen.
> Ezekiel, Daniel, Hosea's lyres
> Swell Joel, Amos, Obadiah's.
> Next Jonah, Micah, Nahum come,
> And lofty Habakkuk finds room, -
> While Zephaniah, Haggai calls.
> Wrapt Zachariah builds his walls;
> And Malachi, with garments rent,
> Concludes the ancient Testament.
> — Anon.

Olive Branch

An emblem of peace which can be an actual branch of the olive tree or anything that is offered up for peace. It was the custom of opposing warriors to display an olive branch when they wanted a truce. When a dove brought Noah an olive branch (Genesis 8:10–11), it was a sign that the Flood was receding and God's wrath had abated. The angel Gabriel held an olive branch to indicate the coming of Christ, the Prince of Peace. Crossed olive branches appear on the flag of Cyprus, where they symbolize peace between Greeks and Turks. An olive branch can also be a child (Psalms 128:3):

> "Your wife will be like a fruitful vine within your house; your children will be like olive shoots around your table."

Omega *see* Alpha and Omega

Omicron

The 15th letter of the Greek alphabet, written *O.* Because it is a circle, it symbolizes unity like the Trinity. The literal meaning of omicron is "small o."

Omobuono, St. *see* Goodman, St.

Onan

The grandson of Jacob. When obliged by the law to marry his brother's widow and begat children, "He spilled the semen on the ground, lest he should give offspring to his brother" (Genesis 38:9). God slew Onan because he did a detestable thing: He prevented procreation, the divine purpose of marriage. Although *coitus interruptus* is what Onan did, the vice of onanism has come to mean masturbation.

> "Because he spills his seed on the ground."
> — Dorothy Parker (1893–1967), upon being asked why her parrot was named 'Onan.'

120 Words

(see also Ten Commandments; Ten Commandments in Rhyme)

When Moses came down from Mount Sinai, he carried two stone tablets upon which were inscribed 120 Hebrew words, the Ten Commandments (Exodus 20:3–17).

One's Days Are Numbered

The conviction that one's life or effectiveness is about to end. It comes from Daniel 5:26:

> "... God has numbered the days of your kingdom and brought it to an end."

Ophir *see* King Solomon's Mines

Orange

A color associated with the Protestants of Ireland. It comes from William of Orange, who derived his title from a principality of that name, which itself came from a Latin word, *aurangia,* that had no connection to the color or the fruit. The word means golden apple. Neither the color nor the fruit is mentioned in the King James Bible (1611). With its white flowers, the orange tree became a symbol of the purity and chastity of the Virgin Mary. The orange was sometimes depicted as the fruit of the expulsion from Eden instead of the apple.

Orans

An image found in the catacombs, a representation of a female praying in a standing position with arms outstretched. It has come to be a depiction of a person in the traditional kneeling position of prayer.

Ordeals

(see also Dei Judicium)

An old Teutonic and Anglo-Saxon custom of placing persons who have been accused of crime before God's mercy, by way of a physical test. It came to be believed that God would protect the innocent by a miracle.

Ordeal by Cold Water: Reserved for common people, this was the ordeal used to detect witches. The accused was thrown into a river. If the person floated, he or she was guilty. If the person sank, he or she was innocent.

Ordeal by Hot Water: This was also for the common folk. The accused would plunge his arm up to the elbow into boiling water to lift out a stone. If the skin blistered, the person was guilty.

Ordeal of Battle: For persons of high rank. The accused and the accuser were required to fight. The winner was judged to be innocent. The loser could live as a *recreant* if he renounced his misdeed.

Ordeal of Fire: For persons of high rank. The accused would be made to walk barefoot and blindfolded among nine red-hot ploughshares placed randomly, or grasp a piece of red-hot iron in his hand. The foot or hand would then be bound for three days and then inspected. Innocence was proven if no injury was sustained.

Ordeal of the Bier: Someone accused of murder would be required to touch the corpse. If he was guilty, the corpse would begin to bleed.

Ordeal of the Cross: In the case of a suit, the plaintiff and defendant would stand with their arms crossed on their breasts. Whoever endured longest was judged the winner.

Ordeal of the Eucharist: An unworthy priest would choke on the elements of the Eucharist. *Corsned* was the word for this ordeal by bread.

Orientation

Finding a position with relation to the points of the compass. The east, or the orient, is where the sun (Christ) rises and is thus the direction from which truth and light emanate. Therefore churches are *oriented*, that is, their altars are placed at the eastern end of the building.

Ostrich
(*see also* Egg)

A large bird, up to eight feet tall and 300 pounds, which inhabits deserts in Asia and Africa. Even the most important worldly concerns take second place when the ostrich gazes to Heaven. Sometimes ostrich eggs were suspended in churches as a sign of God's watchfulness. It was believed that the eggs were hatched by the Ostrich's constant gaze. If the gaze, which symbolized God's watchfulness, was interrupted for even an instant, the eggs would not hatch.

> "The wings of the ostrich wave proudly
> ... she leaves her eggs to the earth, and
> lets them be warmed on the ground"
> (Job 39: 13–14).

Oubliette

A secret dungeon in a medieval monastery or castle with a trapdoor in the ceiling as its only entrance, or a concealed tunnel leading to a river or moat where the bodies of prisoners could be disposed of. Rebellious monks and nuns were thought to have been locked up or even walled up in such places. Whether or not this is true is open to debate. The oubliette may have been nothing more sinister than a sewerage drain.

Our Father *see* Paternoster

Our Lady
(*see also* Virgin Mary)

The common way of referring to the Virgin Mary. It has been in use since at least the eighth century.

Our Lady of Charity *see* Bolivian Navy

Our Lady of Help *see* Army of Andorra

Out-Herod Herod
(*see also* Herod: Herod the Great)

To commit violence on such a scale as to exceed the worst of tyrants. Herod the Great (73–4 B.C.), a very bad tyrant, had the innocent babies of Bethlehem killed. (Matthew 2:1 ff.) In medieval mystery plays Herod was always portrayed as ranting and cruel. The expression comes from William Shakespeare's *Hamlet* (1603–1604):

> "I would have such a fellow whipped for o'erdoing Termagant; it out-Herods Herod..."

Out of the Mouths of Babes and Sucklings

The Lord is praised even by infants. The expression has come to mean wisdom arising from an unexpected or unlikely source.

> "Out of the mouths of babes and sucklings hast thou ordained strength because of thine enemies, that thou mightest still the enemy and the avenger" (Psalm 8:2).

Outer Darkness

Often in the form of "Cast into the outer darkness," this expression means to be cast into hell and to be cut off from the light of God. Nowadays it also has the sense of being a social outcast. It comes from Matthew 8:12:

> "While the sons of the kingdom will be thrown into the outer darkness."

Oversleeping

Those who sleep late can call upon St. Vitus (d. c. 303), their patron saint. Vitus was boiled to death in oil. A rooster, sacrificed as part of a pagan ritual against sorcery, was thrown into the oil with him.

From this comes the saint's association with the prevention of oversleeping.

Owl

A creature of the night which was thought to be blind. On the basis of "the darkness has blinded his eyes" (1 John 2:11), the owl symbolizes the Jews who were too blind to accept Christ as the Messiah. In scenes of the crucifixion the owl represents Christ who came

> "to give light to those who sit in darkness and in the shadow of death" (Luke 1:79).

Ox
(*see also* Boanthropy; Dumb Ox)

Because it was a valuable sacrificial animal, the ox represents, when winged, St. Luke, whose gospel highlights Christ's supreme sacrifice. Its presence with an ass in nativity scenes was considered a proof that Jesus was the Messiah and a fulfillment of Isaiah 1:3: "The Ox knows its owner, and the ass its master's crib." Tradition has it that during the flight into Egypt, Mary rode an ass, while the sons of Joseph by a prior marriage led an ox. The ox is an attribute of St. Thomas of Aquinas (c. 1225–1274), who was called a dumb ox by his contemporaries.

P

Paedobaptist

A Christian who advocates infant baptism as opposed to one who practices adult baptism alone.

Pagan
(*see also* Heathen)

Someone who is neither Christian,

Muslim nor Jew. Someone who has no religion. The word comes from *Paganus*, rustic, a contemptuous term used by Roman soldiers for civilians. The early Christians, calling themselves *milites Christi*, soldiers of Christ, used the soldiers' word and applied it to non–Christians. The word is never used in the King James Bible (1611).

Painting, Religious, Restoration
of *see* Artist's Bill

Palimpsest

In the monasteries of medieval Europe, the monks grew into the habit of ripping apart old books, preferably those of a pagan nature, cleaning off the parchment pages and then using them for Christian manuscripts. The original texts of these works, called palimpsests, can often be seen through ultraviolet light. There are examples of "double palimpsests," pages that were used three times.

Palindrome
(*see also* Sator)

A word or sentence which reads the same backwards and forwards. What did Adam do when he first met Eve? He bowed politely and said, "Madam, I'm Adam." ΝΙΨΟΝ ΑΝΟΜΗΜΑΤΑ ΜΗ ΜΟΝΑΝ ΟΨΙΝ is a Greek palindrome which appears on the fonts in many churches. It means, "Wash my transgressions not only my face." The Book of Genesis can be divided into facetious palindromic chapters:

Chapter 1: Madam, I'm Adam.
Chapter 2: Eve
Chapter 3: Sex at noon taxes.

Palm
(*see also* Palm Sunday; Palmers)

The palm branch was an ancient sym-
bol of victory adopted by early Christians. A palm tree sheltered the members of the Holy Family on their flight into Egypt, and palms were spread before Jesus as he entered Jerusalem. Martyrs will appear before Christ,

> "Clothed in white robes, with palm
> branches in their hands"
> (Revelation 7:9).

Palm Sunday
(*see also* Fig Sunday;
Palm; Palmers)

The Sunday before Easter. A procession in which worshippers carry palm branches recalls the triumphant entry of Jesus into Jerusalem (John 12:12–19). The custom can be traced to fifth century Jerusalem where a bishop, substituting for Jesus, took part in a procession from the Mount of Olives to the Church of the Resurrection.

Palmers
(*see also* Palm; Palm Sunday)

In the Middle Ages those who had made a pilgrimage to the Holy Land were called Palmers. Upon returning, they brought palm branches which were placed on church altars, or fashioned a cross from strips of palm leaves.

> His sandals were with travel tore,
> Staff, budget, bottle, scrip he wore,
> The faded palm-branch in his hand
> Showed pilgrim from the Holy Land.
> —*Marmion*, Sir Walter
> Scott (1771–1832).

Palmistry

Predicting a person's future or revealing his character by studying the crease lines in the palm of the hand. There are several possible references to palmistry in the Bible. "Behold, I have graven you on the palms of my hands; your walls are continually before me" (Isaiah 49:16). "Long life is in her right hand; in her left hand are riches and honor" (Proverbs 3:16). Other names for the practice are chiromancy and chirosophy. Making predictions from lines on the soles of the feet is known as podoscopy.

Paludament

A cloak worn by a Roman general. This was the "scarlet robe" which was mockingly draped over Jesus at the crucifixion (Matthew 27:28).

Pan *see* Satan

Panther
(*see also* Leopard)

A black leopard which is not, as one might expect, always a symbol of evil. It was believed that the panther, after feeding, would sleep for three days in its den, an obvious parallel to the three days Jesus spent in his tomb. When the panther awoke it belched the sweetish odor of allspice, symbolizing the sweet words of the Gospel.

Pants and Panties

Although these words are derived from a saint's name, pants, to say nothing of panties, have only been used in polite company in recent times. The saint was Pantaleone, a Christian doctor who dedicated himself to the poor until martyred in 305. By the 15th century his name, which means "all lion," was considered to be comical. A stock character of the Italian stage soon emerged — Pantaloon, an aged and bespectacled buffoon. His tight breeches, swelling above the knees, were known as pantaloons. From this the words "pants" and "panties" emerged in the 18th century.

The sixth age shifts
Into the lean and slipper'd pantaloon;
With spectacles on nose and
pouch on side;
His youthful hose well sav'd, a world
too wide
For his shrunk shank; and his big
manly voice,
Turning again towards childish
treble, pipes
And whistles in his sound.
—*As You Like It*, William
Shakespeare (1564–1616).

Papal Infallibility
(*see also* Ex Cathedra)

The dogma that the pope is infallible on matters of morals and faith. The doctrine was taught as early as 750, but was not decreed to be an article of faith until 1870. It remains one of the main points of disagreement between Catholics and Protestants. Because he missed his train, Geoffrey Fisher (1887–1972), Archbishop of Canterbury, was overheard apologizing to Pope John XXIII (1881–1963) during a visit to Rome in 1960 when he said, "I'm sorry we're late, we misread the timetables. But there — nobody's infallible."

Papal States
(*see also* Prisoner of the Vatican; Vatican)

Central Italy was awarded to Pope Stephen II (d. 757) in 756 by the Frankish king, Pepin the Short (714–768). The Church sought temporal power to provide itself with the revenues and political independence necessary to carry out its spiritual mission. Papal rule was loose until the middle of the 11th century when Pope Gregory VII (c. 1020–1085) and his successors began to assume more control. By the 15th century the popes ruled as absolute monarchs. The French occupied the Papal States during the Napoleonic Wars, but the Congress of

Vienna (1815) restored them to the papacy. The population of the Papal States, however, had become dissatisfied with what they considered to be a reactionary ecclesiastical regime and there were several uprisings that needed foreign intervention to suppress. Most of the Papal States were united with the Kingdom of Italy in 1860. Thanks to the presence of a French garrison, the area around Rome remained under Papal rule. When the French went home Rome was annexed by Italy in 1870 and the Papal States ceased to exist.

Paradise *see* Earthly Paradise

Paradise Shoots

The only plant descended from the Garden of Eden was the lign aloe, so legend would have us believe. Adam took a shoot of this tree when he was banished from Eden.

Pardoners
(*see also* Indulgence; Treasury of the Church)

Itinerant preachers of the Middle Ages who raised money for crusades, alms and the construction of churches by selling indulgences and the remission of sins. Their methods became rife with corruption. The sale of indulgences was condemned by the Council of Trent (1545–1563).

Parousia *see* Second Coming

Parson's Nose *see* Pope's Nose

Particular Judgment

When a soul in a state of grace leaves the body at death, it appears before God for individual or particular judgment. Souls that are pure enter Heaven immediately; those in need of purification go to purgatory and those in mortal sin to hell. All must submit to the general or last judgment.

Parting of the Way

Deciding between alternatives. It is used in Ezekiel 21:21:

> "For the king of Babylon stands at the parting of the way."

Partridge
(*see also* Quail; St. Partridge Day)

The pheasant. The bird suggests theft and deceit as well as humanity's chief deceiver, the devil.

> "Like the partridge that gathers a brood which she did not hatch, so is he who gets riches but not by right" (Jeremiah 17:11).

Pass Over Jordan

To die and enter Heaven. To cross over the Jordan River was to enter the Promised Land.

Passion Play

The story of Christ's suffering and death developed from medieval mystery plays. The passion play in Oberammergau, Germany, is the best-known survivor. In 1633 plague struck the community and the villagers vowed that if they were spared they would enact the passion every 10 years thereafter. Apart from periods of war and political turmoil, the vow has been kept. The play, which can have a cast of 850, and 100 musicians, takes five hours to perform.

Passionflower

A tropical vine whose flowers supposedly bear a resemblance to the instruments of Christ's passion. The leaf symbolizes the spear that pierced Christ's side; the five anthers represent the five wounds Christ received; the tendrils the scourging whips; the column of the ovary the shaft of the cross; the stamens the hammers that pounded the nails; the three stigmas the three nails; the corona within the flowers the crown of thorns; the calyx the halo; the white flowers are purity; and the blue is heaven. The flower blossoms for three days, symbolizing the three years of Christ's earthly ministry.

> There has fallen a splendid tear
> From the passion flower at the gate.
> —*Maud*, Alfred, Lord
> Tennyson (1809–1892).

Pastoral Staff *see* Crosier

Paternoster

> (*see also* Ape's Paternoster;
> Paternoster-while; Say the
> Devil's Paternoster)

Latin for "Our Father," the first two words of the Lord's Prayer (Matthew 6:9–13) and a name for that prayer. Roman Catholics end the prayer with "but deliver us from evil." Protestants end it with, "For thine is the kingdom, the power and the glory," which some consider to be an interpolation. Every 11th bead of a rosary is called a Paternoster because the Lord's Prayer is repeated then. There is a fishing line which has this name because its hooks are arranged in the fashion of a rosary. Patter, meaning fast insincere talk, is derived from paternoster, probably because some priests were in the habit of reciting it rapidly.

> "A recent government publication on the marketing of cabbage contains according to one report, 29,941 words. It is noteworthy in this regard that the Gettysburg Address contains mere 279 words while the Lord's Prayer comprises but 67."
> —*Quotable Business*, Norman Augustine (1935–).

Paternoster-while

> (*see also* Paternoster)

An antique word which means a short time, the time it would take to recite a paternoster.

Patience of Job

> (*see also* Job's Comforter)

Great patience in the face of adversity, as in the example of Job. "You have heard of the steadfastness of Job" (James 5:11). In fact, Job exhibits patience only in the first two chapters of the book that bears his name. Elsewhere he appears rebellious and angry.

Patmos

A place of solitude or banishment. Patmos is the small Greek island in the Aegean Sea where tradition says St. John, in exile, wrote Revelation.

> "I John, your brother, who share with you in Jesus the tribulation and the kingdom and the patient endurance, was on the island called Patmos on account of the word of God and the testimony of Jesus" (Revelation 1:9).

Patron Saints

> (*see also* Diseases and
> Misfortunes, Patron Saints of)

Accountants Matthew; *Astronauts* Joseph of Cupertino; *Bee Keepers* Ambrose, Bernard; *Bloodbanks* Januarius; *Boot Blacks and Shoe Shiners* Nicholas of Myrna ; *Breast Feeding* Giles; *Bus Drivers* Christopher; *Carnival and Circus Workers* Julian the Hospitaller; *Cemetery Workers* Joseph of Arimathea; *Chastity* Agnes, Thomas Aquinas; *Coin Collectors* Eligius; *Comedians* Vitus; *Customs Officers* Brigid; *Fireworks Makers* Barbara; *Flight Attendants and Stewardesses* Bona; *Gas Station Attendants* Eligius; *Grave-*

diggers Antony; *Greeting Card Manufacturers* Valentine; *Interracial Justice* Martin de Porres; *Jumping and Leaping* Venatus; *Librarians* Jerome; *Lighthousekeepers* Venerius; *Old-clothes Dealers* Anne; *Paratroopers* Michael; *Pasty Chefs* Honorius of Amiens, Macarius the Younger; *Plasterers* Bartholomew; *Playing Card Manufacturers* Balthasar; *Running Water* John of Nepomuk; *Skaters* Lidwina; *Skiers* Bernard; *Soap Boilers* Florian; *Souls in Purgatory* Nicholas of Tolentino, Odilo; *Speleologists* Benedict; *Stamp Collectors* Gabriel the Archangel; *Storks* Agricola of Avignon; *Swans* Hugh of Lincoln; *Taxi Drivers* Fiacre; *Television* Clare of Assisi; *Truss Makers* Foillan; *Unattractive People* Drogo, Germaine Cousin; *Virgins* Blessed Virgin Mary; *Wax Melters and Refiners* Ambrose of Milan, Bernard of Clairvaux; *Whales* Brendan the Navigator

> Saints will aid if men will call:
> For the blue sky bends over all!
> —*Kubla Khan*, Samuel Taylor
> Coleridge (1772–1834).

Paula the Bearded, St. *see* Bearded Women

Pawnbrokers

Pawnbrokers are identified by three golden balls because of the fourth century St. Nicholas of Myrna. When he overheard a poor man say that his three daughters would have to become prostitutes because he could not afford to support them, Nicholas anonymously supplied them with dowries when he threw a golden ball, or bag of gold, through their window.

Peace of God *see* Truce of God

Peacock

Because of its showy tail feathers, this bird is a symbol of pride. It also symbolizes

the resurrection because it was believed that its flesh was incorruptible even after being buried for three days. Peacock is the name of the male bird only. The female is a peahen. Peacocks are mentioned only three times in the King James Bible (1611): 1 Kings 10:22; 2 Chronicles 9:21; and Job 39:13.

> "Remember that the most beautiful things in the world are the most useless; peacocks and lilies for instance."
> —*The Stones of Venice*, John Ruskin (1819–1900).

Pearl of Great Price

Something of great value or importance, specifically the kingdom of Heaven.

> "Again, the kingdom of heaven is like unto a merchant man, seeking goodly pearls. Who, when he had found one pearl of great price, went and sold all that he had and bought it" (Matthew 13:45–46).

Pearls Before Swine

Something costly that is wasted on those incapable of appreciating it.

> "Do not give dogs what is holy; and do not throw your pearls before swine, lest they trample them under foot and turn to attack you" (Matthew 7:6).

Pearly Gates
(*see also* New Jerusalem)

Originally part of St. John's vision of the New Jerusalem. They are now synonymous with entering Heaven.

> "And the twelve gates were twelve pearls, each of the gates made of a single pearl" (Revelation 21:21).

Pelican

According to legend, the pelican becomes angry with its young and kills them.

Three days later the bird returns, opens its breast with its sharp beak, and revives the fledglings with its own blood. In Christian art the pelican became a symbol of Jesus Christ as sacrifice and redeemer. References to pelicans in the King James Bible (1611) can be found at Leviticus 11:18, Deuteronomy 14:17 and Psalms 102:6. In his fourth century translation of the Bible, St. Jerome, thinking that the bird was some sort of woodpecker, named it pelican, which comes from the Greek for "axe beak." Symbolizing self-sacrifice, the state flag of Louisiana depicts the pelican feeding its young with blood from its breast.

Penitent Thief *see* Dismas

Pentagram

A five-pointed star which in Christian art came to symbolize both protection from Satan and the five wounds Christ received on the cross.

Peter, St.

(*see also* Cephas; Peter's Fish; Peter's Pence)

The leader of the 12 apostles. His first name was Simon. Peter was a punning nickname given by Jesus. "And I tell you, you are Peter, and on this rock I will build my church, and the powers of death shall not prevail against it. I will give you the keys to the kingdom of heaven" (Matthew 16:18–19). Peter, the Greek *Petros*, is similar to rock, *Petra*. He was also called Cephas, Aramaic for rock. Roman Catholics interpret the above passage to mean that Peter was given authority over the church, a responsibility passed through the succession of popes. Protestants believe the rock to be all Christians. Peter's attributes are silver and gold keys, usually crossed. An early tradition has Peter preaching in Rome as the city's

first bishop. At his own behest, when he was crucified, he was hung upside down so that he would be lower than Christ.

Peter's Fish

(*see also* Cephas; Peter, St.; Peter's Pence)

A popular name for the haddock. Black spots on either side behind the gills were thought to have been made by Peter's finger and thumb. The apostle obtained tribute money from the mouth of a fish which he had caught (Matthew 17:27). The fact that the haddock, a bottom-feeder, related to the cod, is a saltwater fish not found in the Holy Land is conveniently ignored.

Peter's Pence

(*see also* Cephas; Peter, St.; Peter's Fish)

An annual tribute that was paid to the pope by the people of England. Every family possessing land or cattle to the value of 30 pence had to pay one silver penny at the festival of St. Peter. The tribute was abolished by Henry VIII in 1534. The term came to mean any voluntary contribution of money to the church.

Petrel *see* Mother Carey's Chicken

Pharisees

Anyone who thinks himself better than others or who makes a show of religion can be called a pharisee, as can a hypocrite. The Pharisees were an ancient Jewish religious community of scholars and teachers who believed in a very strict and legalistic form of religious observance. Jesus denounced them many times for emphasizing the outer form of religion while ignoring the inner truth.

"I bear them witness that they have a zeal for God, but it is not enlightened" (Romans 10:2).

Philistines

A seafaring people who lived along the coast of Palestine, the Philistines were enemies of the Israelites. Samson fought them, as did Saul and Jonathan. David made them vassals. In the 19th century, German university students applied the word to the middle class, whose members they considered to be uncultured, narrow minded and materialistic. The reference is to Judges 16: 9: "The Philistines are upon you." Matthew Arnold brought the word into English, where it has come to mean anyone with a bourgeois dislike of literature and art. The Philistines of ancient Palestine were, in fact, a highly cultured people.

> "The people who believe most that our greatness and welfare are proved by our being very rich, and who most give their lives and thoughts to becoming rich, are just the very people whom we call the Philistines."
> — *Culture and Anarchy*, Matthew Arnold (1822–1888).

Phoenix

A symbol of the resurrection, a fabulous red and gold eagle of Arabia. Only one phoenix could live at any one time. Every 500 years the bird would journey to Heliopolis, build a pyre, fan the flames with its wings, and burn itself to ashes. Out of the flames would arise a new, young, beautiful phoenix. Psalm 103:5, "So that your youth is renewed like the eagle's," recalls a phoenix-like legend about the eagle. Once a decade the bird would soar to the fiery regions and then plummet to the sea where it would be reborn.

> Ask me no more if east or west
> The Phoenix builds her spicy nest;
> For unto you at last she flies,
> And in your fragrant bosom dies.
> — *Poems*, Thomas Carew (c.1595–c.1639).

Pietà

Italian for pity or piety. In Christian art a pietà is a sculpture or painting of the sorrowful Virgin Mary cradling the body of Jesus, her dead son. Although it lacks scriptural authority, the pietà image was very popular during the 14th and 15th centuries. The most famous pietà is a marble statue in St. Peter's, Rome, completed by Michelangelo in 1499. When challenged about making the Virgin appear younger than her son, Michelangelo replied that the purity of the Virgin Mary made her youth eternal.

Pilate, St. Pontius
(*see also* Pilate Voice;
Procla, Claudia)

An apocryphal work claims that Pilate sent Emperor Tiberias (42 B.C.–37 A.D.) a letter in which he recounts the miracles of Jesus. It was believed that Pilate must have been a secret convert to Christianity to write such a letter and that he was martyred because of it. The church in Ethiopia has made Pilate a saint.

> "I was at Pontius Pilate's house and pissed against it."
> — *The Unfortunate Traveler*, Thomas Nashe (1567–1601).

Pilate Voice
(*see also* Pilate, St. Pontius)

A very loud voice such as would be possessed by a tyrant like Pontius Pilate.

Pilate's Stair *see* Scala Santa

Pilate's Wife *see* Procla, Claudia

Pillar Saints *see* Stylites

Placemakers Bible

In 1562, in the second edition of the Geneva Bible, a typographical error appeared in Matthew 5:9. Instead of "*peacemakers*" the word "*placemakers*" was used. This resulted in the following:

> "Blessed are the *placemakers* for they shall be called the children of God."

Plagues of Egypt
(*see also* First Born of Egypt)

The expression means any terrible ordeal. The Egyptians had to endure 10 terrible plagues (Exodus 7–12) before Pharaoh freed the Israelites from bondage. The plagues were 1) The water of the river Nile turned to blood; 2) frogs; 3) lice; 4) flies; 5) death of cattle; 6) boils; 7) hail; 8) locusts; 9) darkness; and 10) death of firstborn children.

> "The Lord said to Moses, 'Yet one plague more will I bring upon Pharaoh and upon Egypt; afterwards he will let you go hence'" (Exodus 11:1).

Pomegranate

A thick-skinned fruit with many seeds and juicy red pulp. It symbolizes the joys of heaven because it was promised to the children of Israel (Deuteronomy 8:8). The pomegranate is usually depicted cut in half, with its tightly packed seeds standing for Christian unity. When held in the hand of the Christ Child, the fruit, which returns in spring, predicts the resurrection.

Pontiff
(*see also* Names of the Popes; Pope)

A term that was once applied to any bishop but is now used only of the pope. In ancient Rome it meant someone in charge of bridges, a responsibility of the priesthood. (*Pontus* = a bridge).

Pool of Bethesda

An allusion to unfair advancement or to those held back because of a disability. The pool was a cistern in Jerusalem which had miraculous healing power. In John 5:1–9 a paralytic complains that he has waited for 38 years beside the pool, but others had always stepped down before him. Jesus immediately healed the man.

Poor as a Church Mouse
(*see also* Mouse)

Unlike modern churches, there are no pantries or cupboards in the churches of old. A mouse who lived in an old church would be poor indeed. The expression dates from the 17th century.

Poor as Job's Turkey
(*see also* Job's Comforter; Patience of Job)

To be extremely poor was to be as poor as Job. The devil robbed Job of everything he possessed. As poor as Job was, Job's turkey was even poorer. The bird had but one feather in its tail and had to lean against a fence to gobble. Of course the biblical Job never had a turkey, since the bird is native to North America. The expression was coined by Canadian humorist Thomas Chandler Haliburton (1796–1865).

> "A turkey is more occult and awful than all the angels and archangels. In so far as God has partly revealed to us an angelic world, he has partly told us what an angel means. But God has never told us what a turkey means."
> —*All Things Considered*, G. K. Chesterton (1874–1936).

Poor as Lazarus

About as poor as it is possible to be. Lazarus was a beggar covered in sores who fed from the crumbs left by a rich man (Luke 16:19–31).

Pope

(*see also* English Pope; Fisherman's Ring; Names of the Popes; Pontiff; Pope Joan; Pope's Nose; Power of the Keys; Protestant Pope)

The head of the Roman Catholic Church. In the first centuries of the Christian Church the title was used by many bishops. Leo the Great (c. 390–461) was the first to use it officially. By the time of Gregory VII (c. 1020–1085), it was used only for the bishop of Rome.

> "It often happens that I wake at night and begin to think about a serious problem and decide I must tell the Pope about it. Then I wake up completely and remember I am the Pope."
> — *Wit and Wisdom of Good Pope John*, Pope John Paul XXIII (1881–1963).

Pope Joan

(*see also* Pope)

A woman who, falling in love with a Benedictine monk, reputedly disguised herself as a man. When her lover died, she entered the priesthood, became a cardinal, and in 855 succeeded Leo IV as Pope John VIII. She reigned for two years until her secret was revealed when she gave birth during a procession to the Latern Basilica. Her story inspired a Latin joke, *non papa sed mama*, "not a pope [father] but a mother." Although widely believed in the 15th and 16th centuries, the tale of Pope Joan is complete fiction. Pope Joan was the name of a popular card game played with a deck missing the eight of diamonds, the Pope Joan.

Popeholy

Making a great show of holiness.

Pope's Nose

(*see also* Pope)

In a fowl about to be carved, the fatty rectal bump, which resembles a flattened nose. This insulting term originated during the reign of James II (1633–1701), a time when anti–Catholic feelings were strong in England. It is also known as a parson's nose.

Porta Clausa

(*see also* Virgin Mary)

"Closed gate," in Latin. An attribute of the perpetual virginity of Mary. It comes from Ezekiel's vision of a gate. Sometimes Ezekiel is depicted with a scroll bearing the opening words in Latin, *Porta clausa erit.*

> "This gate shall remain shut; it shall not be opened, and no one shall enter by it; for the Lord, the God of Israel, has entered by it; therefore it shall remain shut" (Ezekiel 44:2).

Potter's Field *see* Aceldama

Power of the Keys

(*see also* Pope)

The ecclesiastical power given to the pope as a successor of St. Peter, it is derived from Matthew 16:19:

> "I will give you the keys of the kingdom of heaven, and whatever you bind on earth shall be bound in heaven, and whatever you loose on earth shall be loosed in heaven."

Powers of Darkness

The devil, or a generalized sense of evil. The phrase is used frequently in the Bible, although in the singular, e.g., Colossians 1:13:

> "Who hath delivered us from the power of darkness, and hath translated *us* into the kingdom of his dear Son."

Powers That Be

A sarcastic reference to the government or established authority. The passage that follows is often used as a justification of the political and social status quo:

> "Let every soul be subject unto higher powers. For there is no power but of God: the powers that be are ordained by God" (Romans 13:1).

Practice What You Preach

You should do what you tell others to do. It is a popular paraphrase of Matthew 23:3, which states the same principle but in a negative fashion.

> "So practice and observe whatever they tell you, but not what they do; for they preach but do not practice."

Praise the Lord and Pass the Ammunition

A popular phrase coined by an unnamed American naval chaplain during World War II.

Prayer

It was once believed that prayer, especially the Lord's Prayer, was more effective if spoken out loud rather than silently meditated upon. The devil, so the reasoning went, could not read minds. He could only judge people based on the deeds he could see and the words he could hear.

> "Father expected a good deal of God. He didn't actually accuse God of inefficiency, but when he prayed his tone was loud and angry, like that of a dissatisfied guest in a carelessly managed hotel."
> — *God and My Father*, Clarence Day (1874–1935).

Prester John

The land of Prester John is any far-off place full of wondrous sights and strange peoples. Prester means priest or presbyter. According to legend, Prester John was a Christian cleric who traveled to a remote country beyond Armenia and Persia, converted its people to Christianity and became their ruler. After the 15th century Prester John became identified with the King of Ethiopia. So widespread was the belief in this fabulous kingdom that both Pope Alexander III (1159–1181) and Louis IX of France (1226–1270) sent emissaries to find it. One of the motives for the Portuguese exploration of Africa was to forge a link with Prester John's kingdom.

> "...I will fetch you a toothpicker now from the farthest inch of Asia; bring you the length of Prester John's foot ..."
> — *Much Ado About Nothing*, William Shakespeare (1564–1616).

Price of Wisdom is Above Rubies, The

A proverb attesting to the supreme value of wisdom.

> "No mention shall be made of coral, or of pearls, for the price of wisdom is above rubies" (Job 28:18).

Pride Goeth Before a Fall

An abbreviation of Proverbs 16:8. God will punish the prideful. The expression goes back to the early 16th century and despite the antique language remains in use:

> "Pride goeth before destruction and a haughty spirit before a fall."

Primer

A child's first reading book. Originally primer was a name for prayer books and devotional works for the laity. Since these were the first books many people read, the word was gradually transferred to ABC books.

Primrose *see* Cyclamen

Printers' Bible

In this Bible, printed in 1702, David appears to be complaining about printers in Psalms 119:161. Instead of *Princes*, "*Printers* persecute me without cause."

Prisoner of the Vatican
(*see also* Papal States; Vatican City)

The Roman Catholic Church exercised temporal control of central Italy until 1870, when its territory was absorbed by the Kingdom of Italy. The papacy refused to accept the annexation, and the popes withdrew into the Vatican in protest. This period when the popes were "prisoners in the Vatican" lasted until the signing of the Latern Pacts with Fascist Italy in 1929. Italy recognized the Vatican as a sovereign city-state with the pope as its head of state. Financial compensation was given for the loss of the Papal States and a guarantee that the Italian government would not interfere in ecclesiastical matters. In return the Church gave up its claim to the Papal States and recognized the existence of Italy with Rome as its capital. The Fascist government of Italy received a valuable boost in prestige and Catholic opposition was placated.

Procession of the Holy Spirit
see Filloque Controversy

Procla, Claudia
(*see also* Pilate, St. Pontius)

In the Bible the wife of Pontius Pilate is not named. Matthew 27:19 records that she spoke of Jesus to her husband, "Have

nothing to do with that righteous man, for I have suffered much over him in a dream." In art her dream is shown as a horrible nightmare. According to the apocryphal Gospel of Nicodemus, Pilate's wife is Procla or Procula. She accompanied her husband to Rome when he explained why Jesus was put to death. When Pilate was condemned to death, he secured a pardon for Procla. At his beheading an angel carried Pilate's head away. Procla witnessed this miracle and fell down dead with joy. There is a Claudia mentioned in 2 Timothy 4:21 whom some have attempted to identify with Pilate's wife.

Procrastination

The patron saint against procrastination and for promptness and expeditious solutions is the aptly named St. Expeditus. A Christian martyr, probably born in Armenia, little is known about Expeditus. A story is told that a package containing a statue and the relics of a saint were shipped to a French convent. The package was marked *spedito*, or special delivery, which in turn became *expeditus*. The saint of prompt solutions has become a cult figure on the Indian Ocean island of Réunion and among Voodoo believers in New Orleans.

> procrastination is the
> art of keeping
> up with yesterday.
> —*archy and mehitabel*, Don
> Marquis (1878–1937).

Procula *see* Procla, Claudia

Prodigal Son

Prodigal means lavish or spendthrift. A prodigal son is a wayward child who repents and returns to his family (Luke 15:11–33). The words "prodigal son" appear as a page heading but not in the biblical text itself.

"...a bankrupt, a prodigal, who dare scarce show his head on the Rialto..."
—*Merchant of Venice*, William Shakespeare (1564–1616).

Promised Land

In modern use "promised land" can mean Heaven or any ideal place. God repeatedly promises the land of Canaan to the seed of Abraham. This is one of the most persistent themes of the Old Testament. Strange to say, but the phrase never appears in the King James Bible (1611). The closest is the "land of promise," mentioned in Hebrews 11:9.

Prophecies of Malachy

A work from c. 1590 which purported to be by St. Malachy (c. 1094–1148). It gives attributes of popes past and future. The last will be the pope at the end of time.

Prophecy *see* Prophecies of Malachy; Prophet Is Not Without Honor; Sibyls

Prophet Is Not Without Honor, A

A person who gets scant respect or honor in his own country. Jesus suffered this fate in his home town of Nazareth.

"And they took offense at him: But Jesus said to them, 'A prophet is not without honor except in his own country and in his own house'" (Matthew 13:57).

Prophet's Gourd
(*see also* Gourd; Jonah)

Something that emerges unexpectedly and quickly grows to immense size. After he is released from the belly of the whale, Jonah preaches in Ninevah. In the King James Bible (1611), a huge gourd grows to protect Jonah but the next day is destroyed by a worm (Jonah 4: 6–10). In more recent translations of the Bible, Jonah is sheltered by a castor oil plant.

Protestant Pope
(*see also* Pope)

A nickname given to Pope Clement XIV (1705–1774), who suppressed the Jesuits because of their influence. The suppression lasted until 1814.

Protestant Rome

Geneva, a canton in the southwestern corner of Switzerland, became the center of Calvinism and was known during the Reformation as the Protestant Rome. Its acceptance of Calvinism alarmed the other cantons of Switzerland and delayed Geneva's admission into the Swiss confederation for generations.

Geneva! My mid flows back to a day in 1916 when I was standing down there, in front of a triumphal arch put up to celebrate the three hundred and eightieth anniversary of Calvin's first arrival in the city. "Since that man came here," said Monsieur Nivelle deliberately and emphatically, "this place has never been the same again." "But anyway," he went on to console himself, "that vulgar electric light along the lake-side has been cut off thanks to this war."
—*Between Niger and Nile*, Arnold Toynbee (1889–1975).

Protoevangelium

A first gospel by St. James the Less supposed by some to be the basis of all the others. If it existed, it has long been lost. The word is also used for the curse put upon the serpent in the Garden of Eden (Genesis 3:15):

"I will put enmity between you and the woman, and between your seed and her seed; he shall bruise your head, and you shall bruise his heel."

Proto-martyr

St. Stephen (Acts 5:7) has been called this because he was the first martyr.

Proud as Lucifer
(*see also* Lucifer)

Extreme pride. Lucifer was the chief of the angels who rebelled against God.

...Pandemonium, city and proud seat
Of Lucifer...
—*Paradise Lost*, John
Milton (1608–1674).

Proverbs and Psalms

Proverbs are short folk sayings that express commonplace truths as well as a book of the Old Testament consisting of moral and religious sayings. Contrasts are drawn between wisdom and folly and between righteousness and sin. Psalms is an Old Testament book containing 150 songs to God. King David, called "the sweet psalmist of Israel" (2 Samuel 23:1), is reputed to have been the author of many of them. A psalter is a version of the Psalms for devotional or liturgical use. Psalmody is the singing of psalms. In Roman Catholic psalters, Psalm 10 to 113 and 115 to 146 are numbered one behind those in Protestant psalters.

Pseudepigrapha *see* Apocrypha

Pudens

A Roman soldier mentioned in 2 Timothy 4:21. A legend grew up that his wife Claudia was British and that because of her he urged Eleutherius, Bishop of Rome in the second century, to send missionaries to Britain.

Purgatory *see* Limbo:
Limbus Purgatorius

Puritan Names
(*see also* Church Organs; Coffee)

Puritan parents visited upon their offspring some imaginative names, including Swear-not-at-all Ireton, Glory-be-to-God Pennyman, Hew-Agag-in-pieces-before-the-Lord Robinson, the Sykes brothers (Lovewell, Dowell, Diewell, and Farewell), Obadiah-bind-their-kings-in-chains-and-their-nobles-in-irons Needham, Praise-God Barebone, Fear-God Barebone, Jesus-Christ-came-into-the-world-to save Barebone, and Dr. If-Christ-had-not-died-for-thee-thou-hadst-been-damned Barebone. (The last named was known as Damned Dr. Barebone.) Faith, Hope, Charity, Prudence, Mercy, Truth, Constancy, Temperance, Honor, Obedience, Rejoice, Endure, Repentance, Humiliation, Humility and Pride were common first or "grace" names. Puritan comes from "pure of heart." The aim of the Puritans was to purify the Church of England of all traces of Roman Catholicism. To call someone a puritan today would be to say that he is narrow-minded and fanatically religious.

"The Puritan hated bear-baiting, not because it gave pain to the bear, but because it gave pleasure to the spectators."
—*History of England*, Thomas Babington Macaulay (1800–1859).

Purple *see* Sacred Purple

Q

Quail
(*see also* Partridge)

A bird belonging to the same family as the partridge. Although it is mentioned in Exodus as providing food for the wandering Israelites, the quail was believed to have unquenchable sexual urges and became a symbol of lasciviousness. Quails are mentioned five times in the King James Bible (1611).

> "The people asked, and he brought quails, and satisfied them with the bread of heaven" (Psalm 105:40).

Quaker
(*see also* Doffing the Hat)

A member of the Society of Friends, a religious sect founded in the 17th century. Members are pacifists and refuse to swear oaths. They are called Quakers because their founder, George Fox (1624–1691), urged them to "quake and tremble at the word of the Lord." The word was originally derisive. The Quakers originally did not use the word *you* because at the time it was the pronoun used when addressing superiors. Stressing the equality of mankind they preferred *thou*, the word used when addressing equals.

> The Quaker loves an ample brim
> A hat that bows to no salaam,
> And dear the beaver is to him
> As it never made a dam.
> —*All Round My Hat*, Thomas Hood (1778–1845).

Quasimodo Sunday

The first Sunday after Easter. It gets its name from the opening of the Latin office for the day, *Quasi modo geniti infantes*, "Like newborn babes" (1 Peter 2:2). It can also be called Low Sunday.

Quick and the Dead

Everyone, without exception, will be judged. As found in the King James Bible (1611), quick is used in the old sense, meaning living. More recent translations use the less memorable "living and the dead."

> "The Lord Jesus Christ, who shall judge the quick and the dead" (2 Timothy 4:1).

Quince

A symbol of sin. A hard, yellowish fruit that resembles the apple, the forbidden fruit. The quince is not mentioned in the King James Bible (1611).

> They dined on mince and slices of quince,
> Which they ate with a runcible spoon.
> —*The Owl and the Pussycat*, Edward Lear (1812–1888).

Quo Vadis?

"Whither goest thou?" in Latin. A legend said that St. Peter, fleeing from Rome to avoid martyrdom, met Jesus on the road and asked this question. Jesus answered, "To Rome to be crucified again." St. Peter immediately saw the error of his ways and returned to Rome where he was martyred. Polish writer Henryk Sienkiewicz (1846–1916) wrote a famous novel called *Quo Vadis* (1896).

> "But now I go my way to him that sent me; and none of you asketh me, Whither goest thou?" (John 16:5).

Quodlibet
(*see also* Dumb Ox)

Any problem of theology or philosophy brought forward as a theoretical exercise in disputation or argument. Medieval philosophers were very learned but some of their problems seem ridiculous to us today:

Whether during Mary's pregnancy if she was seated was Christ seated too? What was the color of the Virgin Mary's hair? When the angel Gabriel appeared before Mary, were his garments clean or foul and of what color? What time of day did he appear? The most famous question: How many angels can dance on the point of a sharp needle without jostling one another?

R

Rabbit
(*see also* Hare)

A small inoffensive mammal with short tail and long ears. It came to symbolize timidity and, because it breeds prolifically, love. The word *rabbit* cannot be found in the King James Bible (1611).

Race Is Not to the Swift, Nor the Battle to the Strong, The

Things do not always turn out the way you expect they will.

"Again I saw that under the sun the race is not to the swift, nor the battle to the strong, nor bread to the wise, nor riches to the intelligent, nor favor to the men of skill" (Ecclesiastes 9:11).

Races of Mankind

Apart from Noah's family the entire human race was said to have perished in the Flood. Noah had three sons, Ham, Shem and Japeth, and postdiluvian humanity was descended from them. Ham is the father of the Hamitic or African peoples, Shem of the Semitic or Asian peoples, and Japheth of the Japhitic or European races. The discovery of the New World posed a problem. Where did the Indians of North and South America fit

into this scheme? One theory maintained that they were the descendants of the lost tribes of Israel; another that their first ancestor was Canaan, son of Ham, cursed by Noah and made a servant (Genesis 9:25).

Raise Cain, To

To cause a disturbance or to make trouble. The reference is to the wicked Cain who murdered his brother Abel (Genesis 4). A joke from the 1840s:

"Why have we every reason to believe that Adam and Eve were both rowdies? Because they both raised Cain."

Rat

Rats are not mentioned in the King James Bible (1611), but Gertrude of Nivelles (626–659) and Martin de Porres (1579–1639) are the patron saints for protection against rats.

Raven

A bird which can represent misfortune or hope. In Genesis 8:7 Noah sent out a raven from the ark, but it failed to bring back good news. But a raven brought food to Elijah.

Take thy beak from out my heart, and take thy form from off my door! Quote the raven, "Nevermore." — *The Raven*, Edgar Allen Poe (1809–1849).

Reap the Whirlwind

To suffer serious consequences from misdeeds or sins.

"For they sow the wind, and they shall reap the whirlwind." (Hosea 8:7).

Rebekah's Camels Bible

In 1823 a Bible was printed in which Genesis 24:61 suggested that, "Rebekah arose, and her *camels* ..." instead of, "Rebekah arose, and her *damsels* ..."

Red
(*see also* Sacred Purple)

Symbolizing blood, red is a liturgical color recalling the blood of martyrs and of the Holy Innocents. The color of fire, red also is used at Pentecost, because fire appeared above the Apostles. Cardinals of the church wear red hats as a reminder that they are willing to shed their blood in the defense of the church.

Red Letter Day

A day when some enjoyable, memorable or very important event occurs. It was the custom, beginning in the 15th century, to mark saints' days in red on calendars to make them more noticeable. Sometimes purple ink was used.

Red Sky in the Morning, Sailors Take Warning; Red Sky at Night, Sailor's Delight

A saying which predicts the weather at mid latitudes in the Northern Hemisphere. Though not the origin of the expression, Matthew 16:2–3 has something similar.

> "When it is evening, you say, 'It will be fair weather; for the sky is red.' And in the morning, 'It will be stormy today, for the sky is red and threatening.'"

Rehoboam *see* Jeroboam

Relic
(*see also* Crucifixion Relics; Multiple Relics; Simony)

A sacred memorial of a holy person. A few of the objects that have been claimed as relics are: a coal that roasted St. Lawrence; the face and part of the nose of a seraph; fingers of St. Andrew, John the Baptist, the Holy Spirit and a thumb of St. Thomas; two handkerchiefs with images of Christ's face; two heads of John the Baptist; the hem of Joseph's garment and the hem of the garment worn by Jesus which was touched by the woman with the issue of blood; a lock of the hair with which Mary Magdalene wiped the feet of Jesus; nails from the crucifixion; a phial of St. Michael's sweat when he fought with Satan; rays from the Star of Bethlehem; a rib from the Word made flesh; the rod of Moses; the seamless coat worn by Christ; slippers worn by Enoch before the flood; the spoon used by the Virgin Mary to feed the infant Jesus; the sword and shield of St. Michael; a single tear shed by Jesus at the grave of Lazarus; and a tooth of Jesus; a water pot used at the wedding at Cana. First class relics are bodies or body parts of saints. Second class relics are things such as clothing and sandals associated with a saint. Third class relics are items brought into contact with first and second class relics and thus rendered holy.

Religious Majesty

In centuries past, the popes addressed kings with special appellations. Thus the king of England was always "His Most Religious"; the king of France was "His Most Christian"; the emperor of Austria was "His Most Apostolic"; the king of Spain was "His Most Catholic"; and the king of Portugal was "His Most Faithful."

Render Unto Caesar

This statement has been used to support the separation of church and state. Some also maintain that it supports the status quo. In response to some Pharisees who asked if it is lawful to pay tribute to Rome, Jesus replied,

> "Render unto Caesar the things which are Caesar's, and unto God the things that are God's" (Matthew 22:21).

The coins, of course, were stamped with the likeness of Caesar.

Rephraim *see* Giants

Rest in Peace *see* R.I.P.

Resurrection Bone

In the Middle Ages it was believed that the human body contained a triangular bone at the base of the spinal column which was incombustible, imponderable and incorruptible. This was the nucleus for the resurrected body.

Resurrection in Two Days or Three?

A fundamental Christian belief is that Jesus was crucified on Friday and on Sunday rose from the dead. Counting inclusively, in the style of ancient times, the time between Friday and Sunday makes three days. The resurrection is reported rather than described. Artistic depictions are based on deductions from accounts of the entombment and the discovery of the empty tomb.

> "For as by a man came death, by a man has come also the resurrection of the dead" (I Corinthians 15:21).

Resurrection Men

Body snatchers of 19th century Britain who robbed fresh graves in churchyards and even murdered to provide bodies for medical dissection. The term was first applied to William Burke and William Hare in 1829. Bodysnatching became such a scourge that relatives of a recently deceased person would stand guard over the grave. Iron coffins and mortsafes, cages of iron bars, were employed to prevent violation.

Revelations
(*see also* Apocalypse; Numbers in Revelation)

A common but an incorrect rendition of the name of the last book found in Protestant Bibles. The correct designation is always singular: *The Revelation to John* or *The Revelation of St. John the Divine*. In Catholic Bibles *Apocalypse* is used.

> *Lord Illingworth*: The Book of Life begins with a man and a woman in a garden.
> *Mrs. Allonby*: It ends with Revelations.
> —*A Woman of No Importance*, Oscar Wilde (1854–1900).

Reverend

The most common title given to members of the clergy. An archbishop is *the Most Reverend*, a bishop is *the Right Reverend*, a dean *the Very Reverend* and an archdeacon the *Venerable*. It is correct to say *the Reverend John Smith* or *the Reverend Mr. Smith* but never *the Reverend Smith*.

Revised Standard Version
(*see also* King James Bible; Septuagint; Vulgate)

A popular Bible translation prepared by American scholars between 1948 and 1952. It avoids words that have not been in use for a century.

Rhabdomancy
(*see also* Dowsing)

The use of divining rods to discover

water or minerals. A possible biblical example of such a rod being used can be found in Hosea 4:12:

> "My people inquire of a thing of wood, and their staff gives them oracles" (Hosea 4:12).

Rice Christians

People who convert to Christianity for material advantage rather than spiritual. The term was specifically applied to converts in India and China as early as 1816.

Rich Man's Comfort
(*see also* Eye of a Needle)

After Jesus says that it is easier for a camel to pass through the eye of a needle than for a rich man to enter Heaven, he goes on to say,

> "What is impossible with men is possible with God" (Luke 18:27).

Ride Abroad with St. George, but at Home with St. Michael

A sexist expression describing a man who is a braggart when not at home but henpecked when he is at home. St. George rode a war horse and St. Michael a dragon. Abroad a man controls a powerful steed but at home he has to fight a dragon.

Right
(*see also* Left)

The side of honor as distinguished from the left, the side of dishonor. This likely stems from the fact that for most people the right hand is the stronger. In the last judgment the sheep will be on the right and the goats on the left. At the crucifixion the good thief was on Christ's right and the bad thief on the left. Right has come to mean justice and virtue.

> "Donald is considerably to the right of our Lord and Savior Jesus Christ!"
> —*A Month of Sundays*, John Updike (1932–).

Right Hand Doesn't Know What the Left Hand Is Doing

An abbreviation of Matthew 6:3–4, from the Sermon on the Mount, a warning against ostentatious charity. It can now be used to describe bureaucratic incompetence:

> "But when you give alms, do not let your left hand know what your right hand is doing, so that your alms may be in secret; and your Father who sees in secret will reward you."

Right Hand of God *see* Dextera Domini

Ring
(*see also* Circle)

A symbol of eternity and of authority. Bishops and cardinals wear signet rings and the pope wears the fisherman's ring, in memory of St. Peter, who was a fisherman. Nuns wear rings on the third finger of the right hand to demonstrate that they are brides of Christ.

Ring the Changes
(*see also* Bell-makers)

An expression which means to try every possible strategy to reach a solution. A charge is the order in which a set of church bells are rung. In a belfry housing 12 bells, there would be 479,001,600 changes without a repetition.

R.I.P.

Commonly seen on gravestones, it means *Rest In Peace*, and comes from the Latin *Requiescat in pace*, the Requiem Mass.

Rivers of Babylon
(*see also* Babylon; Whore of Babylon)

A commemoration of the exile of the Hebrews in Babylon. The expression is often used by those mourning the dead or the destruction of a valued possession.

> "By the waters of Babylon, there we sat down and wept, when we remembered Zion" (Psalms 137:1).

Road to Damascus

A sudden conversion to a belief or cause. Such a thing happened to Saul (later called Paul), an infamous persecutor of Christians. He was on the road to Damascus when "Suddenly a light from heaven flashed about him. And he fell to the ground and heard a voice saying to him, Saul, Saul, why do you persecute me? ... I am Jesus, whom you are persecuting" (Acts 9:3–5). Saul was converted instantly and began preaching the gospel of Christ.

> Whilst I was at Damascus I had my quarters at the Franciscan convent there; and very soon after my arrival I asked one of the monks to let me know something of the spots that deserved to be seen: I made my inquiry in reference to the associations with which the city had been hallowed by the sojourn and adventures of St. Paul. "There is nothing in all Damascus," said the good man, "half so well worth seeing as our cellars." —*Eothen*, A. W. Kinglake (1809–1891).

Robin Redbreast

Fable says that when Christ was carrying his cross to Calvary, a robin plucked a thorn from the crown of thorns. Blood oozed from the wound on Christ's brow and permanently stained the robin's breast red. The bird does not appear in the King James Bible (1611).

Rock of Ages, Cleft for Me

Christ, because he is eternal, is the rock of ages. The title of a well-known hymn, the first verse of which is said to have been written by Montague Toplady (1740–1778) on the 10 of diamonds, between two rubbers of whist. The original expression occurred in a marginal note to Isaiah 26:4, where "everlasting strength" is said to be "rock of ages" in Hebrew. The Revised Standard Version (1952) uses "everlasting rock."

Roman Catholic *see* Catholic

Rome-scob *see* Peter's Pence

Root and Branch

To end something so decisively that it can never happen again. It comes from Malachi 4:1:

> "For behold, the day comes, burning like an oven, when all the arrogant and all the evildoers will be stubble; the day that comes shall burn them up, says the Lord of hosts, so that it will leave them neither root nor branch."

Root of the Matter

The essence of something. The reference is to Job 19:28:

> "The root of the matter is found in him."

Rosary
(*see also* Beadsman)

A string of five large and 50 small

beads used for keeping count during a series of prayers. Each set of one large and 10 small beads is called a decade. The large beads denote the Lord's Prayer or Paternoster and the small beads the Hail Mary or Ave Maria. Between each decade a doxology, such as "Glory to God in the highest," is recited. The rosary is also used for meditation on the mysteries of the faith. Named because of the Virgin Mary's crown of roses, a rosary can also be the name of a rose garden. Rosaries used in the Orthodox Church consist of 100 or 107 beads. The custom of using rosaries is said to have originated with St. Dominic (1170–1221) who, in a vision, received the first rosary from the Virgin Mary.

> With crosses, relics, crucifixes,
> Beads, pictures, rosaries and pixes,
> The tools of working our salvation
> By mere mechanic operation.
> —*Hudibras*, Samuel Butler (1612–1680).

Rose

A flower which is associated with the Virgin Mary because it symbolizes purity. In paradise the rose had no thorns. After the Fall of Mankind the rose acquired thorns (sins). Mary is called the Rose of Sharon (Song of Solomon 2:1) and the Rose Without a Thorn. Blood from the wounds of St. Francis of Assisi (c. 1181–1226) turned to red roses when they hit the ground.

Rose of Sharon

In Song of Solomon 2:1, a bride sings that she is "a rose of Sharon, a lily of the valleys." Sharon was a fertile well-watered coastal plain in Palestine. It is not known what the rose of Sharon was, but the narcissus and the autumn crocus are considered to be the best candidates. The Jerusalem star, a species of St-John's wort, is also known as the rose of Sharon.

Rosin Bible
(*see also* Balm of Gilead;
Treacle Bible)

In a Bible of 1609 the phrase, "Is there no *balm* in Gilead?" (Jeremiah 8:22), was rendered, "Is there no *rosin* in Gilead?"

Rousing Staff
(*see also* Sluggard Waker)

A long pole used by a church official known as a sluggard waker to prod inattentive parishioners.

Rubric

Latin for red ochre or vermillion. Any rule, heading or guide. In Roman custom a law was written in vermillion and called a rubric. Liturgical titles and directions in the Prayer Book are also called rubrics because they are usually printed in red.

Ruth

An example of supreme loyalty and devotion. A Moabite widow, Ruth stayed by the side of her Israelite mother-in-law.

> "Entreat me not to leave you or to return from following you; for where you go I will go, and where you lodge I will lodge; your people shall be my people, and your God my God" (Ruth 1:17).

S

'S
(*see also* Tear God's Body,
To; Zounds)

An abbreviation of *God's*. It is used in such old oaths and expletives as *'Sdeath* (God's death), *'Sheart* (God's heart) and *'Sblood* (God's blood).

Sabbatarians

(*see also* Sabbath; Saturday)

Christians who believe that Saturday, the seventh day of the week, is the true Sabbath. Their claim is that the Emperor Constantine (c. 280–337) changed the day of worship from Saturday to Sunday. The Seventh-Day Adventists are the best known group of Sabbatarians.

> In God's good time,
> Which does not always fall on Saturday
> When the world looks for wages.
> — *Herakles,* Robert Browning
> (1812–1889).

Sabbath

(*see also* Sabbatarians; Sabbath-day's Journey; Sunday)

Derived from the Hebrew "to rest or cease." A divinely ordained day of rest and worship observed by Jews in memory of the day God rested after the creation (Exodus 20:8–11). The Jewish Sabbath begins at sunset on Friday and ends at sunset on Saturday. Most Christians observe the Sabbath on Sunday, the first day of the week, the day creation began and the day of Jesus Christ's resurrection.

Sabbath-day's Journey

(*see also* Sabbath)

The distance that might be lawfully traversed on the Sabbath. It was about seven furlongs, approximately one mile.

> "The Lord has given you the Sabbath, therefore on the sixth day he gives you bread for two days; remain every man of you in his place, let no man go out of his place on the seventh day"
> (Exodus 16:29).

Sabbatical Year

(*see also* Jubilee)

Every seventh year the Hebrews rested the soil, forgave debts and gave to the poor. It is customary in most universities to allow faculty one year out of seven for research and study free of lecturing.

Sackcloth and Ashes

(*see also* Hair Shirt)

To repent for something bad that has been done. In biblical times it was the custom to wear uncomfortable sackcloth woven from hair and to scatter ashes over one's head as an expression of repentance, mourning or humility in the presence of God.

> "They would have repented long ago in sackcloth and ashes" (Matthew 11:21).

Sacra Conversazione

"Holy conversation," in Italian. A type of painting in which the Virgin Mary, holding the Christ-child, is depicted with saints of different eras, often linked by a common theme.

Sacred Purple

(*see also* Red)

The dull red of the hats, stockings and cassocks worn by the cardinals of the Roman Catholic Church. The Tyrian purple of the Phoenicians was obtained from the crushed shells of the murex, a bivalve of the Mediterranean Sea. The dye that resulted was a rare and valuable commodity associated with royalty. The "seller of purple goods" mentioned in Acts 16:14 appears to have been an important person. Because the color purple had regal connotations to the Romans, Jesus was being cruelly mocked at his crucifixion when the soldiers "arrayed him in a purple robe" (John 19:2). To be "Born to the Purple" implies royal status or privilege because only princes and the wealthy could afford to wear purple robes.

Sagallo

A town on the Gulf of Tajura in French Somaliland, now Djibouti, and the site of a short-lived Russian Orthodox colony in Africa. Between 1875 and 1884 the town was occupied by the Egyptians, who built a fort there. In 1889 the Archimandrite Païsi arrived with a detachment of Cossacks and settlers and occupied the fort. The Metropolitan of Novgorod had enlisted Païsi to undertake an evangelical mission for the Abyssinian Orthodox Church. The French considered the presence of the Russians in Sagalo a violation of their territorial rights and dispatched two gunboats. The fort was bombarded and the Russians, after some loss of life that included women and children, surrendered. The would-be colonists were deported to Odessa by way of Suez and their religious colony came to an abrupt end.

St. Agnes's Eve

St. Agnes was martyred (c. 303) at the age of 13. On the night of January 20 some believed that a girl could see who her future husband would be.

> How upon St. Agnes' Eve,
> Young virgins might have visions
> of delight,
> And soft adorings from their
> loves receive
> Upon the honey'd middle of the night,
> If ceremonies due they did aright;
> As, supperless to bed they must retire.
> — *The Eve of St. Agnes,* John
> Keats (1795–1821).

St. Andrew's Cross
(*see also* Christian Imagery on Flags; Crosses on Flags; Union Jack)

An X is always used to represent St. Andrew's cross or the saltire cross. But this is not strictly correct. The cross on which Andrew was martyred was the standard shape.

What was different was that the cross was not fixed upright but rested on its foot and one arm. The saint's hands were fixed to the head of the cross and one of its arms. His feet were fastened to the other end of the cross and its foot. A Roman proconsul, angered because the saint had converted his wife, had Andrew flogged and crucified. Andrew was not nailed to the cross but fastened with cords, the better to ensure a lingering death by thirst and hunger. The following places have a saltire cross on their flags: Scotland, Jersey, Nova Scotia, St. Pierre and Miquelon, Alabama, Florida, Georgia, Mississippi, and Jamaica. The flag of the United Kingdom, the Union Jack, is composed of the saltire crosses of Scotland and Ireland with the St. George's cross of England. The flags of about thirty countries and territories feature the Union Jack as part of the design.

St. Anthony *see* L.S.D.

St. Bernard

From the 15th century, monks at the hospice of Great St. Bernard in the Swiss Alps have been breeding large dogs for use in search and rescue. The St. Bernard dog is known for its strength, docility and intelligence. It is a myth that the dogs carry small brandy kegs.

> "It is, however, not true about St. Bernard dogs rescuing those lost in the snow. Once there was something in the story; but, what with the altitude and the long evenings and one thing and another, the present dogs are of such inclinations that it is no longer reasonable to send them out to work, since they took to eating the travelers."
> — *Home is the Sailor,* Dorothy Parker (1894–1967).

St. Boniface's Cup

An extra glass of wine. Legend says

that Pope Boniface granted indulgences to anyone who would drink a cup of wine to his honor. Generations of thankful tipplers have continued the practice of draining St. Boniface's cup. Since there have been nine popes named Boniface, it is unclear which one is being honored. The first and sixth Bonifaces are the most likely candidates. Boniface I (d. 422) is the only pope of that name to have been canonized. Boniface VI, a reformed wastrel, was pope for only 15 days in 896. Boniface, from a character in *The Beaux' Stratagem* (1707), a comic play by George Farquhar, came to be a name for any jolly tavern keeper.

St. Brendan *see* Brendan the Navigator

St. Catherine *see* Braid St. Catherine's Tresses; Catherine Wheel; Mystical Marriage of St. Catherine; Virgins

St. Crispin's Holiday
(*see also* Crispin and Crispinian, Saints; St. Monday)

Monday. Traditionally a day off work for shoemakers.

St. Crispin's Lance
(*see also* Crispin and Crispinian, Saints)

The awl used by shoemakers.

St. Distaff's Day
(*see also* Distaff Side)

The seventh of January. Women who have kept the 12 days of Christmas return to their ordinary work or distaffs. Distaff means women's work or affairs.

St. Elmo's Fire

St. Elmo (d. c. 303) is the patron saint of sailors because an angel helped him cross the Mediterranean Sea to escape persecutors. St. Elmo's fire is an electrical discharge, often described as a ball of fire, which can sometimes be seen around the mast of a ship during storms. It is also called a corposant, which comes from the Spanish *corpo santo*, holy body. The appearance of St. Elmo's fire is a sign that the saint has taken a ship under his protection. St. Elmo was martyred by having his intestines wrapped around a windlass. He can be invoked against seasickness and bowel trouble.

St. Florian *see* Soap Boilers

St. Francis's Distemper

Having no money. Those in the Franciscan order take a vow of poverty.

St. Gregory the Great *see* God Bless You

St. Grouse's Day
(*see also* St. Partridge Day)

August 12, the first day of the shooting season.

St. James the Less *see* Protoevangelium

St. Mark's Eve

A superstition that if one sits in the church porch on April 24, from 11:00 P.M. until 1:00 A.M., three years in a row one will be "rewarded" with a vision of those who will die during the upcoming year.

St. Martin's Summer
(*see also* Martin Drunk)

In England a period of fine weather between October 18, St. Luke's Day and November 11, St. Martin's Day. The European term for Indian Summer.

> Expect Saint Martin's summer,
> halcyon days.
> —*King Henry VI, Part 1*, William
> Shakespeare (1564–1616)

St. Mary-le-Bow Church *see* Born Within the Sound of Bow Bells

St. Monday
(*see also* St. Crispin's Holiday)

A self-approved holiday of the idle.

St. Partridge Day
(*see also* Partridge; St. Grouse's Day)

September 1, the opening day of partridge-hunting season.

St. Stephen *see* Proto-Martyr; St. Stephen's Loaves

St. Stephen's Loaves

Stones. The reference is to Acts 7:54–60, the stoning of St. Stephen.

St. Swithin's Day

July 15. If it rains on St. Swithin's Day, it is supposed to rain for 40 days more. Swithin was an English saint who died in 862. When his body was removed to a shrine on July 15, 971, heavy rains fell for 40 days. As a result he is sometimes known as the Weeping Saint.

St. Valentine *see* Greeting Card Manufacturers

St. Vitus *see* Oversleeping; St. Vitus's Dance

St. Vitus's Dance
(*see also* Dancing Mania)

St. Vitus (d. c. 300) is the patron saint of mummers and dancers, and is invoked against epilepsy, St. Vitus's Dance (Sydenham's chorea), mad dogs and snake bite. St. Vitus is also invoked by those who have trouble getting up in the morning. In 16th century Germany it was believed that a year's worth of good health could be guaranteed by anyone who danced before a statue of St. Vitus on his feast day.

Saintly Cities

The following large American cities are some of those named directly after saints: San Antonio, San Bernardino, San Diego, San Francisco, San Jose, San Juan, Santa Barbara, St. Louis and St. Paul.

Saintly Countries

The following countries and dependant territories are directly named after saints: St. Kitts and Nevis (also called St. Christopher), St. Helena, St. Lucia, San Marino, St. Pierre and Miquelon, Saô Tomé and Principe, and St. Vincent. The Virgin Islands are named after St. Ursula, the wise virgin. San Marino, only 24 square miles, is located in central Italy and claims to be the oldest republic in the world. It is unique in that it was not only named after a saint but established by one — a fourth century Christian stonecutter named Marinus who was canonized as St. Marinus or San Marino.

Salmanazar *see* Jeroboam

Salome (c. 14–c. 62)
(*see also* Herod: Herod Antipas)

The stepdaughter of Herod Antipas (21 B.C.–A.D. 39) and the daughter of his wife, Herodius (c. 14 B.C.–c. A.D. 40). Herod became so aroused by Salome's dancing that he promised her anything, even half his kingdom. Prodded by her mother, Herodius, Salome requested John the Baptist's head. John the Baptist had angered Herodius by declaring her marriage adulterous. Herod ordered John the Baptist executed and his head was brought to Salome on a platter. Salome has become a byword for treacherous sin. Though her story is related in Matthew 14:6–11 and Mark 6:21–28, Salome is not mentioned by name in the Bible. Her name comes to us from *Jewish Antiquities* by the Jewish historian, Flavius Josephus (37–c. 98). Another woman named Salome was the mother of the apostles James the Great and John the Evangelist. This Salome witnessed the crucifixion (Matthew 27:56–57; Mark 15:40), and was one of the first to learn of the resurrection (Mark 16:1–6).

Salt of the Earth

A common person, or group, exceptionally good or praiseworthy. Salt is a preservative and stood for many things, including friendship, incorruptibility and purity. Jesus said of his disciples,

> "You are the salt of the earth; but if salt has lost its taste how shall its saltness be restored? It is no longer good for anything except to be thrown out and trodden under foot by men" (Matthew 5:13).

Jesus meant that his disciples, if they did not lose faith, would preserve mankind from evil. In the *Last Supper*, by Leonardo da Vinci (1452–1519), Judas Iscariot is identified by the saltcellar that has been knocked over.

Saltire Cross *see* St. Andrew's Cross

El Salvador

"The Savior" in Spanish. El Salvador is the only country in the world named for Jesus Christ the Savior. Despite its holy name, this small Central American republic suffered through a civil war from 1979 to 1992 which killed 80,000 people and displaced a million others, about a fifth of the total population.

Samaritan *see* Good Samaritan

Samson
(*see also* Delilah)

Any strong man can be called a Samson. The Samson of the Old Testament was a man of enormous strength, who killed a lion and battled the Philistines. He was a Hebrew version of Hercules. It is common knowledge that his strength came from his uncut hair which was shorn by Delilah, the evil temptress. In fact, Judges 16:19 indicates that Delilah had a man shave Samson's head and that she was a shrew rather than a temptress. Poor Samson was nagged until "his soul was vexed unto death."

Sanbenito
(*see also* Auto-da-fé)

A yellow cloak or scapular with the red cross of St. Andrew on the front and back. Those whom the Spanish Inquisition had found guilty of heresy were required to wear the *sanbenito* while doing penance. On their heads would be a hat like a dunce cap. Those sentenced to death wore a black *sanbenito* depicting demons and hell fire. The word is derived from the Italian for St. Bernard (1091–1153) and the supposed resemblance to the loose sleeveless garment which he introduced.

Sanctum Sanctorum *see* Holy of Holies

Sangrail *see* Holy Grail

Santa Claus
(*see also* Befana, St.; Kriss Kringle)

For some strange reason Santa, the feminine form of saint in the Romance languages, has been combined with Claus, the Germanic abbreviation of Nicholas. The name goes back to the fourth century St. Nicholas of Myra who, on December 6, his feast day, left presents in the shoes of good children. The transformation of a fourth century ascetic saint from Asia Minor into the fat, jolly de-Christianized Santa Claus was a phenomenon of the 19th century United States.

> "No Santa Claus! Thank God, he lives, and he lives forever."
> — *Is There a Santa Claus?* Francis Pharcellus Church (1839–1906).

Satan
(*see also* Auld Hornie; Beelzebub; Clootie; Cloven Hoofed; Dickens; Old Nick; Serpent; Tutivillius)

A common name for the devil. Satan is portrayed as an adversary but is not mentioned in the earliest Bible narratives. In Job, Satan, the accuser and tempter, can only function with God's permission, and his powers are sharply defined by him. Only in Zechariah 3, Job 1, 2 and 1 Chronicles 21:1 is Satan depicted as being a malevolent spirit. Satan's origins lie in Pan, the pagan god of forests and herds.

Sator
(*see also* Palindrome)

The first line of a Latin palindrome found in the ruins of Pompeii and on a Roman wall in Cirenster, England among other places.

```
S A T O R
A R E P O
T E N E T
O P E R A
R O T A S
```

Read across or down the words mean, "The sower Arepo carefully holds the wheels." The letters of TENET when read up and down or left and right (or down and up and right to left) form a cross, an obvious Christian reference. All the letters of the palindrome can be arranged in the form of a cross, spelling pater noster (our father), with Alpha and Omega (the beginning and end of all things), at both ends. The first and last letters of TENET also suggest a cross.

```
            A
            P
            A
            T
            E
            R
A P A T E R N O S T E R O
            O
            S
            T
            E
            R
            O
```

The letters can also spell, "I pray to you Father, I pray to you, you cure." The words Sator, Arepo and Teneton have been found in ancient murals of the shepherds adoring the Christ-Child.

Saturday
(*see also* Sabbatarians; Sabbath)

The seventh day of the week which was named after the Roman god Saturn. It is the holy day of the Jews of the Old Testament and in Hebrew is called Sabbath. Most Christians have shifted their holy day to

Sunday, the day of the week that Christ was resurrected. The Seventh Day Adventists, among other Christian sects, consider Saturday to be their day of worship.

Satyr
(*see also* Faun)

Greek forest deity, often half man and half goat, devoted to wine and lechery. Because it had cloven hoofs and because of a mistranslation of Isaiah 13:21, where satyr was used instead of he-goat, Christians considered satyrs devils. Some think that the proper translation should be baboon. Because of an incorrect derivation from the Greek word for penis, satyrs were depicted with huge phalluses.

> My men, like satyrs grazing on the lawn,
> Shall with their goat feet dance the
> antic hay.
> —*Edward II*, Christopher
> Marlowe (1564–1593).

Saul *see* Road to Damascus

Saving Grace

Originally a theological term for God's grace which saves sinners. It has entered common speech with the sense of a compensating quality.

Say the Devil's Paternoster
(*see also* Paternoster)

The paternoster is the Lord's Prayer. To say the devil's paternoster is to complain and grumble about providence.

Scala Pilati *see* Scala Santa

Scala Santa

"Holy Stair," in Italian. The name given to a flight of 28 white-veined marble steps in the Lateran Palace in Rome. According to tradition these were the steps Jesus ascended to be judged by Pontius Pilate. They were brought to Rome from Jerusalem by St. Helena c. 326. Indulgence is granted to those who climb the stairs on their knees. When Martin Luther (1483–1546) climbed the steps he heard the words, "The just shall live by faith," and quickly descended. The steps are also called *Scala Pilati*, Latin for "Pilate's Stair."

Scapegoat
(*see also* Goat)

Someone blamed for another's wrongdoing. On the Day of Atonement, Jewish high priests chose two goats by lot. One was sacrificed. The other goat, the scapegoat, had the sins of the people symbolically laid upon it and was driven into the wilderness (Leviticus 16:10).

Scarlet Woman *see* Whore
of Babylon

Scorpion
(*see also* Lash of Scorpions)

A long-tailed venomous creature about five to six inches long. There are 1,400 species worldwide and about a dozen in Palestine. The scorpion was seen by Christians as the symbol of treachery and jealousy. The king of Judah, Rehoboam, threatened to punish his people with scorpions (1 Kings 12:11). According to legend, if a scorpion is surrounded by a ring of fire it will sting itself to death.

Scotus, John Duns *see* Dunce

Scourge of God

Flagellum Dei. The name given by fearful Christians to Atilla the Hun (c. 406–

453), who overran the Byzantine and Western Roman Empires.

Scriptorium

As early as the sixth century a room in a monastery where manuscripts were copied by hand. A good scribe, standing at a sloping desk, could complete five book-sized pages a day. Working at that pace, it took approximately one year to copy out the Bible.

Scrying
(*see also* Urim and Thummim)

Divination by means of patterns of light reflected in a pool of still water or a polished surface such as a mirror. Early Christians foretold the future by using a mirror suspended in a consecrated well. Some maintain that the Urim and Thummim, sacred objects mentioned in Exodus and elsewhere, were used to determine guilt or innocence by means of the light reflected off their shiny surfaces. Joseph may have practiced scrying when he interpreted Pharaoh's dreams with a silver cup filled with liquid (Genesis 44:5,15).

Second Coming
(*see also* Doomsday; Millennium)

The promise that Christ will return in all his glory. Connected with the Second Coming is the Last Judgment or Doomsday, when the dead will be resurrected by Christ and judged. The righteous will dwell in eternal bliss in Heaven. The wicked will suffer eternal damnation in hell. The Second Coming is also associated with the Millennium, a thousand-year period of peace and prosperity that marks the earthly reign of Christ. Some believe the Second Coming will occur at the beginning of the Millennium, some at the end.

See Eye to Eye   *see* Eye to Eye

Seek and Ye Shall Find

Prayers will be answered. Despite the archaic word *ye* this expression remains in everyday use.

> "Ask, and it shall be given you, seek, and ye shall find, knock, and it shall be opened unto you: For everyone that asketh receiveth; and he that seeketh findeth; and to him that knocketh it shall be opened" (Matthew 7:7–8).

Seize the Devil by the Nose

St. Eligius (c. 588–660) was a goldsmith and a blacksmith. One day at the forge the devil taunted him. Eligius lost his temper and seized the devil by the nose with red-hot tongs. The attributes of the saint are hammer, anvil and horseshoe. The last is an attribute because Eligius once cut off the leg of an uncooperative horse brought to him to be shod. He fixed the horseshoe and after making the sign of the cross, attached the leg so that no trace of a wound could be seen.

Selah

A Hebrew word that occurs 71 times in the Psalms and three times in Habakkuk. The meaning of the word is not known but it is thought to be a liturgical or musical direction, possibly signifying a pause.

Separate the Sheep from the Goats

To divide the good from the bad, the valuable from the worthless.

> "Before him will be gathered all the nations, and he will separate them one from another as a shepherd separates the sheep from the goats" (Matthew 25:32).

Septuagint

(*see also* King James Bible; Revised Standard Version; Vulgate)

From the Greek word for 70, often styled LXX. The Septuagint, dating from the third century B.C., is the oldest Greek translation of the Old Testament and Apocrypha. According to tradition, Ptolemy II of Egypt (309–246 B.C.) confined not 70 but 72 scholars in cells on the island of Pharos for 72 days, supplying each with writing materials. When the scholars were released each of their translations was identical, surely an indication of divine inspiration.

Sermon on the Mount

(*see also* Beatitudes; Do Unto Others as You Would Have Others Do Unto You)

A collection of the sayings of Jesus rather than a sermon (Matthew 5). It begins with the Beatitudes in which Jesus describes those who are blessed, beginning with "Blessed are the poor in spirit." Other than that the words were spoken on a mountain, the location is not specified. According to tradition the mountain was Karn Hattin, near the Sea of Galilee. The Sermon on the Mount marks a radical abandonment of the Old Testament's law of retribution, with a law of love so sweeping that we are enjoined to love our enemies.

> "We have grasped the mystery of the atom and rejected the Sermon on the Mount."
> —*Armistice Day Speech*, Omar Bradley (1893–1981).

Serpent

(*see also* Aaron's Serpent; Asp)

Because Eve was tempted by a serpent to commit sin, it is a symbol of envy, cunning and wickedness. The serpent was assumed to be the devil in disguise, who envied Adam and Eve's happiness in Eden. It is an obvious phallic symbol representing sex as the source of evil. At the feet of the Virgin Mary the serpent symbolizes the victory over sin by the Incarnation. When wrapped around a cross, the creature symbolizes Christ lifted up on the Cross, because Moses lifted up a fiery serpent to heal the Children of Israel (Numbers 21:8). As a manifestation of the devil it is one of the evil creatures Christ will overcome. "The young lion and the serpent you will trample under foot" (Psalm 91:13). Because of Psalm 58:4–5, "Like the deaf adder that stops its ear, so that it does not hear the voice of charmers," the serpent has been depicted having one ear pressed to the ground and the other stopped with its tail so that no sound can be heard. The image represents those who refuse to hear God's word.

> "Well, as the serpent used to say, why not?"
> —*Back to Methuselah*, George Bernard Shaw (1856–1950).

Servus Servorum Dei

"The servant of the servants of God," in Latin. A title first used by Gregory the Great, pope from 590 to 604, and used by popes ever since.

Set One's Heart On, To

To be determined to obtain something or to achieve a goal. It comes from Psalm 62:10, where the negative form of the expression is used:

> "Put no confidence in extortion, set no vain hopes on robbery; if riches increase, set not your heart on them."

Set One's Teeth on Edge

To inspire cringing.

"The fathers have eaten sour grapes, and
the children's teeth are set on edge"
(Jeremiah 31:29).

Seth

The third son of Adam and Eve. He replaced Abel, murdered by Cain (Genesis
4:25). Legend has it that Seth placed seeds
under Adam's tongue at his father's death.
From these grew the tree from which the
cross of Jesus was made.

Seven

(*see also* Fourteen; Numbers)

A mystical number. Because it com-
bines four (the earth) and three (the Trinity or Heaven), seven symbolizes completeness or the universe. Creation took place
in seven days, there were believed to be
seven planets, seven seas, the seven kine
and seven ears of corn of Pharaoh's dreams.
The Sacraments are seven in number. For
the Hebrews every seven years was a sabbatical. The major Jewish feasts were each
seven days in duration, the second being
seven weeks after the first. The purification
of the Levites lasted seven days; Baalam
had seven altars with seven rams and seven
bullocks to be sacrificed upon them. The
oath between Abraham and Abimelech featured seven ewe lambs. Naaman dipped in
the Jordan River seven times, Elijah had his
servant look for rain seven times, the exile
of the Israelites in Egypt lasted 10 times
seven years, and there were the same number of elders. Seven priests with seven trum-
pets marched around the walls of Jericho
and did so seven times on the seventh day.
The wedding feast of Samson lasted a full
week and seven locks of his hair were cut
off. There are seven penitential psalms,
seven divisions in the Lord's Prayer, seven
churches of Asia and seven spirits before
God's throne.

Seven Champions

A medieval designation of the champions of seven European countries — St.
George of England, St. Denys of France, St.
James of Spain, St. Anthony of Italy, St. Andrew of Scotland, St. Patrick of Ireland and
St. David of Wales. The mystical number
seven was featured in the stories of each of
the champions.

Seven Churches of Asia

As mentioned in Revelation 1:11, these
places are all in eastern Turkey. They are
Ephesus (now a ruin), Smyrna (now called
Izmir, a city of more than two million peo-
ple), Pergamum (now a small city called
Bergama), Thyatira (the city of Akhisar),
Sardis (a ruin), Philadelphia (the city of
Alasehir), and Laodicea (a ruin).

Seven Deadly Sins

Sins for which the punishment is eternal damnation. The list is non-biblical and
comes from the writings of the early church
fathers. The Seven Deadly Sins are also called
the Seven Mortal Sins, include Pride, Lust,
Avarice. Gluttony, Envy, Wrath, and Sloth.

Seven Gifts of the Holy Spirit
see Columbine

Seven Last Words

In point of fact, the seven last sentences Jesus spoke on the cross.

1. "Father, forgive them; for they
know not what they do" (Luke 23:34).
2. "Truly, I say to you, today you will
be with me in Paradise" (Luke 23:43).
3. "Woman, behold, your son! ... Behold, your mother!" (John 19:26–27).
4. "My God, my God, why hast thou
forsaken me?" (Matthew 27:46).

5. "I thirst" (John 19:28).

6. "It is finished" (John 19:30).

7. "Father, into thy hands I commit my spirit!" (Luke 23:46).

Seven Names of God

El, Elohim, Adonai, YHWH, Ehyeh-Asher-Ehyeh, Shaddai, Zebaot. In the Middle Ages God was sometimes called *The Seven.*

Seven Virtues

The seven virtues are Faith, Hope, Charity, Prudence, Justice, Fortitude, and Temperance.

Seven-year-old Saint

St. Kenelm was a seven-year-old English boy who was murdered in Clent, Worcestershire, by order of his sister early in the ninth century. At the instant of his death a dove appeared miraculously on the altar of St. Peter's, Rome. In the bird's beak was a scroll inscribed:

> In Clent cow pasture, under a thorn,
> Of head bereft, lies Kenelm king-born.

Seventh Commandment Reworded

> Do not adultery commit;
> Advantage rarely comes of it.
>
> — *The Latest Decalogue*, Arthur Hugh Clough (1819–1861).

Shadrach, Meshach and Abednego

An allusion to the retribution that comes to those who would deal harsh punishments to others. When these three men refused to worship a golden idol, Nebuchadnezzar ordered them to be thrown into a fiery furnace. But the Lord rescued them and they emerged unhurt, though their captors perished in the heat (Daniel 3).

Shake the Dust from Your Feet

To sever all connection with someone. It comes from Matthew 10:14:

> "And if any one will not receive you or listen to your words, shake off the dust from your feet as you leave that house or town."

Shakespeare the Author of the Bible?

Misguided numerologists, in love with the number 46, claimed that William Shakespeare (1564–1616) wrote the Bible because the King James Bible was printed in 1610 when Shakespeare was 46. The 46th word of the 46th Psalm is *shake*, and *spear* is the 46th word from the end of the 46th Psalm. They seem to have been unaware of the fact that the King James Bible was published in 1611 when Shakespeare was forty-seven.

Shamrock

The emblem of Ireland. A low plant of the clover family with three leaves growing from a single stem. According to legend, the shamrock was selected by St. Patrick (c. 389–c. 461) as a device for explaining the Trinity.

Shaped Poetry *see* Emblematic Poetry

She Bible *see* He Bible

Shibboleth

In Judges 12:4–6, victorious Gileadites had difficulty identifying Ephraimites crossing the Jordan River. They tested them by asking them to pronounce this word, which means a stream in flood or an ear of grain. The Ephraimites were unable to pronounce *Sh* and spoke the word as *Sibboleth*. Thus identified they were then killed. Shibboleth now means a peculiarity of speech, custom or dress of a group of people. It is also a catch phrase or password used to verify someone's identity. For a long time the police would test a man charged with drunkenness by having him pronounce the words, *truly rural*. If he failed, he was arrested.

Shoemakers

(see also Crispin and
Crispinian, Saints)

St. Crispin is the patron saint of shoemakers. Fleeing persecution, he took up that profession. He was martyred c. 286 by being immersed in a cauldron of molten lead.

Shoes at a Wedding

The custom of throwing old shoes after the bride and groom as they leave the church is very old. It resembles a custom mentioned in Deuteronomy 25:9:

> "Then his brother's wife shall go up to him in the presence of the elders, and pull his sandal off his foot."

Shortest Chapter in Bible

(see also Chapters in the Bible;
Identical Bible Chapters; Longest
Chapter in Bible; Middle
Chapter in Bible)

The shortest chapter in the Bible is Psalm 117.

Shortest Verse in Bible

(see also Identical Bible Verses;
Longest Verse in Bible; Middle
Verse in Bible; Verses in the Bible)

The shortest verse in the Bible and the shortest in the New Testament is John 11:35, "Jesus wept." The shortest verse in the Old Testament is I Chronicles 1:25, which gives three names in a long genealogy.

Shout It from the Housetops

To proclaim something as loudly as possible.

> "What you have whispered in private rooms shall be proclaimed upon the housetops" (Luke 12:3).

Shroud of Turin

A relic dating from c. 1360, which has been preserved at the Cathedral of Turin since 1578. Many revere it as the linen cloth with which Joseph of Arimathea wrapped Christ's body after the crucifixion. There is a figure of a man imprinted on the fabric which believers consider to be an authentic likeness of Jesus.

Shunammitism

Abishag the Shunammite was a young woman employed to comfort the aging King David.

> Now King David was old and advanced in years; and although they covered him with clothes, he could not get warm. Therefore his servants said to him, "Let a young maiden be sought for my lord the king, and let her wait upon the king, and be his nurse; let her lie in your bosom, that my lord the king may be warm." So they sought for a beautiful maiden throughout all the territory of Israel, and found Abishag the Shunammite and brought her to the king. The maiden was very beautiful; and she became the king's nurse and ministered to him; but the king knew her not (1 Kings 1:1–4).

From this passage arose the strange

practice of shunammitism. In 18th century Paris, young girls were used as living hot-water bottles to rejuvenate aging men. The complete cure lasted 24 nights, with three pairs of girls, each a blonde and a brunette, providing the service. They were relieved after eight nights. Only girls of unblemished reputation were employed and the client was required to put up a large deposit as surety that they would remain so. King David's chaste relationship with Abishag foretold the relationship between Joseph and Mary.

Sibyls
(*see also* Augustus)

Priestesses of Apollo who gave prophecies. Two of them were thought to have predicted the coming of Christ. The Sibyl Tiburtine told Emperor Augustus (63 B.C.–A.D. 14) of the birth of a ruler mightier than he. The Sibyl Cuman foretold the Last Judgment. In the Middle Ages sibyls were given Christian attributes. Persica held a lantern which gave off a faint light because she obscurely foretold the coming of Christ. Libyca is depicted with a candle because she predicted that the darkness would be dispelled by the Light of the World. Erythraea predicted the Annunciation and held a lily or rose. Samia is shown with a cradle because of her prediction that a child would be born to a poor maiden and the animals would adore her. Europa holds a sword in memory of the Flight into Egypt and the Massacre of the Holy Innocents. Cimmeria holds a horn symbolizing a feeding bottle. She foretold that a virgin would feed her baby boy with milk. Tiburtine's hands symbolize the hands which struck Jesus. Agrippa holds a scourge recalling the scourging of Jesus. Delphica has a crown of thorns because she predicted that Christ would be crowned with such a wreath. Hellespontica predicted the crucifixion and held a cross. Cuman holds the sponge which, soaked in vinegar, was offered to Jesus upon the cross.

Phrygia has a banner and a cross predicting the resurrection.

> Day of wrath, that day of burning,
> Seer and Sibyl speak concerning,
> All the world to ashes turning.
> —*Dies Irae*, Tomasso di
> Celano (c. 1244–1296).

Sign of the Son of Man

At the end of time, when Christ comes to judge the living and the dead, "then will appear the sign of the Son of man in heaven" (Matthew 24:30). The nature of this sign is not stated. It has been speculated that it will be a cross appearing on high or a blaze of light in a darkened sky.

Sign of the Times

Something that is typical of the time period. It is often expressed in a negative way as it is in Matthew 16:3:

> "You know how to interpret the appearance of the sky, but you cannot interpret the signs of the times."

Signatures *see* Cross-mark

Simon Stylites *see* Stylites

Simony
(*see also* Relic)

The vice of buying and selling sacred things and ecclesiastical offices. Simon was a great magician who was converted and baptized by the Apostles. But when he saw the miracles performed by them, "He offered them money, saying, 'Give me also this power, that any one on whom I lay my hands may receive the Holy Spirit'"(Acts 8:19). Simon was rebuked by Peter. "You have neither part nor lot in this matter, for your heart is not right before God" (Acts 8:20).

Sin Lieth at the Door

The evildoer must bear the fruits of his misdeeds.

"And if you do not do well, sin is couching at the door; its desire is for you, but you must master it" (Genesis 4:7).

Sin-on Bible

In a Bible of 1716, John 5:14 contained a grave misprint. It read "sin *on* more," instead of "sin *no* more."

Sins Be as Scarlet, They Shall Be as White as Snow

No matter how bad the crime, God is prepared to forgive:

"Though your sins are like scarlet, they shall be as white as snow; though they are red like crimson, they shall become like wool" (Isaiah 1:18).

Siren

A mythical being, half woman, half fish, who sings a hypnotic song which lures men to their doom. Even though she was a female, there was a legend that a siren lured Eve to eat the forbidden fruit. The serpent in the Garden of Eden is sometimes depicted as having the face of a beautiful woman.

666

(*see also* Gematria; Mark of the Beast; Mysterium; Numbers)

The mystic number. "Let him who has understanding reckon the number of the beast, for it is a human number, its number is six hundred and sixty-six" (Revelation 13:18). Many theories have arisen about the meaning of 666. One has it that St. John the Divine was referring cryptographically to that cruel persecutor of Christians, the Roman emperor Nero. *Neron Kesar* is the Hebrew form of the Latin Nero Caesar. Hebrew letters had a numeric value except for the vowels *E* and *A* which were not expressed.

N   R   O   N   K   S   R
50 + 200 + 6 + 50 + 100 + 60 + 200 = 666

Skin of Your Teeth *see* By the Skin of Your Teeth

Skull

An obvious symbol of death. When depicted at the foot of the Cross it is the skull of Adam.

"That skull had a tongue in it, and could sing once."
—*Hamlet*, William Shakespeare (1564–1616).

Slender Reed, A

Insubstantial support. It is used in Isaiah and 2 Kings in the form of a "bruised" or "broken" reed to indicate that Egypt was not to be trusted.

Slept with His Fathers *see* Death, Euphemisms for

Slowest Selling Book

David Wilkins published a Latin translation of the Coptic New Testament in 1716. It took 191 years before all 500 copies were sold.

Sluggard Waker
(*see also* Rousing Staff)

An ecclesiastical official whose job it was to wake people who had fallen asleep in church. The sluggard would be poked with a long stick known as a rousing staff.

Smellsmock

A derogatory word for a lustful priest, first used in the 16th century. It is now the name of several plants.

Snake *see* Serpent; Snake Handlers

Snake Handlers

The bizarre practice of handling live poisonous snakes as part of a religious ritual. The practitioners get their justification from Mark 16:17–18:

> "In my name they will cast out demons; they will speak in new tongues; they will pick up serpents, and if they drink any deadly thing, it will not hurt them."

Water moccasins, copperheads and rattlesnakes are the preferred snakes. Participants drape the reptiles around their necks, kiss them and step on them. Needless to say, many snake handlers have been bitten and some have been killed. Some also drink poison and expose their flesh to fire. The snake handling sect survives in a few isolated rural congregations in the eastern United States.

Sneeze *see* God Bless You

Soap Boilers

Soap boilers should be relieved to know that they have their very own patron saint in Florian (d. c. 304). Florian is also associated with firefighting.

Sodom and Gomorrah

Bywords for depravity. These cities at the southern end of the Dead Sea are renowned for their wickedness. The story of Sodom and Gomorrah is told in Genesis 18 and 19. They were so wicked that God destroyed them. The words sodomy and sodomite come from Sodom.

Solomon *see* Wisdom of Solomon

Sons of Belial

Those who are utterly depraved or wicked. The exact meaning of Belial is unknown, but it came to mean evil.

Sophia, St.

The Greek word for wisdom, *Sophia*, called *Sancta Sophia*, "Holy Wisdom" in Latin, was mistaken for a saint named Sophia. A mosque in Istanbul, formerly the Christian church of the Holy Wisdom, is commonly and wrongly called St. Sophia.

Soul

A person's spiritual essence, which leaves the body at death. The soul is depicted in art as a newborn baby carried up to heaven or in a cloth, symbolizing Abraham's bosom. Sometimes the soul is depicted as a butterfly. Babies in an open palm or clutched in a fist illustrate Ecclesiastes 9:1:

> "The righteous and the wise and their deeds are in the hand of God."

Spanish Inquisition *see* Auto-da-Fé

Spare the Rod and Spoil the Child

An expression usually interpreted to mean that a lack of corporal punishment will harm a child in the long run. It is a misquotation of Proverbs 13:24. "He who spares the rod hates his son, but he who loves him

194

is diligent to discipline him." The expression, as commonly used, was first seen in a poem by Samuel Butler in 1664:

> Love is a boy by poets styl'd;
> Then spare the road and spoil the child.

Sparrow

A symbol of the care that God feels for even the humblest of his creatures.

> "Are not two sparrows sold for a penny? And not one of them will fall to the ground without your Father's will" (Matthew 10:29).

Spirit Is Willing but the Flesh Is Weak

Jesus uttered these words, or something close to them, to warn his disciples about the danger of giving in to temptation. They are now used in nearly the opposite sense, as a light-hearted apology for having yielded to temptation.

> "Watch and pray that you may not enter into temptation; the spirit indeed is willing, but the flesh is weak" (Matthew 26:41).

Spy-Wednesday

The Wednesday before Good Friday. On that day Judas Iscariot bargained with the chief priests for the betrayal of Jesus (Matthew 26:3–5; 14–16).

Squint *see* Hagioscope

Stab in the Back

To betray a trusted friend. Abner, cousin of King Saul, was opposed by David and Joab, his general. When Abner went to David's camp to make peace, Joab approached him as if to speak in private and

"smote him there under the fifth rib" (2 Samuel 3:27).

Staff of Life

Specifically bread but any essential foodstuff can be called the staff of life. The expression is based on Isaiah 3:1:

> "For behold, the Lord, the Lord of hosts, is taking away from Jerusalem and from Judah stay and staff, the whole stay of bread, and the whole stay of water."

Standing Fishes Bible

An amusing misprint appeared in a Bible of 1806. Ezekiel 47:10 is rendered "And it shall come to pass that the *fishes* shall stand upon it ..." The correct verse should read, "And it shall come to pass that the *fishers* shall stand upon it."

Star

A symbol of the Epiphany. It was a star that guided the wise men to Bethlehem (Matthew 2:9). The star that will come out of Jacob (Numbers 24:17) was seen as a prophecy of Christ. Christ was "the bright morning star" of Revelation 22:16. The Virgin Mary is symbolized by two stars that always remain bright, *Stella Matutina*, "Star of the Morning," and *Stella Maris*, "Star of the Sea." Satan was "a star fallen from heaven to earth" (Revelation 9:1). God created the stars for light and for telling time.

Star of Bethlehem

The miraculous star which guided the wise men to the infant Jesus (Matthew 2:1–9) has been explained as a supernova, comet, meteor shower or Venus.

Stations of the Cross

A series of 14 paintings, frescos or statues which illustrate Christ's journey along the Via Dolorosa. The devout pray and meditate at each station. Stations 1, 2, 5, 8, 10, 11, 12 and 14 are described in the Gospels. The others come from tradition. The stations are:

1. Christ condemned to death by Pilate
2. Christ bears the cross
3. The first fall under the weight of the cross
4. Christ meets his mother, Mary
5. A passerby, Simon the Cyrene, carries the cross. (According to the Gospels this event occurs at the beginning.)
6. Veronica wipes Christ's face
7. Christ falls a second time
8. Christ speaks to the women of Jerusalem telling them not to weep for him
9. Christ falls a third time
10. Christ's garments are stripped from him
11. Christ is nailed to the cross
12. His death
13. Christ's body is taken down from the cross and presented to Mary
14. The burial

Stella Maris *see* Star

Stephaton
(*see also* Aesop)

At the Crucifixion an unnamed bystander soaked a sponge in vinegar (more accurately sour wine) and put it on a reed for Jesus to drink from (Matthew 27:48; Mark 15:36). Legend gave him the name of Stephaton, a corruption of the Greek word for sponge.

Stiff-necked

Obstinate and self-willed. The patron saint of those suffering from stiff necks is Ursicinus of Saint-Ursanne (d. 625), a missionary among pagan tribes.

"Yet they did not listen or incline their ear, but stiffened their necks, that they might not hear and receive instruction" (Jeremiah 17:23).

Stigmata

Wounds in the hands, feet and side, as well as marks of scourging and the crown of thorns. Stigmata, mirroring the wounds of Jesus, miraculously appear on the bodies of some faithful Christians. The earliest officially recognized stigmata were those of St. Francis of Assisi, who developed wounds in 1224. Stigmata have continued to appear up to and including the present day. Sceptics have suggested self-hypnosis or an altered state of consciousness brought on by prolonged meditation as the cause.

Still Small Voice

The conscience. God speaks to his people with a quiet inner voice. In the midst of a great wind, an earthquake and a fire, Elijah heard "a still small voice" telling him to make Elisha his successor (1 Kings 19:11–13).

Stilo Novo

Anything that is new. It is Latin for "in the new style." When Pope Gregory XIII (c. 1540–1604) reformed the calendar in 1582, it became the custom to include *stilo novo* with the date on correspondence.

Sting Bible

A Bible of 1746 in which "the *sting* of his tongue was loosed and he spake plain" is written, instead of *string*, in Mark 7:35.

Stone of Scone
(*see also* Jacob's Ladder)

Also called Jacob's Stone. The stone upon which Jacob rested his head when he saw the vision of the ladder reaching up to heaven (Genesis 28:11). Upon awakening, Jacob set the stone up as a pillar and consecrated it with oil. It is said to be the Stone of Scone, on which the kings of Scotland were crowned. According to legend the stone was brought to Scotland in 843. In 1296 it was removed to Westminster Abbey in London. In 1996 the Stone of Scone was returned to Scotland.

Stone of Stumbling

A stumbling stone or obstacle.

"He shall be ... for a stone of stumbling and for a rock of offense to both houses of Israel" (Isaiah 8:14).

Storm Petrel *see* Mother Carey's Chicken

Straight and Narrow, The

The path to salvation is difficult and narrow. To stray from the *strait* and narrow is to fall into wrongdoing. This is a common expression which confuses *straight* with *strait* and to some extent changes the meaning from what Christ intended. The word *strait*, found in the King James Bible (1611) as a synonym for narrow, is now used only for a narrow body of water. By substituting the word *straight* we emphasize the importance of a direct path to salvation.

"Enter ye at the strait gate: for wide is the gate, and broad is the way, that leadeth to destruction, and many there be which go in thereat: Because strait is the gate, and narrow is the way, which leadeth unto life, and few there be that find it" (Matthew 7:13–14).

Straining Out a Gnat and Swallowing a Camel

An example of humor in the Bible.

Jesus is criticizing the Pharisees who dispute the trivial but are blind to what is important:

"You blind guides, straining out a gnat and swallowing a camel" (Matthew 23:24).

Stylites

A curious form of Christian asceticism whereby a monk would cut himself off from the world and mortify his body by living atop a pillar. In 423 Simon Stylites of Syria (c. 390–459) began living atop a disused water tank, but was bothered by invalids seeking to be cured by his touch. Simon then moved to a six-foot pillar made from three stone blocks to symbolize the Trinity. There was room for him only to stand on it. The saint lived on a succession of pillars, each taller than the one before. Simon's last pillar, 60-feet high, was his home for 30 years. Many pilgrims came to listen to his preaching. It was said that Simon Stylites could fly like a bird.

Sudarium
(*see also* Mandylion; Volto Santo)

A napkin or head cloth used by St. Veronica to wipe the blood and sweat from Christ's brow as he was led to his crucifixion. Christ's likeness was said to have been imprinted on the cloth.

Suffer Fools Gladly *see* Do Not Suffer Fools Gladly

Suffer Little Children

Jesus rebukes his disciples for complaining about children being brought forth for blessings. The innocence of children is the innocence of souls in heaven.

"Suffer little children to come unto me and forbid them not: for of such is the kingdom of heaven" (Matthew 19:14).

Sufficient Unto the Day Is the Evil Thereof

Trust in divine providence.

> "Take therefore no thought for the morrow: for the morrow shall take thought for the things of itself. Sufficient unto the day is the evil thereof"
> (Matthew 6:34).

We have enough tribulations today without seeking the troubles of tomorrow.

Suicides, Burial of

Forbidden to be buried in consecrated grounds, a suicide was buried at a crossroad and impaled by a stake.

Sun and Moon Stand Still
(see also Jashar)

Joshua quotes from the lost book of Jashar a miraculous event.

> Then spoke Joshua to the Lord in the day when the Lord gave the Amorites over to the men of Israel; and he said in the sight of Israel, "Sun, stand thou still at Gibeon, and thou Moon in the valley of Aijalon." And the sun stood still, and the moon stayed, until the nation took vengeance on their enemies
> (Joshua 10:12–13).

What was originally poetic exaggeration becomes literal in Joshua. A modern legend has it that NASA scientists studying the conjunction of the planets discovered a missing day of 23 hours and 20 minutes and have concealed the truth ever since. Another story has it that a passing comet caused a temporary halt to the earth's rotation.

Sunday
(see also Sabbatarians; Sabbath)

The first day of the week, the Sabbath for most Christians. Although there is no authority for it in the New Testament, Christian worship takes place on Sunday, the Lord's Day, because it was the day on which Jesus rose from the dead. The word comes from the Latin for "day of the sun." Christians adopted it because Christ was "the true sun." Protestants have tended, more than others, to equate Sunday with the Jewish Sabbath, a day not just of worship but of rest.

> On Sunday heaven's gate stands ope;
> Blessings are plentiful and rife,
> More plentiful than hope.
> —*Sunday*, George Herbert
> (1593–1633).

Sunday Best

Your finest set of clothes. It is still customary to wear one's best set of clothes to church on Sunday.

Sunday Saint

A hypocrite. Someone who goes to church on Sunday but otherwise leaves his religion at the church door.

Sunflower

Because it was believed to always face the sun, the sunflower symbolizes the soul seeking God.

> The sunflower turns on the god,
> when he sets,
> The same look which she turned
> when he rose.
> —*Believe Me*, Thomas Moore (1779–1852).

Swallow

A bird that was believed to hibernate during the winter months and emerge in the spring. It was thus a symbol of the resurrection.

Swan and Swan Song

The swan is a symbol of deceit because its beautiful white plumage covers black flesh. In the King James Bible (1611) the swan is mentioned in Leviticus 11:18 and Deuteronomy 14:16. Hugh of Lincoln (1140–1200) is the patron saint of swans and their keepers. The swan's song is symbolic of the end of life. It was a belief that the swan sang only at the time of its death.

Swastika

The bent cross appropriated by the Nazis is in fact one of the most ancient and widespread human symbols. Early Christians used the swastika in the catacombs to represent Christ as the power of the world. The swastika also symbolized Christ as a cornerstone and the evangelists Matthew, Mark, Luke and John with Christ in the center.

Swear on a Stack of Bibles

An exaggerated affirmation of truth-telling. It is customary in courts for a witness to swear on a Bible while answering yes to the following question: "Do you swear to tell the truth, the whole truth, and nothing but the truth?" To swear on a stack of Bibles presumably carries more significance than swearing on just one.

Swiss Guard

The bodyguard of the pope. Composed of recruits from Switzerland, they have defended the Vatican since 1505. On ceremonial occasions they wear a medieval uniform of helmet, tunic, white ruff, breeches and yellow, red and blue striped stockings. The design of the uniform has been credited to Michelangelo (1475–1564). The guard's everyday uniform consists of a black beret, with a blue tunic and trousers.

The strength of the Swiss Guard is four officers, 23 noncommissioned officers, 70 halberdiers and two drummers. Recruits must be Catholics, male, Swiss citizens, less than 30 years of age, at least five feet eight inches tall and have served in the Swiss armed forces. Recently the first nonwhite, a recruit born in India but raised in Switzerland, has joined the Guard.

> "… Those Suisses in striped costumes, are a little disconcerting."
> —*Rome*, Gabriel Fauré (1854–1924).

Swords *see* Not Peace but a Sword; Swords into Plowshares; Take the Sword; Perish with the Sword

Swords Into Plowshares

A commonly used prayer for peace. It was a prediction of peace which will come with the restoration of Zion.

> "They shall beat their swords into plowshares, and their spears into pruning hooks; nation shall not lift up sword against a nation, neither shall they learn war any more" (Isaiah 2:4).

Sydenham's Chorea *see* St. Vitus's Dance

Syllables

There are no words longer than six syllables in the Bible.

Symbols of the Apostles
(*see also* Apostles)

Andrew: A cross because he was crucified on a cross shaped like an x.

Bartholomew: A knife because he was flayed with one.

James the Greater: A staff or a gourd because he is the patron saint of pilgrims.

James the Less: A fuller's pole because he was killed with such an object.

John: A dragon flying out of a cup. Challenged to drink a cup of poison, John made the sign of the cross over it. Satan flew from the cup and the poison was rendered harmless.

Judas Iscariot: A bag because he kept money in one.

Jude: The club with which he was killed.

Matthew: A halberd or hatchet which was used to kill him.

Matthias: The battleaxe used to behead him

Paul: A sword because he was beheaded with one.

Peter: A bunch of keys and a cock. He was given the keys of heaven and denied Christ before the cock's crow.

Phillip: A long staff surmounted by a cross. He was killed by being suspended from a tall pillar.

Simon: A saw because he was sawn in half.

Thomas: A lance because he was killed by one.

T

Take the Lord's Name in Vain, To

Cursing. The Hebrews, in common with most ancient peoples, held names in great veneration and respect. The name of God was so sacred it was not even to be spoken. To use such a sacred name as a curse was unthinkable. This stern commandment against blasphemy has become degraded in popular use. It is often used jocularly when someone's name is mentioned casually or disrespectfully.

"You shall not take the name of the Lord your God in vain; for the Lord will not hold him guiltless who takes his name in vain" (Exodus 20:7).

Take the Sword, Perish with the Sword

Jesus spoke these words when he was arrested and meant them as a warning against violence.

"For all who take the sword will perish by the sword" (Matthew 26:52).

Take Under One's Wing

To offer protection and shelter. It comes from Matthew 23:37. The expression, as in the biblical passage, was originally in the plural:

"How often would I have gathered your children together as a hen gathers her brood under her wings, and you would not!"

Talent

A talent was a unit of weight which could vary from place to place. A talent of silver would be worth several thousand dollars. The modern meaning of a talent, as a natural ability deserving of improvement or cultivation, derives from the parable of the talents (Matthew 25:14–30) in which a man leaves his money in the hands of three servants. The first two invest the money and earn a profit. The third servant buried his money for safe keeping, earned nothing and was berated by the master upon his return.

Tantony Pig

An abbreviation of *St. Anthony's pig*. Anthony (c. 250–350) is the patron saint of swineherds and is usually depicted with a piglet. A tantony pig was the runt of a litter or a pet. It can also be used to describe an obsequious hanger-on. A tantony is a small church handbell. The tantony pig usually has a bell around its neck.

Tawdry

An abbreviation of *to Audry*. St. Ethelreda (c. 630–679), or Saint Audry, was the abbess of the convent of Ely. At the fair of Saint Audry cheap laces were sold under the name of "tawdry laces." Anything cheap and pretentious has come to be called tawdry.

> "Come, you promised me a tawdry lace
> and a pair of sweet gloves."
> — *Winter's Tale*, William Shakespeare
> (1564–1616).

Tear God's Body, To
(*see also* 'S)

Oaths in the Middle Ages featured parts of Christ's body. Collectively these curses were called "Tearing God's body by imprecations."

Tell It Not in Gath

Do not let an enemy gloat over your misfortune. Gath was a town of the Philistines, the sworn enemies of the Israelites and the birthplace of the giant Goliath.

> "Tell it not in Gath, publish it not in the streets of Ashkelon; lest the daughters of the Philistines rejoice"
> (2 Samuel 1:20).

Ten
(*see also* Numbers; 120 Words; Ten Commandments in Rhyme)

A perfect number which represents order. There were Ten Commandments and 10 plagues of Egypt. Joseph had 10 brothers who mistreated him, there were 10 Roman persecutions of the early church, and 10 wise

and foolish virgins. In the Elizabethan era the Ten Commandments was used to denote the 10 fingers or 10 fingernails and the scratches they can make.

> Could I come near your beauty
> with my nails
> I'd set my ten commandments
> in your face.
> — *Henry IV, Pt. II*, William
> Shakespeare (1564–1616).

Ten Commandments *see* 120 Words

Ten Commandments in Rhyme
(*see also* 120 Words; Ten)

> Thou no God shalt have but me;
> Before no idol bow the knee;
> Take not the name of God in vain;
> Nor dare the Sabbath day profane;
> Give both thy parents honor due;
> Take heed that thou no murder do;
> Abstain from words and deeds unclean;
> Nor steal, though thou art poor
> and mean;
> Nor make a wilful lie, nor love it;
> What is thy neighbor's, do not covet.
> — Anon.

Terah
(*see also* White-haired Man, First)

Abraham's father, a maker of idols. Abraham, realizing that there was one true God, smashed his father's idols instead of selling them in the market. According to fable, Terah minted the gold coins that Caspar, one of the magi, gave to the infant Jesus.

Testicle *see* Thigh

Tetragrammaton
(*see also* Jehovah; Yahweh)

From the Greek, "having four letters." A transliteration of the four Hebrew consonants for the unutterable name of God, YHWH (JHVH, IHVH, JHWH, YHUH). In order to ensure that the name remains sacred it is never to be spoken or written with vowels.

> Such was the sacred Tetragrammaton
> Things worthy silence must not
> be revealed.
> —*Britannia Rediviva*, John
> Dryden (1631–1700).

Tetramorphs

The four evangelists, as represented by winged figures of man, lion, ox and eagle. They were derived from visions recorded in Ezekiel 1:4–10 and Revelation 4:6–7. Matthew opens with Christ's human genealogy, so St. Matthew is represented as a man. Mark depicts John the Baptist as "the voice of one crying in the wilderness" (Mark 1:3). Because lions lived in desert wastes, St. Mark, whose gospel begins in the wilderness, is represented by a lion. St. Luke is symbolized by the sacrificial ox because his Gospel commences with Zacharias making a sacrifice. St. John was represented by the soaring eagle because the Book of John carries readers Heavenward with its opening words, "In the beginning."

Thaumaturgis

A title meaning "miracle-worker" given to saints who performed miracles.

Their Name Is Legion

A great number, a multitude, usually used in a negative sense. The phrase stems from Mark 5:9 where Jesus addressed a demon he expelled from a possessed man:

> "And Jesus asked him, 'What is your name?' He replied, "My name is Legion, for we are many.'"

(A legion in the Roman army was a fighting unit of between 3,000 and 6,000 infantry with 300 to 700 cavalry.)

Their Name Liveth for Evermore

This phrase, often found on war memorials, is assumed to be from the Bible but it is not. The phrase is found in the Apocrypha.

> "Their bodies are buried in peace; but their name liveth for evermore" (Ecclesiasticus 44:14).

Theotokos
(*see also* MA DI; Virgin Mary)

The title given to the Virgin Mary by the Council of Ephesus in 431. It comes from the Greek for "To give birth to God." Before the adoption of Theotokas, some contested that Mary was the mother of Christ but not of God.

There Are No Atheists in Foxholes

An atheist is someone who does not believe in God. During World War II an American Army chaplain, Father W. T. Cummings (1903–1944), made the famous remark that "there are no atheists in foxholes." To counter that claim, an atheists' war memorial has been erected in Fearn Park, Alabama. The inscription on the monument reads, "In memory of atheists in foxholes and the countless freethinkers who have served this country with honor and distinction." The early Christians, because they did not believe in the gods of Rome, were called atheists.

> "By night an atheist half
> believes in God."
> —*Night*, Edward Young (1683–1765).

Thief in the Night

Jesus will come unexpectedly. The expression can be used for anything that arrives quietly and unexpectedly.

> "For you yourselves know well that the day of the Lord will come like a thief in the night" (1 Thessalonians 5:2).

Thigh

A biblical euphemism for the testicles.

> "So the servant put his hand under the thigh of Abraham his master, and swore to him concerning the matter" (Genesis 24:9).

This is an example of the ancient custom of holding the testicles as a sign of a solemn oath. Testicle is derived from the Latin *testie*— witness. Related words are *testament* and *protestant*.

Thirteen
(*see also* Numbers)

The superstition that 13 is an unlucky number probably arose from the Last Supper, when Christ and the Apostles numbered 13. The fact that it is indivisible by any other number was probably significant as well. It is considered most unlucky to have 13 at dinner. The French have a word —*quatorzieme*— for an extra guest invited to avoid the number 13. Many streets have no number 13 and many tall buildings have no 13th floor. In 1884 the Thirteen Club was founded in New York to end the superstition. They dined on the 13th of every month, 13 to a table. Everything related to the club was a multiple of 13. In the chapel of the Trindinium Pauperum in Rome is a marble tablet reminding visitors how Pope Gregory the Great (c.540–604) was in the habit of inviting 12 poor men for breakfast each morning. On one occasion Christ came and was the 13th guest. Henceforth 13 should be a lucky number.

> "It was a bright cold day in April and the clocks were striking thirteen."
> —*1984*, George Orwell (1903–1950).

Thirteenth Apostle
(*see also* Apostles)

Matthias, the apostle chosen by lot to replace Judas Iscariot (Acts 1:23–26). Apart from his having been a disciple of Jesus from his baptism and a witness of the resurrection, we know nothing about him. Legend, of course, has stepped in to fill out his story. Matthias was a rich tax gatherer, became a missionary to the land of the cannibals, and after many miraculous occurrences was martyred near Jerusalem.

Thirty Pieces of Silver
(*see also* Judas)

The ultimate betrayal. Judas Iscariot betrayed Jesus for this sum of money (Matthew 26:15). Afterwards he went and hanged himself at the realization of his crime. A piece of silver was probably a denarius, the average daily wage of a laborer. According to John 12:5, Judas had complained that the ointment used to anoint the feet of Jesus was worth 300 denarii.

Thistle
(*see also* Crown of Thorns)

A thorny plant which symbolizes Christ's crown of thorns. It also recalls sorrow and sin because of the curse put on Adam in Genesis 3:17–18:

> "Cursed is the ground because of you ... thorns and thistles it shall bring forth to you."

Thorn in the Flesh

Something that is constantly irritating but not completely disabling. Paul said,

"And to keep me from being too elated by the abundance of revelations, a thorn was given me in the flesh, a messenger from Satan, to harass me, to keep me from being too elated" (2 Corinthians 12:7).

Three times did Paul ask the Lord for relief but was told to call upon divine grace so he could endure it. Although there has been some speculation as to the nature of Paul's infirmity — chronic pain, epileptic fits, poor eyesight, bad temper — it is unknown.

Thorns
(*see also* Crown of Thorns)

Associated as they are with the crown of thorns worn by Christ at the crucifixion, thorns symbolize sorrow and grief. When associated with saints they recall the triumph of martyrdom.

"Some people blame God for putting thorns among the roses. Why not thank God for putting roses among the thorns."
— Anon.

Thou Hast Conquered Galilean
(*see also* Julian the Apostate)

An exclamation put into the mouth of the dying Julian the Apostate by early Christian writers. Galilean was a term of abuse applied to early Christians and Julian had gone so far as to make it illegal to refer to Christians by any other word. At the moment of his victory against the Persians, June 25, 363, Julian received a mortal wound. Realizing that he could not live, Julian was supposed to have cast blood from his wound Heavenward and made the exclamation, "Thou hast conquered Galilean." Jesus was a Galilean.

Three
(see also Numbers)

A mystical number. It represents the Trinity and the eternal God, past, present and future. Christianity abounds in triads. Jonah spent three days in the belly of a whale, there were three Wise Men, Jesus lay in the tomb for three days and Peter denied Christ three times. Body, soul and spirit are the three elements that make up man; knowledge, assent and confidence are the three elements of faith; contrition, confession and restitution are the three elements of repentance; fasting, almsgiving and prayer are the three notable duties; poverty, chastity and obedience the three evangelical counsels. The three virtues are faith, hope and charity.

Batter my heart, three-personed God; for you
As yet but knock, breathe, shine, and seek to men.
—*Holy Sonnets*, John Donne (1572–1631).

Three Kings of the Orient *see* Magi

Three Score and Ten
(*see also* Numbers)

Human life is swift and fleeting. Seventy years has long been considered to be the normal human lifespan.

"The years of our life are threescore and ten" (Psalm 90:10).

Through a Glass Darkly

By glass is meant a mirror, which in biblical times were poorly polished and did not give good reflections. Human perceptions give only a limited degree of truth.

"Now we see through a glass darkly, but then face to face" (1 Corinthians 13:12).

Tidings of Great Joy

The angel of the Lord brought the

good news of Christ's birth to the shepherds in the field:

> "Be not afraid; for behold, I bring you good news of a great joy which will come to all the people; for to you is born this day in the city of David a Savior, who is Christ the Lord" (Luke 2:10–11).

Tiffany
(*see also* Epiphany)

A thin transparent silk. The word comes from the Greek *Theophany*, the Epiphany, the manifestation of Christ to the Gentiles.

Tiphany
(*see also* Epiphany)

The legendary name of the mother of the Magi. It is related to Epiphany.

Tittyvally *see* Tutivillius

To Fall Asleep *see* Death,
Euphemisms for

To-remain Bible

A confusion about punctuation resulted in an amusing misprint in a Bible of 1805. The correct reading of Galatians 4:29 is, "Persecuted him that was born after the spirit, even so it is now." A proofreader wondered if the comma after the word "spirit" was necessary. The compositor answered the proofreader by penciling "*to remain*" in the text. When the Bible was printed, the verse appeared, "Persecuted him that was born after the spirit *to remain*, even so it is now." Amazingly, this error was repeated in two later editions of the Bible.

Toad

A froglike amphibian featured in depictions of the tortures of hell. Toads are shown crawling over the pudenda of lascivious women and wives who denied their husbands their sexual rights. The toad is not mentioned in the King James Bible (1611).

> Squat like a toad, close at the ear of Eve...
> —*Paradise Lost*, John Milton (1608–1674).

Tonsure *see* Make Orders, To

Toothache
(*see also* Dentists)

St. Apollonia (d. 249) is the patron saint against toothache and the patron saint of dentists. Upon converting to Christianity she was seized and had her teeth torn out of her jaw, one by one.

> For there was never yet philosopher That could endure the toothache patiently...
> —*Much Ado About Northing*, William Shakespeare (1564–1616).

Tophet

A place that resembles hell. Tophet was a valley near Jerusalem where children were sacrificed as burnt offerings to Moloch. A fire was kept burning there to consume the dead bodies and filth deposited there.

Totentanz *see* Danse Macabre

Tower of Babel *see* Babel

Traditio Legis *see* Delivery
of the Law

Tre Fontane

"Three Springs." A monastery near Rome constructed on the site of St. Paul's martyrdom. When Paul's head was lopped off it bounced on the ground three times. At each bounce a spring of pure water erupted.

Treacle Bible
(*see also* Rosin Bible)

In a Bible of 1568 the phrase, "Is there no *balm* in Gilead?" (Jeremiah 8:22) was rendered, "Is there no *treacle* in Gilead?" Treacle was used for balm in Jeremiah 46:11, "Go up to Gilead and take *treacle*," and Ezekiel 27:17, "... they exchanged for your merchandise wheat, olives and early figs, honey, oil, and *treacle*."

Treasure in Heaven

True riches are spiritual, not material.

> Do not lay up for yourselves treasures on earth, where moth and rust consume and where thieves break in and steal, but lay up for yourselves treasures in heaven, where neither moth nor rust consumes and where thieves do not break in and steal. For where your treasure is, there will your heart be also (Matthew 6:19–21).

Treasury of the Church
(*see also* Indulgence; Pardoners)

Also the treasury of merits. The store of merits in the Church that were beyond the needs of the salvation of the human race. It was these that were drawn upon for grants of indulgences.

Tree

A poetical allusion to the cross upon which Jesus was crucified. It is frequently encountered in literature, hymns and the New Testament.

> "He himself bore our sins in his body on the tree" (1 Peter 3:24).

Tree Is Known by Its Fruit

You will be judged by what you do rather than by what you say.

> "Either make the tree good, and its fruit good; or make the tree bad, and its fruit bad; for the tree is known by its fruit" (Matthew 12:33).

Tree of Knowledge of Good and Evil
(*see also* Adam; Eve)

A tree in the Garden of Eden which conferred wisdom. Adam and Eve were forbidden to eat its fruit. When they did so they were expelled from Eden. The cross of Jesus was thought to have been made from the preserved wood of this tree. Knowledge that can only be acquired through a loss of innocence is the modern meaning.

> "You may freely eat of every tree of the garden; but of the tree of knowledge of good and evil you shall not eat, for in the day that you eat of it you shall die" (Genesis 2:17).

Trembling Like a Leaf *see* Aspen

Triangle *see* Delta

Triquetra

A decorative detail consisting of three interlaced ovals which represents the Trinity enclosed by a circle, the symbol of eternity.

Truce of God

An attempt by the church to restrict hostilities and feuds. It came into existence about 1033, one thousand years after the death and resurrection of Christ. Nobles would bind themselves by solemn vows not to war against each other between Lent and

Advent, and between Thursday and Monday during festivals. The truce was usually ignored.

Truth Shall Make You Free, The

Salvation and freedom come from the knowledge of God.

"Ye shall know the truth, and the truth shall make you free" (John 8:32).

Turkey *see* Poor as Job's Turkey

Turn the Other Cheek
(*see also* Eye for an Eye)

Jesus goes beyond the principle of retaliation in Mosaic law by saying that we should not pursue vengeance at all. This is often seen as a justification for pacifism.

"You have heard it was said, 'An eye for an eye and a tooth for a tooth.' But I say to you, Do not resist one who is evil. But if any one strikes you on the right cheek, turn to him the other also" (Matthew 5:38–39).

Tutivillius

A name for the devil or Satan. Also Tittyvally. He haunted churches and collected the words of those who gossiped and joked in a big bag, along with the poorly chosen utterances of priests. The bag would be opened at the Last Judgment.

Twelfth Day *see* Epiphany

Twelve
(*see also* Numbers)

A mystical number, 3 × 4, divisible by five of the first six digits, that symbolizes

the chosen people of God. The Trinity gathers people from the four quarters of the globe. There were 12 tribes of Israel, 12 disciples, 12 gates of the New Jerusalem, 12 stars crowning the woman clothed with the sun 12 full baskets of bread.

"Why only twelve?"
"That's the original number."
"Well, go out and get thousands."
— Samuel Goldwyn (1882–1971), during the filming of *The Last Supper.*

Twelve Articles of the Symbol

Legend says that the 12 apostles met for the last time and formulated the confession of faith known as the Apostles' Creed. Each apostle contributed a line as indicated below. There are variants.

I believe in God the Father Almighty, Maker of Heaven and Earth. [Peter]
[And] in Jesus Christ, His only Son, our Lord. [John]
Who was conceived of the Holy Ghost, born of the Virgin Mary. [James the Greater]
Suffered under Pontius Pilate; was crucified, dead, and buried. [Andrew]
He descended into Hell. [Philip]
The third day He rose again from the dead. [Thomas]
He ascended into Heaven, and sitteth on the right hand of God the Father Almighty. [James the Less]
From thence He shall come to judge the quick and the dead. [Matthew]
I believe in the Holy Ghost. [Bartholomew]
The Holy Catholic Church; the communion of saints. [Simon]
The forgiveness of sins. [Matthias]
The resurrection of the body, and the life everlasting. [Jude]

Two
(*see also* Numbers)

A symbolic number which reminds us of the twofold nature, human and divine, of

Jesus. There are many other pairs in the Bible, including Adam and Eve, the two thieves and two of every kind that went aboard Noah's Ark.

Two Thieves, Names of
(*see also* Dismas; Gesmas)

The two thieves crucified with Christ have received many names. The penitent thief has been known as Demas, Desmas, Dismas, Titus, Matha and Vicimus. The unrepentant thief has been named Gesmas, Dumachas, Joca and Justinus.

U

Uncumber
(*see also* Bearded Women)

The English name for Wilgefortis, a saint who never existed. A legend tells of a saint who took a vow of virginity against the wishes of her father, who expected her to marry. She prayed that she would grow a beard and be made so ugly that no man would want her. When this happened, her father had her crucified. Before her death she prayed that all who sought her intercession would be freed from their troubles. She was called Uncumber because women believed that they would be uncumbered or freed from bad husbands if they placed a peck of oats before her image. The legend may have originated in 14th century Flanders where images of a clothed and bearded Christ on the cross were thought to be that of a crucified female saint. The name Wilgefortis was derived from the Latin *virgo fortis*, steadfast virgin.

Unicorn

A fabulous horse with a single white horn growing out of its forehead. The unicorn's horn symbolizes Christ, who "raised up a horn of salvation for us" (Luke 1:69). The horn was thought to purify anything it came into contact with and thus symbolizes the cross of the crucifixion. The unicorn is mentioned nine times in the King James Bible (1611).

Union Jack
(*see also* Christian Imagery on Flags; Crosses on Flags; St. Andrew's Cross)

The Union Jack has been the flag of the United Kingdom since 1801. It is composed of the crosses of the patron saints of England, Scotland and Ireland: the St. George's cross, red cross on a field of white; St. Andrew's cross, white saltire on a field of blue; and St. Patrick's cross, red saltire on a field of white. The following countries and territories have a Union Jack in the upper left canton or other positions on their flags: Alderney, Anguilla, Australia, Bermuda, British Antarctic Territory, British Columbia, British Indian Ocean Territory, British Virgin Islands, Cayman Islands, Cook Islands, Falkland Islands, Fiji, Hawaii, Heard and McDonald Islands, Manitoba, Montserrat, New Zealand, Niue, Ontario, Pitcairn Islands, Queensland, St. Helena, South Australia, South Georgia and the South Sandwich Islands, Tasmania, Tokelau, Tristan da Cunha, Turks and Caicos Islands, Tuvalu, Victoria, and Western Australia. In addition, the flag of the Canadian province of Newfoundland and Labrador consists entirely of a stylized modern representation of the Union Jack.

Unrighteous Bible

The omission of the word *not* caused an alarming misprint to appear in a Bible of 1653. 1 Corinthians 6:9 became, "Know ye that the unrighteous *shall* inherit the Kingdom of God?" In the same edition there was a second misprint. The prefix *un* was left out of Romans 6:13, rendering it, "Neither yield ye your members as instruments of *righteousness* unto sin." For good reason this edition is sometimes called the Wicked Bible.

Urim and Thummim
(*see also* Scrying; Urimancy)

Mysterious objects, possibly precious stones, used in ancient Hebrew worship, most likely for divination (Exodus 28:30; Leviticus 8:8). They were carried in the breastplate of the high priest and probably represented opposites such as yes or no, or life or death. In Mormonism it is believed that Joseph Smith (1805–1844) used the Urim and Thummim in a manner resembling eyeglasses to decipher the golden tablets which became the Book of Mormon.

Urimancy
(*see also* Urim and Thummim)

Divination by the casting of lots. The Urim and Thummim, mysterious objects carried by a high priest, may have been a form of dice. By rolling them, a yes or no answer may have been obtained.

V

Vanity *see* All Is Vanity

Vatican City
(*see also* Papal States; Prisoner of the Vatican)

The residence of the pope in Rome and headquarters of the Roman Catholic Church. Vatican City occupies *Vaticanus Mons*, Vatican Hill, former headquarters of the *vaticinatores*, soothsayers of ancient Rome. At 0.17 square miles, the Vatican City State (Città del Vaticano) is the small-

est sovereign country in the world. It is the sole remnant of the Papal States, a territory of 17,000 square miles in central Italy ruled by the papacy until the middle of the 19th century. Vatican City was established in 1929 under terms of a treaty between Italy and the Holy See, the government of the Church. The Vatican maintains diplomatic relations with most nations, and has its own flag and national anthem. The flag features the keys of St. Peter, the keys to the kingdom of Heaven. St. Peter's Basilica and the Sistine Chapel are in the Vatican.

> "... the occupant of the Vatican (even if he now has a few country houses, his own post office, and a radio station) lives a life as frugal as that of a village priest in some remote hamlet in Wyoming."
> —*Van Loon's Lives*, Hendrik Van Loon (1882–1944).

Vengeance Is Mine, Saith the Lord

A quotation from Romans 12:19 often used as a justification for human vengeance. In fact the complete passage, Romans 12:17-21, states the opposite. Vengeance is for God to administer, not human beings.

Veronica
(*see also* Volto Santo)

A classic move of a bullfighter's cape. The cape is slowly and deliberately waved close to the bull's face. Doing this recalls St. Veronica, who wiped Christ's face on his way to Calvary. Veronica's handkerchief retained an image of Christ.

Verses in the Bible
(*see also* Identical Bible Verses; Longest Verse in Bible; Middle Verse of Bible; Neck-verse; Shortest Verse in Bible)

There are 23,214 verses in the Old Testament and 7,959 verses in the New Testament for a total of 31,173 verses. The modern division of the chapters of the Bible into numbered verses is attributed to the Dominican scholar Sanctes Pagnini (1470–1541) in his Latin Bible of 1528.

Vesica Piscis
(*see also* Aureole; Mandorla)

Latin for "fish's bladder." A pointed upright oval shape, so named because of its presumed resemblance to a fish bladder. It is another name for a mandorla or aureole, a feature enclosing sacred figures in medieval sculpture and painting.

Via Dolorosa

Latin for "sorrowing road." A street in Jerusalem believed to be the one traversed by Jesus from the hall of judgment to the site of his crucifixion at Calvary. Any prolonged torment or suffering can be called a via dolorosa.

Vials of Wrath

To vent anger or exact vengeance is to empty the vials of wrath. The vials of wrath were plagues recalling the plagues of Egypt.

> "And one of the four beasts gave unto the seven angels seven golden vials full of the wrath of God ... and I heard a great voice out of the temple saying to the seven angels, Go your ways, and pour out the vials of the wrath of God upon the earth" (Revelation 15:7, 16:1).

Vicar of Bray

Someone who changes his principles and beliefs to suit changing circumstances. The Vicar of Bray was reputed to be a 16th century Church of England clergyman who lived during a period of religious turmoil. To suit the current circumstances, the Vicar

of Bray was twice a Roman Catholic and twice a Protestant. The unnamed vicar of the town of Bray, Berkshire, was mentioned in T. Fuller's *Worthies* (1662):

> "This vicar, being taxed by one for being a turncoat and an inconsistent changeling, 'Not so,' said he, 'for I always kept my principle, which is this,— to live and die the Vicar of Bray.'"

Vine of Sodom *see* Dead Sea Fruit

Vine of the Lord

A vine in a corner of the Vatican garden which was traditionally tended by the pope himself. The vine was reputed to produce a wine of exquisite character. Legends said that the Vine of the Lord originated in the Garden of Eden and produced the wine served at the wedding feast at Cana.

Vinegar
(*see also* Aesop)

In Matthew 27:48, Mark 15:36 and John 19:29 an unnamed bystander soaks a sponge in vinegar and offers it to Jesus to quench his thirst as he hangs on the cross. To modern eyes this appears to be a cruel thing to do to a dying man, but in biblical times vinegar was sour wine, probably spiced or diluted with water. It was the drink of the common folk and Roman soldiers. To offer it to Jesus was a kindness.

Vinegar Bible

A name given to a Bible edition of 1717. Due to a misprint, the page heading for "The Parable of the *Vineyard*" (Luke 20:9-16) reads, "The Parable of the *Vinegar*."

Vinium Theologicum

The best wine. It was commonly believed that churchmen reserved the best wine for themselves.

Violet

The color violet symbolizes suffering and sorrow. The flower symbolizes humility.

> Then let me to the valley go,
> This pretty flower to see,
> That I may also learn to grow
> In sweet humility.
> — *The Violet*, Jane Taylor (1783–1824).

Virgil (70–19 B.C.)

Though a poet of Rome, Virgil was considered something of a prophet in the Middle Ages because in his *Fourth Eclogue* he predicted the coming of the Messiah. The poem tells of the birth of a child who will usher in a glorious era of peace. In the *Aeneid*, Virgil described Rome as a holy city from which religion would uplift the world.

> "A debt to Virgil is like a debt to Nature."
> — *Victorian Literature*, G. K. Chesterton (1874–1936).

Virgin Mary

(*see also* Assumption of the Virgin; Betrothal and Marriage of the Virgin Mary; Candlemas Day; Carnation; Education of St. Mary the Virgin; Lily of the Valley; M; MA DI; Marigold; Mariolatry; New Eve; Orange; Our Lady; Porta Clausa; Theotokos)

As the mother of Jesus, Mary is the greatest Christian saint. She personifies purity, patience and sympathy for human suffering. After being visited by the Holy Spirit she conceived Jesus (Luke 1:26-38). She wed Joseph and had other children. She gave birth to Jesus in a humble manger in Bethlehem (Luke 2:1-20). In order to escape the Massacre of the Innocents (Matthew 2), Mary and her family fled to Egypt. She sought out Jesus when he was discoursing with the priests in the temple (Luke 2:41-51) and suffered his rebuke at the marriage at Cana (John 2:1-5). Mary witnessed the crucifixion of her son (John 19:25-27).

> Of wedded maid and virgin mother born,
> Our great redemption from above did bring.
> — *On the Morning of Christ's Nativity*,
> John Milton (1608–1674).

Virgins

(*see also* Catherine Wheel; Mystical Marriage of St. Catharine)

Catherine of Alexandria is the patron saint of virgins. Catherine lived a holy life, considered herself to be the mystical bride of Christ and was martyred for her faith. A French proverb applied to spinsters says, "She has dressed the hair of St. Catherine." It was a superstition that a woman who dressed a bride's hair would soon be a bride herself. Thus, to dress the hair of the patron saint of virgins was to die unmarried.

Vitus, St. *see* St. Vitus's Dance

Voice Crying in the Wilderness

Someone who gives a warning that goes unheeded. John the Baptist, wandering in the wilderness, predicted the advent of Christ and how his coming was prefigured in the Old Testament.

> "In those days came John the Baptist, preaching in the wilderness of Judea, 'Repent for the kingdom of heaven is at hand.' For this is he who was spoken of by the prophet Isaiah when he said, 'The voice of one crying in the wilderness.'"
> (Matthew 3:3).

Voice of the Turtle Is Heard in the Land, The

The coming of spring. The turtle mentioned here is a turtledove.

> "For, lo, the winter is past, the rain is over and gone. The flowers appear on the earth; and the time of the singing of birds is come, and the voice of the turtle is heard in our land" (Song of Solomon 2:11-12).

Volto Santo

(*see also* Abgar's Letter to Jesus and Jesus' Reply; Mandylion; Sudarium; Veronica)

Italian for "Holy Face." There are several relics which claim to bear an authentic image of Christ. The most famous is the Holy Shroud preserved in Turin since 1578. St. Luke was said to have painted the baby Jesus in Mary's arms and Nicodemus to have carved a likeness of Jesus in a crucifix. St. Veronica and King Abgar were rewarded with miraculous imprints of the holy face on napkins. From the 11th century onwards there was a cult of the Holy Face. In the earliest days Christ was not depicted at all. But in order to counter the heresy that Jesus only "seemed" human, his human image began to be shown. But how? One tradition was that the savior must be ugly. "He had no form or comeliness that we should look at him, and no beauty that we should desire him" (Isaiah 53:2). But gradually Jesus came to be depicted as a handsome young man. "You are the fairest of the sons of men" (Psalm 45:2).

Vulgate

(*see also* King James Bible; Revised Standard Version; Septuagint)

From the Latin, *vulgata (editio)*, "spread among the people." The Vulgate is the Latin translation of the Bible. It was prepared principally by St. Jerome during the fourth century. Subsequently revised, it became the authoritative Latin text of the Roman Catholic church. The Gutenberg Bible of 1456, the first printed Bible, was a Vulgate. The word also means common speech, or the accepted text of any work.

W

Wages of Sin, The

(*see also* Earn the Wages of Sin, To)

A powerful statement of sin and redemption. Now used in an almost light-hearted or ironic sense to describe twinges of moral guilt. Wages was often treated as a singular noun until the 19th century.

> "For the wages of sin is death, but the free gift of God is eternal life in Christ Jesus our Lord" (Romans 6:23).

Walk on Water

To perform a miracle or accomplish a seemingly impossible task is to walk on water. The reference is to the famous miracle of Jesus when

> "he came to them, walking on the sea" (Matthew 14:25).

Walls Came Tumbling Down

An expression which means a victory achieved without a fight. In Joshua 6:1–20 we learn how the mighty walls of Jericho came tumbling down after a miraculous trumpet blast. The biblical passage reads, "As soon as the people heard the sound of the trumpet ... the wall fell down flat ... and they took the city" (Joshua 6:20).

> "Ancient Jericho is not very picturesque as a ruin. When Joshua marched around it seven times, some three thousand years ago, and blew it down with his

trumpet, he did the work so well and so completely that he hardly left enough of the city to cast a shadow."
— *The Innocents Abroad*, Mark Twain (1835–1910).

Wandering Jew

A legend from the Middle Ages about a man who refused to allow Christ to rest on his doorstep and was condemned to wander until Christ's second coming. In one version he was Cartaphilus, the doorkeeper of Pontius Pilate. Leading Jesus from the judgment hall, Cartaphilus struck him, sneering, "Get on faster, Jesus!" Jesus answered, "I am going fast, Cartaphilus, but you shall wander the earth until I come again." Eventually Cartaphilus was baptized and received the name Joseph. He is thought to fall into a trance at the end of each century and reawaken as a man of about 30. In another version he is Ahasuerus, a cobbler who refused Christ permission to sit and rest on his way to Golgotha. Wracked by remorse he is constantly on the move, unable to find a peaceful grave. It was not until the early 17th century that the wanderer was identified as a Jew. There have been numerous sightings claimed and the legend has sometimes given rise to anti–Semitism.

"I'll rest," said he "but thou shalt walk";
So doth this wandering Jew
From place to place, but cannot rest
For seeing countries new.
— *Wandering Jew*, Anon.

Wash One's Hands, To

To refuse to take part in some action or accept responsibility. Pontius Pilate literally washed his hands to demonstrate that he was innocent of the condemnation of Jesus (Matthew 27:24).

Water Into Wine

Accomplishing a seemingly impossible task. At the wedding celebration at Cana the wine ran out. Jesus averted this disaster by taking six stone jars of water and changing them into wine. The chief steward tasted the result and said,

"Every man serves the good wine first; and when men have drunk freely, then the poor wine; but you have kept the good wine until now" (John 2:10).

The water into wine symbolizes the inferiority of the Old Testament to the New.

Way of a Man with a Maid, The

The imbalance of power between the sexes. This phrase, which does not sound biblical, is often used today to refer to a man's sexual conquests.

"There be three things which are too wonderful for me, yea, four which I know not: The way of an eagle in the air; the way of a serpent upon a rock; the way of a ship in the midst of the sea; and the way of a man with a maid" (Proverbs 30: 18–19).

Way of All Flesh
(*see also* Death, Euphemisms for)

Death. A paraphrase of 1 Kings 2:2 and Joshua 23:14, where the expression is written as "the way of all the earth."

Weaker Vessel

Nowadays an unflattering term for women. It comes from 1 Peter 3:7 in the King James Bible (1611). Women were weaker physically and socially, but as vessels, waiting to be filled with the "grace of life," they were equal to men.

"Likewise, ye husbands, dwell with them according to knowledge giving honor unto the wife, as unto the weaker vessel, and as being heirs together of the grace of life."

Weasel

(*see also* Cockatrice)

According to Leviticus 11:29, an animal that is unclean. It was believed to give birth through the mouth and conceive via the ear. It could revive its young with an herb called rue. The weasel was the enemy of the cockatrice and symbolized Christ's triumph over the devil.

Weather *see* Red Sky in the Morning, Sailors Take Warning; Weather Vane

Weather Vane

Because it swings every which way, it symbolizes wavering faith. However, because of its role in Peter's denial of Christ (John 13:38), the cock on a weathervane denotes vigilance against the approach of Satan. Each of the directions found on a church weather vane has a guardian angel: North — Urial; South — Michael; East — Raphael; and West — Gabriel.

Weeping and Gnashing of Teeth

(*see also* Gnash One's Teeth)

An expression which has come to mean grief and frustration. In a prophecy of the end of time, Jesus contrasts the faith of a Roman soldier, a foreigner, with the unbelief of His own people.

"I tell you, many will come from east and west and sit at table with Abraham, Isaac, and Jacob in the kingdom of heaven, while the sons of the kingdom will be thrown into outer darkness; there men will weep and gnash their teeth" (Matthew 8:11–12).

Weeping Chancel

The chancel is the easternmost part of a church, where the altar is placed. When a chancel is not in alignment with the nave, the main part of the church, it has been described as weeping. It is said to symbolize Christ's head turned toward his right shoulder, in the moments before he died on the cross. In fact, the misalignment is due to centuries of rebuilding and renovation. Churches represent the cross, not Christ's body on the cross.

Weeping Statues

A phenomenon whereby a statue, most often of the Virgin Mary, appears to be weeping tears. Many of these have been shown to be hoaxes or to involve the seepage of water through a porous material by capillary action. But a few have no known rational explanation.

Weighed in the Balance and Found Wanting

To be examined and found to be inadequate. The expression comes from Daniel 5:27, where the plural is used.

"You have been weighed in the balances and found wanting."

Wesley, Charles *see* Why Should the Devil Have All the Good Tunes?

Whale

(*see also* Jonah)

In the story of Jonah he was swallowed by a great fish, probably a whale. Jonah spent three days in the whale's belly before being vomited out. This represents the three days Jesus spent in the tomb and the resurrection. A whale could surface luring the unwary sailor into believing it was an island before submerging and pulling the seaman under the waves. This symbolizes the deceitful powers of the devil. The patron saint of whales is St. Brendan the Navigator (c. 485–575), who is reputed to have once celebrated the Mass on the back of a whale, mistaking it for an island.

What Hath God Wrought!

A phrase which appears in Numbers 23:23, expressing awe in the presence of God's great works. It is also famous as the first message ever sent by telegraph, on May 28, 1844, by Samuel Morse.

What is Truth?

In the New Testament (John 18:37–8), this question was asked by Pontius Pilate of Jesus but never answered because Pilate left the room. In the Apocryphal Gospel of Nichodemis (3:10–14) the question is answered.

> Pilate said, Art thou a king then? Jesus answered, Thou sayest that I am a King; to this end I was born, and for this end came I into the world; and for this purpose I came, that I should bear witness to the truth; and every one who is of the truth heareth my voice. Pilate saith to him, What is truth? Jesus said, Truth is from heaven. Pilate said, Therefore truth is not on earth. Jesus saith to Pilate, Believe that truth is on earth among those who, when they have the power of judgment are governed by truth and form right judgment.

Wheel

Because of Ezekiel 1:1–28 and its vision of flaming wheels carrying the throne of God, the wheel represents the power of God the Father. The wheel is an attribute of St. Catherine of Alexandria, who was martyred on a spiked wheel. Wheels can contain the Seven Deadly Sins or the Works of Mercy, thereby transporting a man to Heaven or to Hell.

Wheels Within Wheels

Complex, often hidden, motives that interact with each other. The expression sounds of recent origin but, in fact, it comes from a slight misstating of Ezekiel 1:16. Since about 1750 the plural *wheels* has been used.

> "As for the appearance of the wheels and their construction: their appearance was like the gleaming of a chrysolite; and the four had the same likeness, their construction being a wheel within a wheel."

When in Rome Do as the Romans Do

A common proverb which advises people to follow the local customs. Probably the earliest rendition was in the fourth century when St. Augustine, discovering that people in Rome fasted on Saturdays, asked St. Ambrose what he should do. St. Ambrose replied that at home in Milan he did not fast of Saturday either, but when in Rome he followed the Roman custom.

> "When I am here I do not fast on Saturday; when at Rome I do fast on Saturday."

White

The color of the purified soul, joy and virginity. White is worn at baptism, confirmation, first communion and marriage. White is associated with virgin saints and saints who did not suffer martyrdom.

White-haired Man, First
(*see also* Abraham-man; Abraham's Bosom; Terah)

Abraham, the father of the Jewish people was the first of the Old Testament patriarchs (Genesis 11:27–25: 10). He lived early in the second millennium B.C. Because he is traditionally depicted with white hair, legend arose that he was the first white-haired man. Abraham is, of course, a central figure in one of the Bible's best-known stories, his near-sacrifice of his son, Isaac.

Whitsunday

The seventh Sunday after Easter is White Sunday, which commemorates the descent of the Holy Spirit at Pentecost. Between Easter and Pentecost it was the custom for the newly baptized to wear white robes. For some the day stood for wit or wisdom and recalled the day when the Apostles were filled with the wisdom of the Holy Spirit.

Whore of Babylon
(*see also* Babylon; Rivers of Babylon)

The scarlet woman. A sinful woman who sits upon a scarlet beast with 10 horns and seven heads. The whore is probably an allegorical representation of the Roman Empire. Upon her head is written,

> "Babylon the great, mother of harlots and of earth's abominations" (Revelation 17:5).

Whoring After Other Gods

Nowadays this is a metaphor for selling-out. But in the Old Testament it is a literal reference to the Hebrews when they turned to the worship of foreign gods,

> "...for they played the harlot after other gods and bowed down to them" (Judges 2:17).

Why Should the Devil Have All the Good Tunes?

A saying of Charles Wesley (1707–1788) from about 1740. Wesley wrote religious lyrics to popular tunes of the day. He composed more than 6,500 hymns, including such standbys as "Hark! The Herald Angels" and "Christ, the Lord, is Risen Today."

Wicked Bible *see* Adulterous Bible; Unrighteous Bible

Wicked Prayer Book

In an edition of the prayer book printed in 1686, the lack of *not* in the Epistle for the Fourteenth Sunday after Trinity resulted in a grave error:

> "Now the works of the flesh are manifest, which are these; adultery, fornication, uncleanliness, idolatry ... they who do these things *shall* inherit the kingdom of God."

Widow's Cruise

A small measure, which, by careful management, can be made to go a long way. A cruise is an earthenware jar or pot. In 2 Kings 4:1–7, a poor widow receives a miraculously refilling jar of oil.

Wife-hater Bible

In a Bible of 1810 the word *wife* occurs in Luke 14:26 instead of "*life*." The result:

> "If any one comes to me and does not hate his own father and mother ... and even his *wife*, he cannot be my disciple."

Wild Huntsman

A medieval legend of a ghostly hunter with a pack of spectral dogs who haunts lonely forests. One version of the tale has him as a Jew who, refusing Jesus a drink of water from a horse trough, indicates a puddle in a hoof print as being good enough for "such an enemy of Moses."

Wild Men

Wild forest creatures sometimes called wodewose who resembled men but were unable to speak. They carried clubs, were covered in green hair, and abducted women and unbaptized children. Saints Abdon and Sennen could overpower them.

Wilgefortis, St. *see* Uncumber

Will No One Free Me of This Turbulent Priest?

In 1162 Thomas à Becket (1118–1170) reluctantly became the archbishop of Canterbury. His erstwhile friend, King Henry II (1133–1189), became so angry at Becket's defense of the Church from temporal authority, that the archbishop had to flee to France. Upon his return, the king made his infamous outburst. Shortly after, three or four armed knights cut Becket down as he knelt in prayer at the altar of his cathedral. The turbulent priest became a saint just three years after his murder in the cathedral. There is little justification for the "à" in Becket's name. His parents were plain Beckets and in his lifetime he was always Thomas Becket without the "à."

Wine *see* Abstemii; New Wine into Old Bottles; Water into Wine

Winepress *see* Mystical Winepress

Wisdom *see* Price of Wisdom Is Above Rubies, The

Wisdom of Solomon

The son of David and Bathsheba, Solomon ruled Israel from 960 B.C. to 922 B.C. He is famous for his wealth, his many wives and his wisdom. The most famous example of his wisdom occurred when two women disputed who was the mother of a child. Solomon suggested that the child be cut in half and each woman receive an equal part. One of the women immediately renounced her claim. Solomon judged that woman to be the true mother and she was given the child.

Wise Men of the East *see* Magi

Wit's End, At One's

When someone has tried everything and doesn't know what to do next he is at his wit's end. Although in use in English since the 14th century, the modern use of this expression comes from Psalms 107:27.

> They reeled and staggered like drunken men and were at their wit's end.

Wodewose *see* Wild Men

Wolf *see* Wolf in Sheep's Clothing

Wolf in Sheep's Clothing
(*see also* Aesop)

An enemy who masquerades as a friend. The wolf represents greed and lust. The she-wolf symbolizes a lewd woman or prostitute who preys on men. As a result, hypocrites, heretics, greedy clergy and false monks have all been depicted as wolves. The devil is shown as a wolf disguised in a sheep's skin. Because of a belief that it was unable to turn its head, the wolf represented the proud and the stiff-necked.

> "Beware of false prophets, who come to you in sheep's clothing but inwardly are ravenous wolves" (Matthew 7:15).

This warning suggests that Jesus was familiar to some extent with Greek literature. It is similar to an animal fable by Aesop (c. 620–c. 560 B.C.).

Wood of the Cross

A legend says that when Adam died in Hebron, three trees grew from his body. The trees were transplanted by David in Jerusalem where they fused into one, an obvious symbol of the one god in the Trinity. Solomon attempted to use the tree as a support for the Temple but it was too short. From the tree was made the cross upon which Christ was crucified. The wood was then buried for three hundred years until discovered by St. Helena (d. 330), the mother of Constantine (c. 280–337).

Woodpecker

A bird associated with heresy and the devil. As the woodpecker destroys a tree bit by bit, so does the devil destroy a man and plant heresy in the Church. There are no woodpeckers in the King James Bible (1611).

Word, The   *see* In the Beginning Was the Word

Word of God

Scripture or divine revelation.

Words in the Bible

In the King James Bible (1611), there are 593,493 words in the Old Testament and 181,253 words in the New Testament for a total of 774,746 words.

Wormwood and Gall
(*see also* Gall of Bitterness)

The most bitter and disagreeable things imaginable. The herb known as wormwood, *Artemisia absinthium*, is a bitter herb from which absinth and vermouth are made. A legend says that wormwood sprang up in the track of the serpent as it was driven out of paradise. Gall is a bitter alkaline liquid, usually yellow or greenish, secreted by the liver and stored in the gallbladder. It aids in the digestion of fats and is now called bile.

> "Behold I will feed them with wormwood, and make them drink the water of gall" (Jeremiah 23:15).

Worst Metaphor

The Bible is famous for its stirring and memorable metaphors, but the one found in Ecclesiastes 11:1—"Cast your bread upon the waters, for you will find it after many days"—isn't one of them. It encourages us that if we are generous without thought of reward, the reward will be given. There is nothing wrong with the message, but what good is soggy bread many days old? A modern restating of the phrase was made by Elbert Hubbard in 1911:

> "Cast your bread upon the waters and it will come back to you — buttered."

Would You Adam and Eve It?
(*see also* Adam; Eve)

Cockney rhyming slang for "would you believe it?"

Writing on the Wall
(*see also* Belshazzar's Feast)

A warning. By the time the writing on the wall is visible, all is probably lost. In Daniel 5, the feast of Belshazzar, king of Babylon, is interrupted by a disembodied hand which writes, "Mene, mene, tekel, upharsin," on the wall. The words are Aramaic and no one could read them. Daniel was summoned and interpreted the words to mean that Babylon would be weighed, measured and divided. That very night the

Medes invaded Babylon and Belshazzar was killed. The literal meaning of the words has to do with units of measurement. Daniel's interpretation plays on clever puns which are not apparent in translation.

> Look at a branch, a bird, a child, a rose,
> Or anything God ever made
> that grows,—
> Nor let the smallest vision of it slip,
> Till you may read, as on
> Belshazzar's wall,
> The glory of eternal partnership.
> —*Sonnet*, Edwin Arlington
> Robinson (1869–1935).

Wyvern

A mythical beast symbolizing pestilence or Satan. The creature was a flying serpent or dragon with a barbed tail coiled in a knot and the legs of an eagle.

X

X
(*see also* St. Andrew's Cross)

Symbolic of the saltire cross upon which St. Andrew was crucified, the X has also symbolized Christ since the 12th century. As a stylized image of two mouths touching, X represents a kiss. An illiterate would sign his name with an X, really a St. Andrew's cross, and then kiss it to show good faith.

ΞΣ

A sacred monogram. The first and last letters of the Greek word ΞΡΙΣΤΟΣ, Christ, pronounced, "Christos."

ΞΙ

A sacred monogram, the initial letters of the two Greek words ΞΡΙΣΤΟΣ

ΙΗΣΟΥΣ, "Christos Jesous," Christ Jesus. The two letters are often superimposed.

X-mark *see* Cross-mark

Xmas
(*see also* Christmas)

The X of Xmas is the first letter of the Greek word for Christ and resembles a cross. Xmas, regarded as a vulgar abbreviation for Christmas, should never be written in formal contexts and never pronounced as "exmas." In fact, Xmas is not an abbreviation and has been recorded as early as 1551.

ΞΡ
(*see also* Labarum)

A sacred monogram called Chi-Rho. It comes from the first two letters of the Greek word ΞΡΙΣΤΟΣ, Christ. The two letters are often superimposed.

Y

Υ [Y]

Made with three strokes of the pen, the letter Υ symbolizes the Trinity. Known as the Thieves of Calvary's cross, the Υ depicts the human figure. The foot represents the innocence of the infant. The divergent arms symbolize free will, the paths to virtue or vice. Υ is called upsilon, in Greek, and is roughly equivalent to Roman Y.

Yahweh
(*see also* Jehovah; Tetragrammaton)

A transliteration, and presumed vocalization, of the Hebrew name for God in the Old Testament, YHWH. It means "He that is," or "He that brings everything into existence." In the English Bible the word became Jehovah. Scholars prefer Yahweh.)

Yellow

Yellow can symbolize revealed truth, the sun or divinity. However, dull yellow can suggest treason, deceit and jealousy. Judas is often depicted with a yellowish beard and clad in a yellow garment. Victims of the Inquisition wore yellow. Jews were sometimes forced to wear yellow because they had betrayed Christ. The color is mentioned four times in the King James Bible (1611).

Yew

An evergreen tree often found on the south side of British churchyards. It symbolizes death and the promise of eternal life. Branches of yew were sometimes carried in place of palms on Palm Sunday. The day was sometimes called yew Sunday. In medieval Wales, yews were given the names of saints and the penalty for cutting one down was 15 pence. The tree is not to be found in the King James Bible (1611).

> Strew on her roses, roses,
> And never a sprig of yew!
> In quiet she reposes;
> And would that I did too!
> —*Requiescat*, Matthew
> Arnold (1822–1888).

YHWH *see* Jehovah;
Tetragrammaton; Yahweh

Yves, St. *see* Lawyers

Z

Zion *see* At Ease in Zion

Zodiac Interpretations

There have been attempts to interpret the gospel message in the stars.

Virgo the virgin — the Virgin Mary; Libra the scales — the price of sin; Scorpio the scorpion — the death that comes from sin; Sagittarius the archer — demonism; Capricorn the goat — earthly corruption; Aquarius the water carrier — Noah's flood or living water; Pisces the fish — the remnant of God's people; Aries the ram — sacrifice; Taurus the bull — resurrection; Gemini the twins — Christ human and divine; Cancer the crab — the gathering of the saved; Leo the lion — Christ the king.

Zounds
(*see also* 'S)

An oath or expression of anger. A corruption of "God's wounds." Similar expressions are, 'Sdeath (God's death); 'Slid (God's lid); and 'Sblood (God's Blood).

> Zounds! I was never so bethumped
> with words
> Since I first called my brother's
> father dad.
> —*King John*, William Shakespeare
> (1564–1616).

Bibliography

Ammer, Christine. *The Facts on File Dictionary of Cliches.* New York: Checkmate Books, 2001.

Apostolos-Cappadona, Diane. *Dictionary of Christian Art.* New York: Continuum, 1994.

Avis, Walter S., et al. *Gage Canadian Dictionary.* Toronto: Gage, 1983.

Barber, Richard, and Anne Riches. *A Dictionary of Fabulous Beasts.* London: Macmillan, 1991.

Brewer, Ebenezer C. *Brewer's Dictionary of Phrase & Fable.* Rev. ed. London: Cassell, 1967.

Briggs, Katherine. *Abbey Lubbers, Banshees & Boggarts.* Harmondsworth: Kestrel Books, 1979.

_____. *A Dictionary of Fairies.* Harmondsworth: Penguin, 1976.

Burnham, Tom. *The Dictionary of Misinformation.* New York: Thomas Y. Crowell, 1975.

Cavendish, Richard, ed. *Man, Myth & Magic: The Illustrated Encyclopedia of Mythology, Religion and the Unknown.* New York: Marshal Cavendish, 1995.

Ciardi, John. *A Browser's Dictionary.* New York: Harper & Row, 1980.

_____. *A Second Browser's Dictionary.* New York: Harper & Row, 1983.

Cohen, J. M. and M. J. Cohen. *The Penguin Dictionary of Modern Quotations.* Harmondsworth: Penguin, 1980.

Compact Edition of the Oxford English Dictionary. Oxford: Oxford University Press, 1971.

Cooper, J. C. *An Illustrated Encyclopaedia of Traditional Symbols.* London: Thames and Hudson, 1978.

Cresswell, Julia. *The Penguin Dictionary of Clichés.* Harmondsworth: Penguin, 2000.

Cross, F. L., ed. *The Oxford Dictionary of the Christian Church.* Oxford: Oxford University Press, 1997.

Davidoff, Henry, ed. *The Pocket Book of Quotations.* New York: Pocket Books, 1952.

Durant, Will. *Our Oriental Heritage.* New York: Simon and Schuster, 1954.

_____. *Caesar and Christ.* New York: Simon and Schuster, 1944.

Fahlbusch, Erwin, et al. *Encyclopedia of Christianity.* Grand Rapids, MI: William B. Eerdmans, 1999.

Ferguson, John. *An Illustrated Encyclopaedia of Mysticism and the Mystery Religions.* London: Thames and Hudson, 1976.

George, Leonard. *Crimes of Perception: An Encyclopedia of Heresies and Heretics.* New York: Paragon House, 1995.

Gerwig, Henrietta. *University Handbook for Readers and Writers.* 1925. Reprint, New York: Thomas Y. Crowell, 1965.

Harding, Les. *A Book in Hand Is Worth Two in the Library.* Jefferson, NC.: McFarland, 1994.

Hargrave, Basil. *Origins and Meanings of Popular Phrases and Names.* London: T. Werner Laurie, 1925.

Harvey, Paul, ed. *The Oxford Companion to English Literature.* Oxford: Oxford University Press, 1960.

Hendrickson, Robert. *The Facts on File Encyclopedia of Word and Phrase Origins.* New York: Checkmate Books, 2000.

_____. *The Wordsworth Book of Literary Anec-*

dotes. Ware, England: Wordsworth Editions, 1997.

Lass, Abraham H. David Kiremidjian, and Ruth Goldstein. *The Wordsworth Dictionary of Classical and Literary Allusion*. Ware, England: Wordsworth Editions, 1994.

Latham, Edward. *A Dictionary of Names Nicknames and Surnames of Persons, Places and Things*. London: George Routledge & Sons, 1904.

Lurie, Charles N. *Everyday Sayings*. New York: G. P. Putnam's Sons, 1928.

McKenzie, John L. *Dictionary of the Bible*. Milwaukee: Bruce, 1965.

Manser, Martin H., comp. *The Westminster Collection of Christian Quotations*. Louisville: Westminster John Knox, 2001.

Metford, J. C. J. *Dictionary of Christian Lore and Legend*. London: Thames and Hudson, 1983.

Morley, Christopher, ed. *Familiar Quotations by John Bartlett*. 11th ed. Boston: Little, Brown and Company, 1943.

Muir, Frank. *An Irreverent and Thoroughly Incomplete Social History of Almost Everything*. New York: Stein and Day, 1976.

Neil, William, comp. *Concise Dictionary of Religious Quotations*. Grand Rapids: William Eerdmans, 1974.

Partridge, Eric. *The Wordsworth Book of Usage & Abusage*. Ware, England: Wordsworth Editions, 1995.

Paulos, John Allen. *Innumeracy: Mathematical Illiteracy and its Consequences*. New York: Vintage Books, 1990.

Pepper, Margaret, ed. *The Macmillan Dictionary of Religious Quotations*. London: Macmillan, 1996.

Phyfe, William Henry P. *5000 Facts and Fancies*. New York: G. P. Putnam's Sons, 1901.

Rawson, Hugh. *A Dictionary of Euphemisms and Doubletalk*. New York: Crown Publishers, 1981.

Shaw, Eva. *The Wordsworth Book of Divining the Future*. Ware, England: Wordsworth Editions, 1997.

Speake, Jennifer. *The Oxford Dictionary of Foreign Words and Phrases*. Oxford: Oxford University Press, 1997.

Strong, James. *The New Strong's Exhaustive Concordance of the Bible*. Nashville: Thomas Nelson, 1996.

Tabori, Paul. *The Natural History of Stupidity*. London: Prentice-Hall, 1962.

Thody, Philip. *Don't Do It! A Dictionary of the Forbidden*. New York: St. Martin's, 1997.

Walsh, William S. *Curiosities of Popular Customs*. Philadelphia: J. B. Lippincott, 1925.

_____. *A Handy-Book of Curious Information*. Philadelphia: J. B. Lippincott, 1913.

_____. *A Handy-Book of Literary Curiosities*. Philadelphia: J. B. Lippincott, 1892.

_____. *The International Encyclopedia of Prose and Poetical Quotations*. Philadelphia: John C. Winston, 1931.

Webster's Biographical Dictionary. Springfield, MA: G. & C. Merriam, 1966.

Weideman, Hugh. *The Rapid Fact Finder*. New York: Thomas Y. Crowell, 1958.

Williams, William F., ed. *Encyclopedia of Pseudoscience*. New York: Facts on File, 2000.

Yapp, Peter. *The Travellers' Dictionary of Quotations*. London: Rutledge, 1988.

Znamierowski, Alfred. *The World Encyclopedia of Flags*. London: Hermes House, 2001.

Index